Sandy Jaccksch

The Evaluation
and Treatment of
Marital Conflict

THE EVALUATION AND TREATMENT OF MARITAL CONFLICT

A Four-Stage Approach

PHILIP J. GUERIN, JR.

LEO F. FAY

SUSAN L. BURDEN

JUDITH GILBERT KAUTTO

Basic Books, Inc., Publishers   New York

Library of Congress Cataloging-in-Publication Data

The evaluation and treatment of marital conflict.

  Bibliography: p. 275
  Includes index.
  1. Marital psychotherapy.   I. Guerin, Philip J.
RC488.5.E94 1987   616.89'156   85–73889
ISBN 0–465–02112–3

To

Thomas F. Fogarty, M.D.,

our colleague, friend, and teacher

whose wisdom, ideas, and insight

made a major contribution

to this work

CONTENTS

The Evaluation
and Treatment of
Marital Conflict

The names and identifying details in all the case material in this book have been changed. Many of these cases represent common sets of symptoms.

Introduction: A Model of Marriage and Marital Conflict

MARRIAGE is a struggle, a constant struggle to relate intimately to another human being without being controlled or taken for granted. It can be a playful struggle that enriches both spouses and fosters their growth, or it can be a deadly struggle, in which one or both spouses are convinced that their emotional—even physical—survival is at stake.

Treating dysfunctional marriages is also a struggle, and it too can be either playful and enriching or deadly and draining. Therapists often complain about the difficulty of listening to people's marital woes and the discouragement in seeing them stuck in the same place week after week. But the fascination of helping couples deal with their problems is supplemented by the intellectual excitement of testing and evaluating the varied approaches to marital therapy that have evolved over the years.

Our own approach has found something valuable in all these therapies. It is presented as one way of doing marital therapy. We make no claim that it is the final word, but only that we have found this approach useful.

Development of Our Approach

Our model for treating dysfunctional marriages is the product of thousands of hours of clinical work over our combined experience of nearly fifty years. In addition, it has been refined and enriched by our analysis of treatment plans and clinical tapes in the Marital Project at the Center for Family Learning (CFL).

Our work began informally in 1978, when Guerin and Kautto began to meet regularly at CFL to discuss issues that were arising in the treatment of marital conflict. This informal work continued in chart rounds, in case conferences, and in the education program for family therapy trainees.

In the fall of 1981 a more formal approach to the work was taken with the formation of the Marital Project. Burden and Fay joined Guerin and Kautto, and Burden was appointed director of the Project. A format was devised for the one-day-a-week Project, consisting of one hour of chart rounds, two hours of case conference, and four to five hours of clinical work by each member of the Project. The two-hour case conference consists of a consultation with a family in the clinic, which is taped one week and reviewed the following week.

It has been in these sessions that Guerin's idea of staging, first presented formally at a workshop in 1978, has been fleshed out. Through our work with the couples in the Marital Project, we identified four stages of marital conflict according to the duration and intensity of the conflict.

BASIC ASSUMPTIONS

Our clinical experience with dysfunctional marraiges has led us to formulate a therapeutic approach based on several assumptions relating to the various spheres in which a couple acts and interacts—the social context and the extended family, the dyad, various triangles, and the spouses as individuals.

The Social Context and the Extended Family

Marriage exists in a two-ply envelope: the social and cultural context in which the couple lives and the extended families from which the partners come. The extended family can be and often is a source of significant strength for a marriage, in providing support, feelings of belonging, and a greater range of relationships. A changing social context can be a source of opportunity and a challenge to personal growth. But both the social context and the extended family can also be, and usually are, the sources of chronic and acute stress for a marriage. That stress is most difficult to absorb and handle when spouses are emotionally caught by the context in which they operate—that is, when they feel constrained to act and react in the same old ways and cannot see any new, creative ways of responding.

Efforts to increase people's emotional freedom to operate more functionally in their contexts pay handsome dividends in marital therapy. People become better partners, lovers, and companions; they learn to recognize what they believe in, not just what they are against. Emotional freedom does not cure them of their character deficits, behavioral idiosyncrasies, or emotional or physical illnesses, but they become aware of and better able to accept their own assets and limitations as well as those of their marriage and of the multigenerational family system of which they are a part.

The Dyad

Although marriage operates in a social and cultural context, it is still a relationship between two people. In interacting with each other, married people tend to get locked into scripts. These scripts, involving such things as the ways they communicate with each other, the time they spend with each other, and their movement toward and away from each other, are often dysfunctional and need to be addressed in therapy.

We believe that a couple's behavior with each other is a product of the degree and quality of the bonding between them. We have yet to find a satisfactory way of defining the bonding process, but we are absolutely convinced of its importance. We find that people who are rushing to escape their extended families tend to bond too closely with their marriage partners, creating a sticky, dysfunctional cocoon, while people who are too tied to their extended families tend to develop a tenuous marital bond.

It is important to note, however, that all sorts of dyadic relationships work. Our own conceptions of what marriage ought to be are too narrow. People find a wide variety of marriages to be functional.

Triangles

All married couples are constantly involved in triangles—with children, with in-laws, with friends, and so on. In severely dysfunctional marriages, triangles are the central fact of life. We believe that triangles should be a focus for all family and marital therapy; in severe marital conflict they should receive most of the therapist's attention.

The Spouses as Individuals

The well-being and level of functioning of individual spouses and the premorbid state of their family systems are important factors in how well they do as partners, companions, and intimates in a marriage. People's experiences of themselves and others are often quite narrow because of their personal and family histories. We believe that therapy must try to expand the partners' view of themselves and of the other in order to increase their level of functioning, reduce their bitterness, and help them achieve appropriate self-focus—that is, a focus on one's own part in the dysfunctional marital process rather than on one's spouse's part. The ability to achieve self-focus and the extent of bitterness are predictive of how well a couple is likely to do in marital therapy.

We find that people come to marriage with a double set of expectations: they expect their spouses both to duplicate the good things from their families of origin and to make up for the hurts and deficits from those families. The interesting thing about these expectations, however, is that, especially in times of stress and conflict, they are most often directed toward a partner's limitations rather than his or her strengths.

Although the four areas (the social context, the dyad, triangles, and the individual) are conceptualized separately, in therapy one weaves them together all the time, moving back and forth freely according to one's own operating style, the individual case, and one's beliefs about marriage and what makes it better.

THE STAGES OF MARITAL CONFLICT

Marital conflict differs substantially from one couple to another, not only with respect to the specific issues around which the conflict is organized but, more importantly, with respect to the *duration and intensity* of the conflict. We believe that treatment must be tailored to the level of severity of the conflict. Our method calls for assigning a stage to the conflict, so that a treatment plan based on the intensity and duration of the conflict can be developed.

We have observed that couples in the throes of marital conflict can be classified into four groups:

Group 1 couples demonstrate a preclinical or minimal degree of marital conflict and respond favorably to education about how marriages work and don't work. They are able to take that information and use it to change their relationships for the better.

Group 2 consists of couples who have been in active conflict for less than six months. The conflict includes a significant degree of projection and loss of self-focus. When the therapist dissects the conflictual marital process, however, both spouses can generally move to self-focus within six to eight sessions, and the intensity of the conflict is substantially reduced.

Couples in group 3 present clinically with severe marital conflict. The conflict has been going on for over six months, and the projection is intense. Each spouse blames the other, and both are totally unable to obtain or maintain self-focus. In these cases the clinician is almost exclusively concerned with trying to control the couple's instantaneous reactivity—their tendency to react to each other emotionally and without thinking. Moreover, when a positive result is obtained through therapy, a recycling of the conflict inevitably occurs within six to eight months. Such recycling is a common phenomenon at all levels of marital conflict. In a significant percentage of cases in this group, however, when recycling occurs both spouses and the marital relationship itself have lost their resilience and are unresponsive to further treatment.

In Group 4 are the couples who present to treatment after one or both spouses have engaged an attorney. At this stage, the situation is adversarial rather than potentially conciliatory. In a high percentage of cases, any attempt to keep the marriage from dissolution appears doomed. The work of therapy is then more profitably aimed at diminishing emotional damage to the spouses, their children, and their extended families.

Several characteristics of these groupings have parallels in certain types of cancer and their treatment. Oncologists identify the severity of a malignancy according to certain cellular characteristics and the degree of invasion of surrounding healthy tissue. Stage 1 is often a precancerous lesion that requires no specific treatment or just simple excision, plus instruction in watching for signs of a recurrence. The more advanced stages require more invasive treatment. Chemotherapy often produces an initially positive result, even in the most advanced cases, only to be followed by a recurrence within a relatively short period of time, at which point the patient's biological defenses have often lost the ability to join forces with chemotherapeutic agents to produce another remission.

The observation of the similarities between marital conflict and certain types of cancer in their responsiveness to treatment raised the following questions in our minds: Would an attempt to identify the stages of marital conflict through levels of severity improve our precision in applying existing techniques and stimulate a creative effort to develop new techniques for the more severe cases? Would a successful effort at identifying the stages of marital conflict also assist in the evaluation of treatment results and the formulation of more accurate prognostic guidelines? We believe that it would.

PLAN OF THE BOOK

The goal of this book is to give clinicians a conceptual structure with which to understand what they see clinically and a treatment method tied to that structure. The first part of the book, which is both clinical and theoretical, presents in detail the background for our treatment methods. Chapter 1 discusses the social context and the multigenerational family system, especially as sources of stress for marriages. Chapter 2 presents our view of the dyad, focusing on the couple's own interaction. Chapters 3 and 4 are detailed treatments of triangles. Chapter 3 presents the theory of triangles and a clinical discussion of triangles with outsiders, and chapter 4 deals with triangles within the family. Chapter 5 presents our view of the individual in marriage and our ideas about how individual problems need to be dealt with in marital therapy.

The second half of the book is completely clinical. Chapter 6 offers a method for evaluating a couple when they first present for treatment, including how to determine the stage of the conflict. Chapters 7 through 10 then offer specific guidelines for treating each of the four stages of marital conflict.

PART ONE

The Nature and

Causes of

Marital Conflict

1

Sources of Marital Stress

DON AND SUSAN, a couple in their mid-forties, came for marital therapy shortly after Susan had received a call from Don's mistress informing her of their three-year affair. Susan had known for over four years that things were not right in the marriage. She had occasionally suspected that Don might be involved in an extramarital relationship but had always dismissed the thought as paranoid.

In their first meeting with the therapist, Susan recalled her agonized thoughts as she waited for Don's return home the evening of that call. They had been married for eighteen years after a three-year courtship. The first seven years had been close to perfect: much love and affection, good sex, many things done together while they also maintained separate groups of friends. They had bought a lovely home and had produced a healthy son and daughter.

Perhaps it had been too perfect. Seven years ago Don had received an offer of a job in New York City that he could not refuse. With some reluctance, he and Susan left his comfortable job in Indianapolis, both sides of the extended family, and their lifelong social network, to take on the challenge of New York. A home in Westchester and a daily commute to the city for the "seven-to-seven shift" required considerable adjustment by both spouses. For Don the grind was wearing, and this job was much harder than his old one. His New York colleagues were used to playing hardball, and Don found himself wondering if the money and the career advancement were worth the price. Susan felt isolated without family and old friends, and it took a long time before she felt she belonged in the rather cliquey town into which they had moved. She also felt that her new environment undervalued her decision, made long ago in Indiana, to be a wife and mother at home.

Everyone had seemed to manage quite well until one morning five years ago, a morning Susan could remember as though it were yesterday. Don's mother called to say that Don's father had lung cancer. The course of his father's illness, through surgery and chemotherapy, and the trips back to Indiana were upsetting, but Don seemed to take them all in stride. When his father died ten months later, the entire family went to the funeral and stayed on for a week to comfort and support Don's mother.

During this time and in the months that followed, they seemed to draw even closer together as a family. Then gradually Don seemed to change. He stayed at work later, slept more when he was home, and seemed less tolerant of the demands of the children and more critical of Susan. This phase lasted about six months, and then he seemed to snap out of his doldrums. He joined a racquetball club. He also stopped going to church and became openly cynical about his previously deeply held values, especially about the importance of family life, self-sacrifice, and the ultimate rewards for a life lived according to moral rules.

Although Susan did not know it at the time, Don had come under a new influence. One afternoon, when his partner did not show up for their usual racquetball game, Carole, a single, twenty-eight-year-old attorney, offered to substitute, and thus began a three-year relationship that Susan finally learned about from the phone call.

Don and Susan's case typifies the profound effect that social forces are having on married people's lives in our time. Shifting ideas of the meaning of marriage and its obligations, new roles for women in society, new ideas about sexual morality, and new expectations of sexual satisfaction, as well as value shifts and economic forces that affect marriages and families, are all present in Don and Susan's story. Their story, especially Don's father's death, also illustrates the impact that events in the multigenerational family have on marriage.

These social forces and the events in their family stressed Don and Susan's marriage in many ways. In our work with marital conflict, we have found that the most important sources of stress on a marriage are societal change and the developmental and situational transitions that occur in all multigenerational family systems. This chapter deals with these sources of stress and with the mechanisms by which they trigger the onset and affect the course of marital conflict.

The Social Context

Numerous observers both within the family therapy field and outside it have focused on economic problems, racial and religious oppression, and major shifts in cultural values as social forces that directly affect the family. Nathan Ackerman, in numerous papers throughout his career (for example, 1954, 1955, 1965, 1967), pointed to the need to combine insight into individual psychodynamics with an understanding of the effects of the social context on the mental health of children and their families. As early as 1938, he observed the effects of the Great Depression on the power hierarchy in coal miners' families in eastern Pennsylvania. He reported how fathers, out of work and thus deprived of the only socially legitimate role they could play in the family, were pushed out of their families and rendered powerless in them (1967). Robert Coles's *Children of Crisis* (1967) provides us with a description of the effects of racial oppression and changes in race relations on black children and families in the United States. Andrew Greeley, in his account of the social history of Irish Americans (1981), documents vividly the impact of British oppression on Irish family life.

Social forces are most stressful to the marital relationship during times of sociocultural change. Change is a natural and inevitable process that presents both the opportunity for growth and adaptation and the potential for chaos and disintegration. Either way, social change is almost always stressful to individuals, to relationships, and to families. By challenging the way things are "supposed to be," it increases anxiety, modifies people's expectations of themselves and of their way of life, including their marriages, and sets them up for relationship problems.

In our work with marital conflict, we have consistently found three aspects of the present social context to be relevant to the study and treatment of marital conflict: the changing meaning of marriage, the women's movement, and the sexual revolution.

THE THREE MEANINGS OF MARRIAGE

The way people think about marriage to some extent determines the way they behave when they are married. Sociologists who have studied this area think that most ideas about the meaning of marriage can be classified into three categories: (1) the religious, or sacred, meaning of marriage; (2) the communal, or social, meaning; and (3) the personal, or individualistic, meaning (Eshleman, 1981).

One must remember that classifications such as this exist in their pure form only in the minds of the scientists. They are no more than abstractions of complex natural processes. In real life, the categories overlap, combine, and recombine in numerous blends and appear inconsistently and sporadically. When we look at the attitudes of the people we see clinically, we do not find total consistency. People give more than one meaning at a time to marriage and family. They hold on to one meaning while they are moving toward another, and they shift from one meaning to another according to circumstances. It is this shift, as we shall see, that is of particular interest to clinicians.

The Sacred Meaning of Marriage

In the sacred view, marriage and the family are divine institutions, founded by God and governed by religious leaders. People who hold this view in its extreme form maintain that personal or earthly considerations in marriage (such as money, sexual attraction, and personal satisfaction) must be subordinated to God's will and purposes. Everything about a marriage, including whether and with whom it may take place, how it should be lived out, and whether and under what conditions it may end, is to be decided according to the laws of religion.

This meaning of marriage, even in its purest and most extreme form, has had a very long history and has often been combined with the social meaning of marriage, as in the Middle Ages of Western Europe. It is widely perceived to be the view of marriage held today by Orthodox Judaism and by traditional Roman Catholicism.

Couples for whom this is the prevailing meaning of marriage are likely to view their marital difficulties on a right-wrong axis and to take the problem to a clergyman for resolution. When such couples present for marital therapy, their views must not be deprecated, explicitly or implicitly, by the therapist. These couples should be treated by someone with religious credibility; if the therapist is not from the same belief system, the therapy should be conducted in consultation with someone with the couple's religious beliefs. Lack of such credibility can result in a conflict between therapist and couple that sabotages the process of therapy.

In working with these couples it is important for the therapist to validate the worth of their values while at the same time working to increase the degree to which they allow room for changes in their belief systems. Perhaps most important, the therapist must help them put aside the right-wrong axis and replace it with a more psychological perspective, without undermining their views of God and religion. Therapy of any kind that attempts to undermine clients' religious beliefs and replace them with the therapist's more "enlightened" view of the world is overly invasive and not productive. People need to be helped, in gentle and respectful ways, to consider how they may be misusing God and religion to avoid improving their individual and marital functioning.

Clinical problems in marriage can occur when one partner believes in the sacred meaning of marriage and the other does not. An example was provided by Dennis and Anne Nolan, a couple in their early thirties who had been married for three years. Both Catholics, they were in conflict about the practice of birth control. Anne had used a diaphragm since she was in college. Dennis had always been uncomfortable with this practice, believing it to be morally wrong and contrary to Church teaching. A year before, his entreaties had finally worn Anne down, and she had agreed to try natural family planning (an elaborate version of the "rhythm method"), a method of birth control approved by the Church. A pregnancy had ensued, which Anne terminated by an abortion after much agonizing and often acrimonious discussion with Dennis. Dennis, horrified at this break with Catholic moral norms, questioned whether he could stay married to Anne. It was at that juncture that they decided to seek treatment.

The Social Meaning of Marriage

The second meaning of marriage defines it in terms of its social obligations. A couple's marriage is seen primarily as the business not of God, nor of the couple, but of their families and community. The rules and wishes of the families and the community govern who may marry whom, how they are to live, and whether or not the marriage may end. Considerations such as family property, lineage, and appropriate race, religion, or ethnic background are all-important. The obligations of the bride and groom to their parents and to the rest of their extended families are seen as paramount —even more important than their obligations to each other.

Throughout human history, this has probably been the most common and enduring view of marriage, and it continues to be held by most traditional societies. A good example of it is found in family life in rural Japan, where traditions hundreds of years old still regulate marital interaction (beautifully depicted in the film *The Japanese, Part III: Farm Song,* produced by John Nathan and distributed by the Japan Society).

A more modern version of this view presented to CFL's clinical service for treatment just a few years ago. Peter and Donna Ghessian, both forty-three, had been married for twenty-five years and had four children ranging in age from twenty-four to seventeen. Peter had founded a real estate development firm specializing in commercial real estate and now operated shopping centers in twelve states. He was a very successful, driven man who failed totally to comprehend his wife's complaints. Although he felt somewhat guilty about his frequent brief affairs, he clearly did not understand why his wife could not overlook them. Donna complained not only about his infidelity but also about his emotional distance from her, his preoccupation with work and with his own extended family, and his lack of interest in what she was doing with her life in returning to school for an MBA.

Peter was an old-fashioned patriarch, who valued that position very highly in both his own and Donna's extended families. He had provided well-paid jobs in his real estate concern for both his brothers, for his sister's husband, for Donna's brother and brother-in-law, and most recently for his eldest daughter's fiancé. In the case of two of these people, the jobs were make-work positions for men who were not especially competent. Peter did not complain about that, however, for he valued the respect and debts of gratitude owed him by the entire family. For him, this was the meaning of marriage and family, and his wife's demands for a more emotionally satisfying marriage puzzled and offended him.

The Individual Meaning of Marriage

For those who hold the social or religious meanings of marriage, the social and religious contexts provide a powerful source of support for the couple and their marriage. That advantage is balanced, of course, by the disadvantage that these views of marriage do not give much weight, if any, to the emotional and interpersonal satisfactions that ought to be part of long-term relationships.

In recent years, a third view of the meaning of marriage and family has made its appearance, especially among the middle classes of the industrial nations of the world. This view holds that the demands of marriage and family life are subordinate to the well-being and happiness of the individual. Happiness and personal fulfillment become the criteria for deciding whom to marry, by what rules to live as a family, and if and when to terminate the marriage. The authority for these and all other decisions concerning family life is not God or clergy, not extended family or community, but oneself.

Almost all observers would agree that the overwhelming trend in American society, especially on the East and West coasts, is toward the individual view of marriage. For example, a study of Roman Catholics in a semirural diocese in New England (Fay, 1980) found that approximately 65 percent of the sample were primarily individualistic in their ideas about the meaning and purpose of marriage. Between 20 and 25 percent appeared to see marriage principally in sacred terms, and about 10 percent indicated at least some adherence to a social meaning for marriage. These findings are quite striking when we remember that the population being investigated was nonclinical, entirely Roman Catholic, and living in a rural area.

Another way of looking at the meanings of marriage is to talk about levels of commitment. In both the social and sacred views of marriage, a blind commitment, whether to God, the Church, the extended family, or the community, tends to be the operative attitude with which men and women approach marriage. The stakes, in terms of both this world and the next, are very high, and the people involved directly and indirectly in the marriage are numerous. High stakes and a large number of involved people raise the level of commitment with which couples approach marriage, sometimes to a point where they are unable to recognize their own and their spouses' emotional needs and limitations.

Although the individual meaning of marriage maximizes the emotional stakes, it minimizes both the worldly and eternal commitments and cuts to two the number of people who are thought to be involved. Marriage thus becomes a contract to which two people commit themselves, but with an explicit or implicit understanding that the marriage is subject to termination if either or both do not have their needs met.

These three views of marriage need not be mutually exclusive nor present people with irreconcilable conflict. They may do so, of course, when spouses hold different views and adopt all-or-nothing attitudes about them. But couples can choose to understand their own and their spouses' beliefs, to be open to change in their own values, and to tolerate differences of opinion and belief with their spouses. It is the therapist's task to help them move away from the all-or-nothing approach to a more integrative meaning of marriage.

An understanding of the meanings of marriage is of more than academic interest for therapists, for clinical problems in marriage frequently occur when one spouse shifts from a traditional view to an individual one while the other spouse does not. Such a shift in Donna Ghessian's view made her dissatisfied with a marriage that for many years had been acceptable to her.

It is not unusual to find a shift in view at a critical turning point in a person's life—for example, after the death of a parent. Ron and Arlene Philips, a couple in their late forties, came to therapy for treatment of marital conflict that appeared to have been provoked by Ron's anger and depression. Ron had always been cheerful and hardworking, someone who seemed to take great pleasure in helping members of the family and in being seen as dependable, the family's leader. His personality seemed to change drastically, however, soon after his parents died, within several months of each other.

When the Philipses were first seen in treatment, Ron was clinically depressed and could talk about little except his feelings that no one cared about him, no one admired him, no one paid any attention to him. He said many times that he could no longer see any purpose in his marriage.

The contrast between Ron's definition of marriage and family while his parents lived and his definition after their deaths could not have been sharper. He had moved from a traditional, socioreligious kind of belief, in which obligations to God, family, and community had been paramount, to one in which his own feelings of dissatisfaction took on an importance he had not allowed them to have for over twenty years. A man like Ron is usually overly compliant with the expectations of the extended family, locked into living his life in a way that his parents approve. He buries a lot of resentment about the oppressive aspects of his family's expectations. When his parents die, he is confronted with his own mortality, the buried resentments surface, and there is a reactive move to noncompliant, even oppositional behavior. This happened to Ron. His distress at his mother's death was displaced onto his marriage, and his perceptions about how marriage was supposed to work shifted.

This shift confused and upset Arlene. She did not know what it meant and had no idea how to deal with it. She complained that anything she tried to do to please Ron met with his scorn. Arlene's views of marriage had not changed. For her, God, children, and extended family were still essential ingredients in her life.

In a case like this, the therapist outlines for the couple exactly what has happened to them and how the changes in their relationship are linked to changes in the social context. The couple can begin the task of working through the implications of these changes in their marriage. Ron can discover how his radical rejection of former beliefs is an emotional reaction to his parents' deaths. Arlene can explore a view of marriage more compatible with present-day circumstances. Both can work to establish better ways to tolerate and deal with their differences.

THE WOMEN'S MOVEMENT AND THE SEXUAL REVOLUTION

The dramatic shift from sacred and social to individualistic marriage is an outgrowth of what has been termed the age of cultural narcissism, born in the social turmoil of the 1960s and early 1970s. The women's movement and the sexual revolution, also outgrowths of this period, have been even more dramatic in their influence on marriages.

Karen and Nathan McCollum had one child, a three-year-old daughter. They had conceived Bertie when they had been married for less than a year. They were both twenty-seven years old and overwhelmed with their responsibilities. Karen had begun law school on a scholarship and found that, although a good student, she was under a good deal of internal pressure to do very well. Nathan had been in favor of Karen's attending law school because he thought that the life style they aspired to would require them to be a two-income family. Nevertheless, he had many misgivings, fearing that Karen would become too absorbed in school. He had recently bought into a business that kept him at work six days a week from ten to twelve hours a day. As if that weren't enough, the couple had also purchased an old house in need of many repairs that they planned to do themselves on weekends.

Karen and Nathan had planned to have an "egalitarian" marriage, a partnership in which each would parent and run the house on a fifty-fifty basis. However, as Nathan pushed the shopping cart through the grocery store or prepared dinner for Bertie, he found himself increasingly angry at what he saw as a lack of responsibility and caring on Karen's part. Karen on the other hand complained that Nathan was never around to do his share and was full of criticism for her when he was around. By the time they were seen by the therapist in an evaluation interview, Nathan had left the house after an explosive exchange in which the couple had become physically violent.

This example, although somewhat extreme, presents issues around which a good deal of the conflict we see clinically is organized. The changes in roles and responsibilities that this young couple were battling over are the result of a process that has been going on at least since the beginning of the Industrial Revolution. As long ago as 1848, which marks the beginning of the women's suffrage movement, women have been trying to achieve a social status in which they could vote, work, and earn money, just as their male counterparts do. In the years since the publication of Betty Friedan's *The Feminine Mystique* (1974), women have been actively trying to make that dream a reality. Today, when women think about their lives, more and more of them consider not only marriage and motherhood but also careers, personal development, and their place in the world.

Society has begun to respond, however reluctantly, to this shift. For example, it is now against the law in some states for a husband to rape his wife. A battered wife is permitted to press criminal charges against her husband. The Equal Opportunities Act has made it less possible for women to be denied employment and equal pay because of their sex. Sexual harassment on the job has finally been identified as a real problem for women, and a woman can now bring suit against an employer who attempts to blackmail her sexually.

Hand in hand with the social and political changes occurring because of the women's movement are changes in the way women view themselves sexually. Just as they have discovered their intellectual and economic potential, women have also begun to discover their sexuality. As they have come to view themselves as individuals with legitimate needs, women have become more explicit about their sexual needs. Not only are they more interested in having orgasms, but they are also better able to say no to their husbands when they are not interested in having sex. No longer do women universally see it as their duty to have sex when their husbands request it, as their mothers and grandmothers did in past generations. Sex is not something to be endured or tolerated; it is to be pleasurable, or not to be at all. Some women we have seen clinically are so disappointed by what they see as men's insensitivity and selfishness that they have chosen female partners in their second "marriages."

How have these changes that women have been making affected the men in their lives? For an answer, one has only to look at the nature of the problems their husbands are bringing into therapy. Husbands complain that their wives are never around, that they are having affairs, that they are not taking care of the home or the children. Men also report an increase in their own sexual dysfunctions. As women have altered their expectations of themselves, their expectations of the men around them have also changed. Having seen themselves as undervalued in the traditional female role and feeling powerful for the first time in their lives, with a "sisterhood" behind them, many women have been demanding that men make up to them all the injustices from the past or at the very least applaud their new directions.

The enlightened male intellectually subscribes to the idea of equality between himself and his wife. He agrees that fathers can and should be just as nurturing as mothers. He says it isn't fair for the woman to do all the shopping, laundry, cleaning, and cooking. "After all," he reasons, "I live here, too." That, however, is in theory. In practice even the most liberal of men often run headlong into their emotional conservatism. Sometimes with a good deal of guilt, a man will apologize for his anger and hurt when he explains why life has fallen apart at home. As Nathan McCollum told the therapist, "I can't help it. I know it's wrong, but I want a hot meal when I get home from the office at the end of the day." Nathan's recognition of his dilemma may have identified a major issue for him in his marriage, but it did little to resolve the conflict for him. Instead he seethed. "Karen comes in after I get home, doesn't even say hello, and wants to be left alone. Well, hell, I wasn't playing tiddlywinks all day!" In one of her lighter moments, Karen noted, "What we need is a wife or a maid or something, maybe a mother, to take care of both of us."

The impact of the women's movement and the resultant shift in sexual behavior in many marriages present the marital therapist with a complicated and emotionally charged situation, which demands artful handling. It is important for the therapist to be aware of his or her own biases and assumptions that may be activated during the therapy. For example, if the therapist's wife has returned to school or work and is no longer as available to him as she was earlier in the relationship, the therapist may have to monitor his reactions to a wife in a clinical case who is in a similar position. The sex of the therapist could have added meaning for the couple in a case where the issue of equality between the sexes is intense. It is often useful to raise this subject early in therapy rather than wait until it becomes an issue. The therapist can do so with the use of gentle humor, poking fun at his or her own biases. If humor is not appropriate, discussing the issue explicitly will usually be sufficient, but the subject may have to be brought up from time to time when the therapist notices that gender is becoming an issue.

When dealing with couples who are engaged in the power struggles that emerge from these male-female issues, the therapist must spend time eliciting the grievances of each partner. Tying these grievances to the expectations the husband and wife have of each other is an important place to begin. Where do their expectations come from? From their social network? From their parents? Or from some abstract ideal? It is the issue of trust, or the lack of it, that is often at the bottom of the conflict. In the case of Nathan and Karen, Karen's not being where she used to be and doing what she used to do created for Nathan an intense experience of loss. This process was outside his awareness and was played out by his anger and lack of interest in her "law school stories." The husband's camouflaged reaction to his sense of loss and the wife's disappointment at her husband's indifference to her "problems" set the stage for the battle over women's versus men's rights.

Carol and Peter Allen came to therapy in the throes of a struggle over her efforts toward greater independence. Carol had been married and had two children by the age of twenty-one, and she had spent the next decade concentrating on home and family. In her early thirties she decided she wanted the college education she had never had and then a career in business; she called it her "Five-Year Plan." Peter intellectually supported her desire for a college degree. His family put a premium on education, and Carol's lack of it had often been a source of embarrassment to him. He also thought she was an intelligent woman who deserved her chance in the outside world.

Shortly after Carol began to implement her plan, however, conflict in the marriage escalated dramatically. She had been excited about the courses she was taking and wanted to be able to talk about them with Peter. Initially he had been receptive, but as he felt himself losing his place on her list of priorities, his resentment grew and his tolerance for her new enthusiasm decreased. He complained that she had become a ruthless, self-centered woman with little regard for her children, house, or husband. Carol felt she had supported Peter for ten years and that it was now his turn to be supportive. She accused him of showing his true chauvinist colors.

In this kind of case one of the things we do is to evaluate the *way* in which the wife is moving in a new direction. Is she moving too quickly? Is it an overcorrection? These are not questions of right and wrong, but rather questions of degree. The system might be better able to support her change if she slowed her pace just a bit, or if she found a way to be more sensitive to the repercussions in the family. Overcorrection is a relative term. The same pace might be very functional in one family and destructive in another. In order to evaluate the wife's move, the therapist must look at the way it is affecting the system. Carol had gone from full-time mother and wife to full-time student with literally no time for the family, and the family was reeling. The therapist supported her goals for a college education and a career but worked with her to achieve them in a way that enabled her to remain sensitive to the family.

Behind an overcorrection there is usually a significant amount of fear and ambivalence about the steps one is taking. These feelings must be dealt with in the therapy. Wives in Carol's position need to learn that conflict organized around an overcorrection detours them away from the desired goals. Husbands in Peter's position need to understand the feelings that are driving their wives and at the same time must take responsibility for their own behavior, which is driven by a sense of loss, fear, and mistrust.

The Multigenerational Family System

Every marriage exists within a multigenerational family system, which is the source of the biological and psychological endowment of both spouses. Placing the marriage in that context enables the therapist to begin to make an assessment of the stage of the conflict and to make some preliminary judgments about intervention.

THE PREMORBID STATE OF THE FAMILY

The premorbid state of a family, its level of functioning prior to the emergence of symptoms, is an index of the amount of stress likely to be funneled to the marriage from the extended family, as well as a good predictor of how much stress a marriage can absorb and dissipate without producing symptoms. Marriage is a joining of two family systems, and the best markers of the premorbid state of the family are the number and severity of individual dysfunctions in the multigenerational family system and the number of conflicts and cutoffs in the relationships in that system. The Petersen wedding is a good illustration of how the joining of two systems, and the types of relationships that exist in those systems, start a marriage off at a given level.

Carl and Anne Petersen had a big wedding. The ceremony took place in the Roman Catholic parish church to which Anne's Italian parents had belonged for nearly thirty years. This locale for the wedding had caused some consternation for Carl's parents, who were Episcopalians, but they got over it by telling themselves that, after all, the custom in America is that a wedding takes place in the bride's church. The cost of the reception was borne equally by both families at the insistence of Carl's father and was held in the country club where Anne's boss was a member. One hundred and fifty people were invited.

The couple had met in college during their junior year, dated off and on until graduation in 1978, and then begun to see each other exclusively. Anne took a job as a secretary and Carl took a test to become a police officer in their hometown of New Haven, Connecticut. When he was hired, he and Anne announced their engagement and set the date for the following August—slightly more than two years after their graduation from college.

The wedding was a happy affair. When the day arrived, all the issues between the families that had cropped up in the previous several months had been amicably resolved. Carl's parents had reconciled themselves to seeing their son married in a Catholic church. Since the Petersens were paying for half the cost of the wedding, each family invited exactly half the guests. Most of Anne's allotment was taken up by relatives, while the Petersens, a geographically and emotionally distant family, invited more friends.

There had been other, less simple issues. One of the most troublesome was what to do about Carl's brother, Bill, who had a long history of manic-depressive illness. He had moved in and out of his parents' home countless times over the past ten years and was currently in Colorado. Carl had hated him since Carl was twelve and he was seventeen. Everyone decided that the best solution was to invite him, but as a guest rather than as a member of the wedding party. Carl hoped and believed—correctly, as it turned out—that he would not come.

Anne was worried about her father's drinking. He had been "falling asleep" every night after dinner for years, and although the word *alcoholic* was never used, Anne's parents had been fighting about his drinking for as long as she could remember. She decided to confront the issue head-on and extracted from her father a promise not to drink at the wedding.

The ceremony and reception went very well. Everyone professed to have had a wonderful time. A detached observer of the Petersen wedding, however, would have had no difficulty in seeing that this wedding was itself a stressful event. The conspicuous absence of Carl's brother, Anne's father's unusual abstemiousness, the clannishness of Anne's large family in contrast with the social orientation of the more formal Petersens, all suggested that two families who never would have pursued a social acquaintance were being joined in a permanent relationship that neither of them ever sought. The clinician would note the history of bipolar illness, the presence of alcoholism, Carl's cutoff from his brother, the intrusiveness of Anne's family, and the emotionally distant rather than personal connections among Carl's relatives as markers of a premorbid family state that would potentially add stress to this marriage.

Cohesive and Fragmented Family Systems

In every multigenerational family, the relationship system and patterns of interaction have both direct and indirect impact on marital relationships in the system. Understanding the relationships in the extended family system is therefore an important part of understanding the origins, course, and eventual outcome of marital conflict.

In one pattern, the couple is embedded in the multigenerational family unit. Members of the family live close together, and there is substantial, even daily, contact between the married couple and other family members. We call this a *cohesive family system*. When this kind of system is seen clinically, the therapist usually has little difficulty making the connection between problems in the marriage and stresses in the larger family system. Typically there is substantial and often obvious leakage of anxiety from the extended family into the marriage. Although there are usually cutoffs, the influence of cohesive systems on marriage comes primarily from their intrusiveness.

Ted and Patty Mead, a couple in their late twenties, came to the clinic two weeks after they had initiated a voluntary separation. They had been married two and a half years, and there was one child, Anna, aged thirteen months. Ted was the only child of an Irish father and a Hungarian mother. Patty was the middle child of three girls in an Italian family. Ted's father, to whom he had been very close, had died suddenly two years before Ted and Patty were married. His mother's response to her husband's death had been to move toward her son emotionally with great intensity. He managed to keep her at bay with semiabusive behavior and somewhat malignant neglect. He admired and respected Patty's family, especially their closeness, but he had expected Patty and himself to be "pretty much independent" of both families when they married.

Beginning with the wedding plans, things did not go as Ted had hoped. First, his mother felt slighted by Patty's family and refused to attend the wedding. When the wedding day came, she went to the church but refused to go to the reception. She had continued to alienate herself from Patty and her family, especially in refusing to come to the baby's baptism. Ted was angered and embarrassed by his mother's behavior, but he never really dealt with her or with his wife's and in-laws' reactions to her. He just hoped the problem would go away and focused on trying to get Patty to be less involved with her family.

Part of the treatment plan for this couple called for Ted to confront his overly negative view of his family and to begin to develop relationships with key family members. Meanwhile, Patty was to work on effecting a better separation from her cohesive family without cutting them off or damaging her relationship with them.

While the pattern of physical closeness and overinvolvement is by no means extinct in our culture, it is becoming less and less common. In the more usual pattern, seen clinically in connection with marital conflict time after time, the marriage has ended up cut off from both spouses' families of origin. The couple is, in effect, on its own, without people in the multigenerational family system to turn to for support or emotional connectedness. We call this constellation a *fragmented family system.*

There are two kinds of cutoff that can be seen in this situation. The first is a *complete cutoff,* in which the couple have little or no contact with one or both sides of the multigenerational family unit. Sometimes such a complete cutoff is the result of a dramatic conflictual event that has alienated everyone from everybody else. One couple, for example, had had no contact at all with the husband's family of origin for several years because of a bitter fight over his father's estate.

A complete cutoff can also be the result of a less dramatic process in which the members of the multigenerational family unit drift out of contact with one another because of physical distance and perhaps because of the death of the "family switchboard": the person who had held the family together by acting as the information exchange and by taking the initiative for getting people together. For instance, one couple who lived 800 miles from their families of origin only realized how cut off they were when they were asked how long it had been since they had spoken to their families. It turned out that there had been no dramatic conflict, in fact no overt conflict of any kind in the family, but that since the wife's mother had died, there "just hadn't been any reason" to call or go home.

This kind of drift away from contact is often related to a second kind of cutoff, the *ritualized cutoff*, in which families manage their conflicts by placing a rigid structure around their time together. They may celebrate holidays, birthdays, and other family events by coming together for dinners, parties, and cookouts. They may have regular patterns of telephone or personal contact (for example, the daughter who calls her mother faithfully at noon on the fourth Sunday of every month). But nothing of personal significance ever happens in these contacts, and when stress hits, the members of the family cannot turn to each other for support, advice, or a sense of belonging.

Although it is harder to make a clinical connection between this type of structure and marital conflict than it is with the cohesive structure, the connection is there. For example, it is very common for a marriage in this kind of extended family structure to present in what we refer to as the *cocoon phenomenon,* cut off from other segments of the multigenerational family unit and turned in on itself. This isolation serves to cut down the leakage from the extended family's problems, of course, but it prevents the development of sufficient relationship options: the couple does not have the choice of turning to family members for help in dissipating anxiety and upset in times of stress and for emotional support over time.

TYPES OF FAMILY STRESS

Stress from the multigenerational family unit is of several types. In this section we will consider the relevance and impact of two types: *situational* and *developmental stress.* In addition we will offer the simplified concept of transition times as our way of demonstrating how events in the extended family create situational and developmental stress.

Situational Stress

The literature abounds with analyses of both situational and developmental stress. The work of Holmes and Rahe (1967) is of particular relevance to our view of situational stress. Their study focuses on the impact of the stressful events in a person's life—events that call for adaptive or coping behavior, which we refer to as situational stress. Their findings have consistently shown the importance of clusters of these events: "this clustering of social or life events achieves etiologic significance as a necessary but not sufficient cause of illness and accounts in part for the time of onset of disease" (p. 213).

Our clinical experience parallels that of Holmes and Rahe. Like them we do not propose a cause-and-effect relationship between documented situational stress and dysfunction (which in their work is physical illness, in ours marital conflict). Rather, we contend that a simultaneous occurrence of many such stressors, combined with one or more transition times (to be discussed in the next section), forms a period of *cluster stress.* This cluster stress sets off a series of interconnected emotional processes in the individuals and couples in the multigenerational family unit. If these processes are allowed to escalate without intervention, symptom development —in the form of physical or emotional dysfunction in the system's most vulnerable individuals or relationships—is inevitable.

The amount of stress required to produce symptoms depends on the vulnerability of the particular family system. In the less vulnerable system whose stress threshold is only moderately exceeded, the conflict flares up and moves around from one relationship to another (husband-wife, sibling-sibling, parent-child, and so on). The conflict is of moderate intensity and of relatively short duration, and the system ultimately rights itself and reestablishes its prestress equilibrium. In the more vulnerable unit, the conflict comes to rest in the most vulnerable individual or relationship in the system and goes through repeated escalating cycles, until a rupture of the relationship is imminent. The result is either a distancing with chronic conflict or a search for therapeutic assistance.

Catherine and Edward Sullivan came to therapy originally because of Catherine's difficulty in dealing with the behavior of their three children, an eight-year-old girl and two boys, aged two and one. The two-year-old, Kevin, had just undergone surgery and radiation therapy for a malignant brain tumor and was now in chemotherapy. The family had come to New York three years earlier when Ed got a job there, but their families were still in the Midwest. Both Ed and Catherine were depressed. At the beginning of therapy, Catherine was by far the more dysfunctional, unable to control her behavior with the children and almost constantly crying. As she improved, Ed's depression deepened and he was placed on antidepressants. The medication worked quickly in relieving his symptoms, but at that point young Kevin began to show personality changes, and his physicians shortened the time between his checkups in obvious concern about a recurrence of the tumor. It was then that marital conflict surfaced explicitly.

The severe situational stressors that fed into the picture of cluster stress in this case are obvious. They included migration, job change, physical distance from extended family, and especially Kevin's illness.

Developmental Stress

Like the individual, the multigenerational family system goes through a series of predictable developmental changes, frequently termed the family life cycle. Sociologists used the concept of the family life cycle in the 1950s, and by the 1970s the idea had become explicit in the language of the family therapy movement.

Our approach to the multigenerational life cycle focuses on changes. Like changes in the social context, changes in the family life cycle increase anxiety and can create significant emotional damage, particularly in families that are vulnerable. The evaluation of families in order to predict the potential for damage can be extremely complex, however, because the multigenerational family life cycle is so complex. At any given moment, numerous individuals and subsystems within the multigenerational unit are going through developmental life cycle changes of their own, and in a particular family system the picture can become extremely complicated, cumbersome, and difficult to remember in clinical interviews. For example, elderly parents can be dying, the husband can be experiencing disappointment at the course of his career, and children can be struggling with adolescence.

For this reason we suggest that the clinician use the concept of *transition times,* which are defined as any addition to the family system, subtraction from it, or change in the status of a family member. The most important are marriage, birth, adolescence, midlife, retirement, and death. Watching the extent to which these transition times have accumulated in a particular multigenerational family unit will give the clinician a good diagnostic and prognostic reading of the potential for emotional damage and its possible sources in that family. Although a particular clinical situation may necessitate getting involved in the content of the particular life cycle stages the multigenerational family is going through, simple assessment of the *level* of stress impinging on a marriage and showing its impact is greatly simplified by the concept of transition times.

It is obvious that painful transition times such as death and divorce will be stressful and raise anxiety. It is equally true that potentially joyful transitions can be the source of considerable stress and anxiety. People usually have unrealistically high expectations for family relationships when the transition is defined as joyous. The arrival of a new infant is the classic example of this phenomenon. Mother was counting on having a daughter and is presented with her sixth son; Father throws his back out on the way to the hospital; at the christening the grandmothers battle over who the baby looks like and Father's childless sister drinks too much.

Often, a number of transition times take place simultaneously. This cluster stress can set off a pattern of automatic relationship behaviors in the family. A frequent combination consists of death in the grandparental generation, midlife crisis for the parents, and adolescence and leaving home for the younger generation.

When the Washburns presented at CFL, they had suffered the loss of both grandmothers within the past eighteen months. Marjorie Washburn had returned to work. The Washburns' fourth child had just left for college, and their youngest was a high school senior. The family requested treatment for marital conflict and for the youngest daughter, Janet, whose behavior had become antisocial.

The therapist's awareness of the impact of cluster stress provided him with a starting point for opening up the emotional process in this family. Making the connection between stress and conflict without making it a cause-and-effect connection can be validating and comforting. The following is a segment from an early session with Marjorie and Ted Washburn, who were focused on their concern about their adolescent daughter's antisocial behavior.

THERAPIST: Janet, your parents think you have a problem. Do you?

JANET: How should I know?

THERAPIST: I guess they're worried about the shoplifting charge.

JANET: They don't understand.

THERAPIST: What?

JANET: Nothing.

THERAPIST: Do you ever worry about them?

JANET: Sometimes.

THERAPIST: What worries do you have about your Dad?

JANET: He works too hard, and he isn't the same since my grandmoth-
            ers died.

THERAPIST: Was he close to both of them?

JANET: Yeah, but especially my mother's mother.

THERAPIST: How is he different?

JANET: He's quiet, no fun, never laughs.

THERAPIST: Do you miss that?

JANET: I used to, but I don't anymore.

THERAPIST: How come you don't care anymore?

JANET: It doesn't matter. Ask her—she's the one who's never home.
            If she really cared she would be.

THERAPIST: You mean you're angry at your mother for going back to work.
            How come you're not relieved?

JANET: What?

THERAPIST: You know, she's not there to check up on you.

JANET: I don't want to talk any more. Ask them some questions.

THERAPIST: Who should I ask first?

JANET: I don't care.

THERAPIST: Ted, what have you been thinking while Janet's been talking?

TED: She's just making up a lot of excuses for totally unacceptable
            behavior on her part. I'm not happy because of her behavior,
            and Marjorie and I fight over how best to handle it.

THERAPIST: The deaths of your mother and mother-in-law, your wife's
            returning to work, and Sally leaving for college haven't had
            much of an emotional impact on you, then.

TED: Not that I'm aware of. Why?

THERAPIST: I don't know, I guess with all that stress in such a short period
            of time, I'm a little surprised there hasn't been more emotional
            fallout than just Janet.

TED: Well, my wife has to go into the hospital next week for an
            upper GI series.

This brief segment demonstrates how the therapist, aware of the
many transition times in this family, was able by tracking the accumulated stress through Janet and Ted Washburn to begin to spell out
the emotional process that was feeding into Janet's symptoms. At the
same time he was able to validate the understandable nature of the emotional repercussions.

Stress and the Marital Relationship

High levels of anxiety and emotional arousal in a family are the result of a combination of cluster stress and the premorbid state of that family. Symptoms develop when the amount of stress is beyond the system's ability to dissipate or manage it. The point at which this happens varies from family to family. Some families are so chronically dysfunctional and vulnerable that any stress is enough to send them into a tailspin and produce symptoms. For example, the father's return a few minutes late from work can set off in one or more members a frenzy of worry and thoughts of catastrophe. On the other hand, there are some stresses that are so severe and even catastrophic—the death of a child, for example—that their occurrence in any family, no matter how functional, is enough to produce symptoms.

Stress is a demand that the organism (an individual or a family) must respond to. It raises the levels of anxiety and emotional arousal in the individual and the family system. Once the levels are sufficiently high, it operates in three distinct but related ways to produce symptoms in a marital relationship.

First, stress heightens the vulnerabilities already in the system. This process has been well documented in the literature on children as the symptom bearer—for example, in Minuchin's famous study of the rise and fall of free fatty acid levels in diabetic children in response to stress (Minuchin et al., 1975). The same process results in marital conflict when the marriage is the most vulnerable point in the system.

Second, when anxiety and emotional arousal are high, stress triggers emotional reactivity and automatic behavior. It is very difficult to think things through when one is anxious and the emotions are fully engaged. If one is not free to consider new approaches to a situation, the only behavior available is the reactive, automatic behavior learned long ago, which serves no other purpose than to aggravate an already stressful situation. Then the spiral of reaction and anxiety continues to escalate until symptoms that can confine and organize the anxiety begin to appear.

Third, because people under stress become more needy, whether the need is to be held or just to be left alone, stress ensures a heightening of the expectations that the partners have brought to the marriage. Expectations are the "wish list" with which people approach marriage and their spouses, the acknowledged, unacknowledged, and even unconscious desires that they anticipate marriage will satisfy. Marital therapist Clifford Sager thinks of expectations as the "individual contract" that each partner brings to a marriage without informing the other of all its terms and without even being aware of some of those terms (Sager 1976).

Thus far we have considered the premorbid state of the multigenerational family system and social context as the sources of stress for a marital relationship. We have seen how the premorbid state of the family influences the impact of situational and developmental stress. The genogram, a multigenerational diagram of the family, is the best tool developed to date for organizing these data in a clinically useful way. It is discussed in full in chapter 6. We turn now to a consideration of the dyad and how patterns of interaction within it feed marital conflict.

2

The Marital Dyad:
A Theoretical Overview

OUR conceptual framework for looking at the marital couple is divided into four categories. First we look at the emotional climate that surrounds the couple. Second we look at the ways in which communication, relationship time, and activity together are used to maintain the relationship. Third, we examine aspects of marital fusion, including personal boundaries, the operating styles of emotional pursuers and emotional distancers and the ways they relate to each other, and reciprocal functioning, patterns of functioning in which one spouse functions better when the other functions poorly. Finally we look at the way power and influence are distributed and used in the relationship, approaching this area through a consideration of the major issues around which marital conflict is organized: sex, money, parenting, and in-laws.

The Emotional Climate

The emotional climate that surrounds the marital relationship can be described in terms of safety, temperature, and turbulence. In an atmosphere of safety, people are relaxed and open rather than tense and guarded. There is little threat of an overreactive response or loss of control. It is safe to be oneself, to be vulnerable, to be emotionally open.

The temperature of a marriage can range from frigid to superheated. In severely troubled marriages, temperature extremes often occur in repetitive cycles. When the emotional climate is frigid, family members move rapidly away from one another toward their own private domains within the home. When they infrequently emerge for meals or other family functions, there may be a rapid shift to an overheated, actively conflictual atmosphere, and the family members quickly retreat to their own domains.

Turbulence refers to the presence of active conflict. In an unstable atmosphere, almost any stimulus can bring on marital conflict. In a typical case of a turbulent climate, a couple is seated in a restaurant. The waitress hands both menus to the husband, and he fails to pass one on to his wife. She berates him. The waitress does not return promptly to take their order, and the wife gets in a huff about the service. Her husband attempts to quiet her by yelling at her. She decides to wait in the car and asks for the keys. He moves to oblige but cannot seem to find the keys. She erupts in a boisterous rage and leaves the restaurant.

In dealing with turbulence clinically, the therapist develops a kind of personal radar to pick up the areas of instability and uses it to avoid ill-timed or inappropriate responses.

THE EMOTIONAL CLIMATE IN THE THERAPY SESSION

One goal of therapeutic intervention is to lower the tension and create a safe, warm, and calm climate in the therapy sessions, with the hope that the family will eventually be able to carry that atmosphere over into the home. Among the means of establishing this climate, we have found three to be especially important: (1) the therapist must maintain his or her own emotional stability in the face of shifts in climate; (2) the therapist must connect with both marital partners; and (3) the therapist must work to bring out and neutralize toxic issues.

Maintaining Emotional Stability

At any time during evaluation or treatment, something may be said that will set off a rapid shift in the emotional climate of the therapy session. In the following excerpts, Bill and Dorothy Howard, a couple in their late forties, are in the middle of an evaluation session. All has been calm and reasonable until the therapist asks an apparently benign question about how long they had been married before the conflict between them began.

DOROTHY: We had six years, and it wasn't a peaceful relationship.

BILL: What do you expect?

DOROTHY: Then the animal has to come out, all the nastiness, all the . . . everybody is human.

BILL: You mean you have some statements about the first six years? You can look back and say they weren't a good six years?

DOROTHY: I'm not saying that they weren't a good six years.

BILL: They were a six years that had a few problems.

DOROTHY: What I am saying is that your disposition hasn't changed. It was rotten then, and it still is.

BILL: What?

DOROTHY: He was a lousy bastard.

THERAPIST: Was he born like that, or did his mother make him that way?

DOROTHY: Well, I think she was very difficult when she was young, according to his sister.

THERAPIST: All you gotta do is wait it out. He'll mellow as he gets older.

DOROTHY: Well, I'm not waiting until he is eighty-four years old.

THERAPIST: You're going to change him now?

The therapist attempts to avoid getting caught up in the shift of the emotional climate and to handle it with playful banter. This can be a useful way for the therapist to maintain stability, but the intensity of the shift may make it unwise and even inappropriate to use playful attempts at humor. When an intense flare-up of anger and mutual blaming occurs in a session, the therapist may first give it a chance to burn itself out, observing how each partner handles it. If the conflict appears on the verge of getting out of control, however, the therapist may have to call for a time out and ask one partner to listen while the other one talks, alternating and balancing "air time" between the two. If this technique fails, one spouse may have to be asked to leave for a while, to be given time with the therapist later in the same session. In order to make judgments about how best to proceed, the therapist must develop a tolerance and stability in the presence of intense expressions of affect.

Connecting with Each Spouse

In marital therapy, as in any other effective form of intervention, it is essential that the therapist make a connection with each person from the very beginning. The therapist assumes and maintains control of the climate and flow of the therapy session, listens effectively, interviews creatively, and validates the emotional experience of each of the participants. Another excerpt from the session with Bill and Dorothy Howard demonstrates some of these techniques.

THERAPIST: You think he could be nicer if he really wanted to be?

DOROTHY: Absolutely. I am really convinced of that, I really am, I really feel that.

THERAPIST: Well, if he didn't have the kids to get bugged at you about, what would he get bugged about?

DOROTHY: He can't pick on my weight any more, or my eating habits, because they're together.

THERAPIST: You changed all that for him?

DOROTHY: No.

THERAPIST: You just changed it for you, and he happened to like it?

DOROTHY: Yeah, and he happened to like it. I am not very good at changing things just for him, because he is not pleased even when I do it.

THERAPIST: No matter how you do it, he is not pleased?

BILL: Oh, that's . . . come on, come on.

DOROTHY: Bullshit, then you try something else. You are going to give me a two-week reprieve here, until you start with the cigarettes, and then you are going to start on that.

THERAPIST: Two main complaints about Bill here would be his criticalness of you and the kids, and your being unable to get underneath his expertise to the real him.

DOROTHY: Number one is right. Number two, you might be right, but I haven't ever given it much thought.

THERAPIST: Well . . .

DOROTHY: It went through my mind last week about how much I rely on Bill and his expertise, and how much I need his strength and approval.

In this part of the session, a connection has been made with Dorothy, and she is gaining some self-focus. The same method—process questions and statements by the therapist—can be used to connect with Bill and help him form his self-focus.

Bringing Out and Neutralizing Toxic Issues

Money, sex, parenting, and in-laws are all potentially toxic issues in a marriage. When communication on the issue is closed, the tension and anxiety around it may become high, creating a significant impact on the relationship.

Mary and Bert Hazen were a couple in their late thirties. They came to the clinic when the wife, cheered on by her co-workers, decided she had had enough of Bert's abusive behavior. Bert had committed the unforgiveable sin of appearing at Mary's place of business and berating her, in front of several colleagues, for what he considered an outrageous credit card bill. On the surface and in fact, money was a toxic issue for this couple; the overt struggle that went on between them most often centered around it. The covert struggle, however, was linked to Bert's desire for frequent sexual contact and Mary's adept and creative ways of avoiding it. In addition, Bert's father had died twelve months previously, and the emotional impact of his death on both of them was a closed issue.

In order to begin neutralizing these issues and creating a safer climate, the therapist had to establish a hierarchy of the issues, judging which of them the couple could handle with the least distress. On the basis of the clinical presentation of this couple, the therapist chose to approach first the struggle over money. When communication on that had been opened, he proceeded to talk about Bert's irritability as possibly being linked to the loss of his father, and finally brought to the surface the issue of sex, revealing Mary's part in the problems this couple was experiencing. A more detailed consideration of each of these important issues and how they play a significant part in the treatment of marital conflict is presented later in this chapter.

Maintaining the Marital Relationship

Relationships, like other living structures, will not survive unless time and effort are invested in their care. The marital relationship is no exception, yet couples routinely ignore the need to nurture their marriages. Even couples who are successful and productive in their professional lives, who recognize the need to invest creativity and time to ensure their occupational and social success, will admit that they make little effort to maintain their relationships. It seems to be an automatic human reflex to expect one's spouse to make one happy. Naive as this expectation is, each marriage does in fact have a division of investment and responsibility for making the relationship work. The more functional the relationship, the more that investment and responsibility are equally distributed. The less equally distributed they are, the greater is the chance for marital conflict or for dysfunction in one spouse. Sometimes neither spouse is doing much to nurture the relationship, and this too is a harbinger of trouble. Clinically it is always useful to help couples evaluate and improve the effort each is expending on the relationship.

In studying the process of nurturing the marital relationship, we have found that effort is best expended on two areas: (1) *communication* of both factual information and the personal thoughts and feelings that might be categorized as "self-disclosure," and (2) improving the quality and quantity of *relationship time and activity together.*

COMMUNICATION

Let us look at John and Betty Tracy, a couple in their late thirties, seated in the therapist's office. Betty sits alone on a couch built for two, while John occupies the chair most distant from the couch. John stares out the window, legs crossed, his arms folded tightly across his chest. The look on Betty's face clearly expresses her anxiety and hurt. In all this, John and Betty are engaged in nonverbal communication. As the therapist begins to probe the process that brought them in, he asks for information, which John provides, though with an astonishing economy of words. This is an example of one type of verbal communication, *information exchange.* Betty speaks of her hurt and anger at John, another kind of verbal communication, called *self-disclosure.*

Let us observe another example of communication as John and Betty are about to begin Sunday dinner with their two children. John is watching television, and he comes promptly but glumly when Betty calls him to the table. Sally, aged thirteen, is in her room and has to be called three times before she comes. John Jr., aged eight, is outside playing and rushes into the dining room as soon as he is called. He begins talking nonstop to anyone who will listen (and no one really does) about the soccer game he was having with friends. Betty nervously begins to serve the dinner and spills gravy on the tablecloth. John looks at her with disgust but says nothing. Betty scolds Sally for her slowness in coming to the table. It is obvious that more is being communicated in these scenes than just what is said.

Communication is a very broad topic. Our clinical experience has led us to concentrate on five aspects of marital communication that we have found to be crucial to our clinical model:

1. The degree of openness in the verbal communication around toxic issues
2. The type of verbal communication the couple engages in: whether

they limit themselves to information exchange or whether they engage freely in self-disclosure

3. The character of the verbal communication: the degree to which it is critical, laudatory, or affectionate
4. The credibility of the verbal communication: each spouse's trust in the truth of the other's communication
5. Nonverbal communication: especially tone, facial expression, and body posturing.

Open and Closed Communication

The degree of openness in a couple's communication is best determined by tracking their ability to exchange information and discuss their thoughts and feelings about toxic issues. Every family, and every marriage, has its toxic issues—that is, emotionally charged issues or topics that provoke intense emotional reactions from family members. These issues vary from family to family, from couple to couple, and couples vary in how they communicate about them. Some people, whom we describe in chapter 5 as *emotional pursuers,* handle toxic issues by talking about them over and over again in a somewhat ritualized manner. The issues never become closed off, but the emotionality surrounding them is never dealt with. This type of pseudo-open communication about a toxic issue has much the same effect as pouring salt on an open wound: the wound never heals and is the source of constant emotional pain.

Other people, *emotional distancers,* handle toxic issues by closing them over, putting them away in a "safe" compartment. The anxiety about these issues is unacknowledged but always present below the surface. The tension created often triggers displaced conflict in the relationship or emotional dysfunction in one of the spouses.

What issues become toxic in a marriage depends on the family background and individual history of each spouse. For example, one wife found it difficult even to inform her husband about the medical appointments of their seriously ill child: the fact that her husband had given her all the responsibility for dealing with the child's illness, never accompanying them to the clinic or speaking to the doctors himself, had made her so angry and resentful that she could not even share information with him about the child's ongoing care. Another husband confided to the therapist that he had been afraid to "open up his insides" to anyone, including his wife, lest such intimate self-disclosure make him vulnerable to a recurrence of the Chron's disease (ileitis) from which he had been in remission since his senior year in college.

Types of Verbal Communication

The two types of communication we are most concerned with are information exchange and self-disclosure. Both are important in a functioning marriage.

A relationship begins with an initial exchange of information between the principals. A young man meets a young woman at a party. Initially they exchange a series of nonverbal courting behaviors that communicate that the interest is not one-sided but mutual, and they then begin a verbal exchange of information. Information exchange continues over time and leads to a proposal that they have dinner together. Activities undertaken together foster a stability in the relationship which, reinforced by continued success in information exchange, eventually creates a climate in which self-disclosure becomes safe and appropriate.

This second step—self-disclosure—initiates a process of serious emotional investment in expectations of each other. Self-disclosure is the beginning of trust; it involves risk-taking and creates a vulnerability to disappointment and hurt.

Information exchange and self-disclosure continue to be interwoven in any relationship as long as the bonding remains intact. The better a marital relationship is functioning, the more open and fluid is the information exchange and the more likely that self-disclosure will consist of genuine thoughts and feelings, delivered in a way that enables the partner to understand and respect them without feeling threatened by them.

Bob and Karen Denton, a professional couple in their late forties, provide an example of the clinical usefulness of these ideas. Bob and Karen were able to communicate relatively openly about many of the things in their lives that required a simple exchange of factual information. There were, however, several toxic issues that invariably compromised even simple information exchange; religion, Bob's analyst, and Karen's commitment to a painting class appeared to be the most toxic. When these topics came up, as they sometimes had to, Bob acted depressed and confused and had difficulty finding words, while Karen became furious and started screaming.

Self-disclosure was considerably more compromised with these two than information exchange, but it was not entirely closed over. Bob had been in analysis for many years and had an ideological commitment to openness, and Karen was temperamentally inclined to self-revelation and expected it from Bob. This combination sometimes worked, but the usual pattern was that in the middle of a conversation Bob's voice would trail off; he would lose his train of thought, forget what he was going to say, and in general look depressed and dysfunctional. Karen's "self-disclosure" would often be criticism of Bob, whose pained silences infuriated her. Most of their attempts at self-disclosure therefore ended in acrimony and bitterness.

Attempts to attain openness and honesty of communication, especially of personal thoughts and feelings, are fraught with potential difficulty. Much of what gets passed off as openness and honesty in a relationship is either a critical emotional reaction or a demand for disclosure so that it can be picked apart. Functional openness and honesty, in the form of sincere expression of personal thoughts and feelings without blame or a demand for reciprocation, take a lot of work. Without feelings of tenderness, especially about those characteristics of others that are most difficult to tolerate, openness and honesty can quickly deteriorate into blaming and criticism.

The Character of Communication

All marital communication usually contains some mixture of affectionate, laudatory, and critical components. The proportions of that mixture, and specifically how much is criticism, are important to the overall picture of a dysfunctional marriage.

Criticism increases distance, feeds bitterness, and dampens libidinal impulses. It often represents the external expression or projection of hurt and anger. Criticism can take both *explicit* and *implicit* forms.

Explicit criticism is relatively easy to identify. "You're frigid" and "I wish you wouldn't tell the same stories every time we go to a party" are explicitly critical statements. Implicit criticism can appear in many guises, including withdrawal and withholding of sex or companionship.

Cultural background and individual temperament determine whether criticism is expressed explicitly or implicitly. Some cultures disapprove of explicitness; it is the norm to keep emotions and criticism implicit. In other cultures, however, openness and explicitness are valued, and a person who is closed and expresses feelings only implicitly is seen as deviant and unfeeling.

The concepts of *emotional pursuer* and *emotional distancer*, which will be elaborated in chatper 5, are relevant to understanding criticism in communication. The emotional pursuer tends to make criticism explicit while the emotional distancer prefers to keep it implicit. Any attempt to force the emotional distancer to become explicit is likely to have the unintended effect of closing off communication even further.

Jeanne and Walter Warren, a couple in their late forties with one son, aged twelve, presented for treatment of marital conflict after having tried three previous therapists. Walter was Jewish, and Jeanne had been raised a Baptist but no longer practiced. It was clear from the first session that certain subjects, notably the religious training of their son, could not be raised without resulting in intensely emotional conflict.

Levels of criticism in this couple's communication were extremely high. In fact, it appeared that they had reached the point where they equated communication with criticism. Walter's criticisms of Jeanne tended to be implicit; for example, Jeanne perceived as hostile and critical his habit of withdrawing from certain conversations by losing his train of thought. Jeanne's criticisms of Walter were much more explicit, though couched in terms of constructive suggestions. Both were so unhappy that most of their verbal and nonverbal communication conveyed their dissatisfaction with the relationship.

Credibility

In the absence of credibility, much of what is communicated in a marriage becomes irrelevant. In general, the more severe the marital conflict, the lower the levels of credibility in the marriage. But we have been surprised by some striking exceptions to this rule. One or both people in a very conflictual marriage may claim, "He has never lied to me" or "I trust her completely and am inclined to believe anything she tells me."

Jeanne and Walter Warren, in spite of the severe impairment of their communication, had high credibility with each other. Both reported that lying or cheating had never been part of their lives, and they seemed somewhat puzzled when the therapist asked questions about credibility. Although the therapist must take such reports with a certain amount of skepticism when there is so much dysfunction in a couple's communication, Jeanne and Walter's sense of high credibility was a favorable prognostic sign.

By contrast, Jane Samuelson told her therapist that she couldn't trust her husband "as far as she could see him." He had been having an affair with a coworker, had promised many times to give it up, and had assured Jane that he had given it up, but she repeatedly discovered that the affair was still going on. This lack of credibility was a negative prognostic sign.

Metacommunication

Metacommunication refers to the unspoken message tied to a verbal communication or expressed in nonverbal behavior such as facial expression, tone of voice, and body posturing. An example of the former is the classic bedtime statement, "I have a headache." Here the not-too-disguised message is "I'm not interested in sex." An example of the latter is seen in the case of John and Betty, described earlier. John's sitting in the far corner of the office, half turned away, arms and legs folded, communicated clearly at least part of his attitude toward Betty and her wish to be in therapy.

The therapist must develop an ability to pick up and read those communications. They can enrich one's understanding of how conflict develops in marriage and can also be used clinically by being made explicit to the couple during the course of therapy. It is important to develop clinical judgment and a sense of timing about making interventions around nonverbal communication, however. Earlier in the development of family therapy, when the study of body language was at its peak, confrontational tactics concerning it were overused.

RELATIONSHIP TIME AND ACTIVITY TOGETHER

"Don't tell me how much you love me; tell me how much time you have for me." Time is perhaps the most important currency in relationships in general, and time and sexual compatibility are the two most important currencies in the marital economy.

Two kinds of time are important to the marital relationship: activity together—time spent in some shared activity such as going to a movie or washing the car—and what we call relationship time—time spent working on the relationship by "being there" for each other and interacting on a personal level.

Two extremes are often encountered in dysfunctional marriages. At one extreme, the partners spend little if any relationship time together, and their activity-centered time is minimal. There are no shared interests, and the couple is so reactive to each other that time spent together is unpleasant. At the other extreme, the spouses are constantly together, clinging to each other and allowing no separate interests or activities. Such a couple is usually moving away from productivity, avoiding conflict with others outside the marriage, and in effect overdoing the function of marriage as a refuge and a haven. In more functional marriages, the couple finds a balance between common interests and separate interests. Each partner is able to leave the other and live a life outside the marriage and then return to derive comfort and pleasure from the company of his or her spouse.

Joseph and Alice Weston, a couple in their early thirties and married for eight years, had no children. They came for therapy complaining that their marriage was "dying": they seemed to have less and less in common and were growing away from each other at a steady and disturbing rate.

They were spending less time with each other and investing more time in separate interests and activities.

In the time they did spend together, there was a significant difference between activity together and relationship time. Although the quantity of activity together was relatively small, the quality of it was good. Relationship time was a dramatically different story. Alice always initiated these times, while both of them initiated activity together. Alice complained that during relationship time Joseph got restless almost immediately and always seemed to find a reason to cut it short. He agreed with Alice's perceptions and gave as the reason for his behavior that these "hanging-out" times frequently ended in a fight.

When asked by the therapist how their time spent together had changed over time, the couple's response was eager: "That's the whole point! It was nothing like this at the beginning!" They went on to describe the first two or three years of their marriage as a time when they shared an intense togetherness. There were phone calls to one another during the day; every problem was discussed in some depth; neither ever went anywhere without the other. As they both began to grow in their jobs and developed separate social networks through work, they missed their former togetherness, but they resented being corralled back into it. This resentment increased the distance between them and made it more difficult to spend time together, especially when there was no activity to be the focus of their attention.

Fusion

The degree of marital fusion is one of the most important variables in the genesis and course of marital conflict. Fusion, as we use it in this model, has its roots in the work of Murray Bowen (1957) and Thomas Fogarty (1977). Fusion is the opposite of differentiation. It can best be understood by considering its components: personal boundaries, the styles of emotional pursuers and distancers and the way they move together, and reciprocal emotional functioning.

PERSONAL BOUNDARIES

When we speak of boundaries in a relationship, we mean the point at which one partner interacts with the other. A boundary is not a rigid cell wall but a membrane of varying degrees of permeability. The notion of such a membrane is suggested by two consistent clinical observations: (1) marriage partners give different degrees of access to personal emotional space, and (2) patterns of affinity and repulsion occur reactively between spouses as they go through alternating cycles of connection and distance.

This concept of boundary is closely tied to the distinction between emotional pursuers and emotional distancers. The emotional pursuer in a low-stress environment has a personal boundary that is relatively open to the sharing of personal thoughts and feelings and allowing access to his or her inner world. In times of high stress, the emotional pursuer may well have an overly permeable boundary, inviting others into his or her personal space almost at random while spilling anxiety and emotional upset on anyone within reach. (An exception occurs under extreme stress, when the pursuer may reverse movement, retreat to an island of invulnerability, and close up emotionally.)

The emotional distancer in a low-stress environment is also relatively open. Access to his or her inner world is possible but limited to a select few. Under high stress, even the select few are shut out. Again, however, there is an exception at the extreme. For example, when an emotional distancer has been left by his wife, the tightly sealed membrane at his personal boundary may involuntarily burst, and with a rush of emotion long-held personal thoughts and feelings will pour out almost uncontrollably. Interestingly, however, as the emotional distancer regains stability after such an occurrence, the memory of the event is lost, and there is no recall of what was said.

These two kinds of personal boundary greatly influence the kinds of connections and repulsions that occur when they meet in a marriage. The semiautomatic, emotional interaction at the boundary is the essence of fusion. We believe it is best understood in terms of operating styles and reciprocal functioning.

PURSUER AND DISTANCER STYLES

A person's operating styles are determined by the individual's constitutional temperament as it is shaped by the family of origin and by the marital relationship. The key components of operating styles are:

1. Affinity for relationship time (pursuer) vs. affinity for alone time and/or activity together (distancer)
2. Expression of affect and of personal thoughts and feelings (pursuer) vs. avoidance of them (distancer)

3. Relatively nonselective permeability of personal boundaries (pursuer) vs. overly selective permeability (distancer)
4. Fast vs. slow personal rhythm. The pursuer moves through life at extremes of high speed and dead stop, while the distancer is more deliberate.

These characteristics have been organized into the descriptive categories of the emotional pursuer and the emotional distancer. Although everyone has a predominant operating style, a person's style can vary from one relationship to another and from one issue to another. For example, a wife may be an emotional pursuer with her husband and son and at the same time an emotional distancer from her mother and from her lover in an extramarital affair.

When one spouse operates as a pursuer while the other operates as a distancer, their complementary behavior patterns to a certain extent provide a balance and stability to the relationship. In a low-stress environment, when the spouses are functioning fairly well, the pursuer's energy and intense emotionality toward the relationship provide a counterpoint to the distancer's cool, logical steadiness. The impatience of the pursuer provides impetus, and the reliability of the distancer provides staying power to accomplish the shared tasks of the relationship. The emotional personalism of the pursuer fills a perceived lack in the distancer's life, and the distancer's calm reasonableness is a reassuring check on the pursuer's impulsiveness.

Pursuit and distance thus operate in a satisfactory balance in which both partners can be comfortable. The pursuer is usually the first to notice when distance is becoming too great and acts to narrow the distance and keep the connection. The distancer acts as a kind of governor to ensure that the relationship does not heat up too much and that boundaries are respected.

When stress rises and produces a critical level of tension and emotional arousal in the family, however, the very characteristics of operating styles that provided the balance become the stimuli for escalating cycles of reaction in the relationship. Instead of balance and stability they create conflict. These behavior patterns can be tracked in a series of steps that we call the *interactional sequence.*

THE INTERACTIONAL SEQUENCE

It has been our clinical observation of conflictual marriages that movements for closeness and distance between husband and wife follow a

TABLE 2–1

The Interactional Sequence

	The Emotional Pursuer	The Emotional Distancer
Step 1	Moves toward the distancer	Moves away, usually toward objects
Step 2	Pursues the distancer intensely	Distances more intensely
Step 3	Tires of pursuit, moves away from the distancer, in reactive distance	Moves tentatively toward the pursuer, then away
Step 4	Attacks the distancer, defending self	Attacks the pursuer, defending self
Step 5	Remains at a fixed distance, not moving toward distancer	Remains at a fixed distance, not moving toward pursuer

predictable sequence of steps. The five steps in the sequence are shown in table 2-1. Let us see how this sequence occurs in a couple in which the wife is the emotional pursuer and the husband the emotional distancer.

Step 1 is marked by the introduction of significant stress, such as several transition times occurring simultaneously. Both spouses react by moving in the direction of restoring their own levels of internal emotional comfort, becoming more like themselves: the wife as pursuer moves toward her husband, the distancer, for emotional connection in an attempt to restore her inner calm, while the husband moves away toward objects and activity, also in an effort to restore inner calm.

In step 2 of the sequence, the response with which each spouse tries to restore his or her own calm has the unintended but completely predictable effect of raising the anxiety and upset in the other. At the very moment when the pursuer needs connectedness more than ever, her spouse is distancing even more than usual. Just when the distancer needs to be left alone to calm down, he sees his wife coming at him spilling prodigious amounts of anxiety and emotion. This pattern creates additional anxiety for both spouses, raises their level of emotional arousal, and intensifies still further their emotional reactivity to one another. The cycle of pursuit and distance intensifies even more.

The first and second steps in this sequence happen over and over again in most marriages. As stresses come and go, whether singly or in clusters, the cycle repeatedly begins, intensifies, and subsides. After each episode the couple may reestablish a stable connection in the dyad, or triangulation may produce a stabilizing effect. If the stress and anxiety remain high, however, and this pattern recycles more and more rapidly, the disappointment, anger, and hurt begin to accumulate. Eventually the emotional pursuer tires of moving forward for connection with only limited success, feels a loss of self-respect, and begins to withdraw. The anger and resentment intensify and build toward bitterness. This movement of withdrawal into what we call *reactive distance* is step 3. When it occurs, the emotional distancer, sensing the shift, is provoked into a reactive pursuit of his wife. He moves toward her, asking "What's wrong?" The typical response from the emotional pursuer is "Nothing."

At this point, the emotional pursuer, still in reactive distance, can respond to her husband's pursuit in one of two ways. She may be so thrilled that she finally has his attention that she moves back toward him, almost immediately closing off most of her distance. This movement relieves the tensions and narrows the emotional distance, but it represents a return to the baseline without any new awareness of what has happened or any increase in their ability to cope with stress. The interactional sequence is now primed for more severe escalation when next it recycles.

If the emotional pursuer does not close off the distance in response to the emotional distancer's first move, the other likely response is to take refuge behind a wall of hurt, to communicate to the distancer that his attention and interest are too little and too late, and to attack him with a wave of old and new criticism about his coldness, indifference, and lack of caring. If the emotional distancer responds to this attack with his own counterattack of criticism, the couple has moved to step 4. At this point in the sequence, the reactive pursuit and reactive distancing are so rampant that it is difficult to tell who is the pursuer and who is the distancer. In fact, the therapist's difficulty in distinguishing between them is a marker for this step in the interactional sequence.

When the spouses have been worn out by the attack-counterattack posture, or when the emotional distancer moves away, often saying "I don't know what you want from me," the sequence moves to step 5: a fixed distance occurs in which there are no attempts at resolution, and over time anger and resentment are replaced by emotional numbness and indifference. Phrases like "I'm numb," "I don't feel anything anymore," and "I just don't care anymore" are the markers for this step in the sequence.

It is relatively easy to discover where in this interactional sequence a couple is located. Steps 4 and 5 are the most immediately evident. In the first interview with William and Anne Gorman, the therapist was hard-pressed to control the bickering and criticism with which the couple attempted to provide information. Both spouses were sullen and resentful, tossing angry accusations at one another and bitterly defending themselves. By contrast, Arthur and Michelle Friedrichs had little to say. They both described themselves as having no hope for their relationship, and Michelle said that she was frightened by the fact that she didn't care anymore about Arthur or about their marriage. William and Anne were in step 4 of the interactional sequence; in their intense conflict it was difficult to tell who was the pursuer and who was the distancer. Arthur and Michelle, on the other hand, were in step 5, as evidenced by their statements of numbness and indifference.

If steps 4 and 5 are ruled out, the couple can be asked questions that differentiate between steps 1, 2, and 3. The answers should clarify whether the present movement in the relationship continues or intensifies a long-standing pattern of pursuer moving toward distancer (steps 1 and 2) or whether the present movement represents a change that began when the pursuer got fed up and pulled back into a reactive distance (step 3). The former was the case with Tom and Yolanda Wallace. From the very first interview, Yolanda spoke of her frustration and anger at Tom's long punitive silences and at her own willingness to do anything at all to get him to speak to her. By contrast, Ken Carpenter made the initial call for therapy for himself and his wife and said in the first interview that he had had a hard time persuading Judith to come. Judith announced that she was fed up with doing all the work in their relationship and that for several months she had been too angry and resentful to try further. Tom and Yolanda were at step 2, and Ken and Judith were at step 3 in the interactional sequence.

RECIPROCAL FUNCTIONING

Over time, people can come to depend on the way their marital partners operate. Becoming dependent on the strengths of one's spouse can cause those same abilities to atrophy or fail to develop in oneself. In time of crisis, if one of those abilities is called upon, nothing is there to respond, and the dependence on the other to fill that void is further intensified. A simple example is the marriage in which one spouse handles all the financial affairs of the household, and the other "can't even balance the checkbook." This increasing interdependence builds to the point where functioning becomes reciprocal: when one spouse functions well, the other functions poorly. The reciprocity may move back and forth like a seesaw, or it may become relatively fixed. The fixed states produce the most emotional dysfunction.

A clear example of reciprocal functioning and of how that reciprocity can shift over time can be found in most marriages in which one spouse is alcoholic. Very often the nonalcoholic spouse overfunctions in many areas of the family's life. When the husband is the alcoholic, for instance, the wife performs all parenting, household, and sometimes even economic tasks for the family, while her husband underfunctions in most if not all of these areas. If and when the alcoholic husband stops drinking, joins AA, and begins to raise his level of functioning, his wife often becomes depressed. The reciprocity thus shifts, as he becomes the functioning partner.

The following vignette provides a more subtle example. Sarah Blackston, a woman in her forties in treatment for mild depression, described a day she had recently spent. She had taken the day off from work, gone shopping in the city with friends, had a facial, and returned home. After supper, she took a long bath and got into bed with a book she had been looking forward to reading. She felt wonderful. Then she heard her husband, returning home late from the office, come into the house and start to climb the stairs. At once she could feel the anxiety that emanated from him. He came into the bedroom looking glum, and Sarah asked him what was wrong. "Nothing," he replied. She became anxious now and pressed him to tell her what was wrong. He avoided her at first. Finally he sat on the edge of the bed and poured out his anger and frustration at his boss and several colleagues, who had made his day miserable. He then slipped under the covers and fell peacefully asleep, while Sarah, no longer feeling wonderful, lay staring into the darkness, her insides churning about her husband's boss.

Bringing out a couple's reciprocal functioning is therapeutically important, because by learning about the process they are caught up in people see hope for change. Understanding the way reciprocal functioning swings back and forth over time can validate the emotional experience of the spouse who is currently underfunctioning and can sometimes serve to motivate an attempt at change. It is the one who is overfunctioning, however, who has the easiest time changing his or her part in the process.

Major Issues in Marital Conflict

The first three parts of this chapter have dealt with processes that play an integral part in the genesis and maintenance of marital conflict. Most often, however, marital discord presents clinically organized around a particular issue. These conflictual issues must be dealt with effectively by the therapist in order for the underlying process in the marital relationship to change. There are many such issues, but we have found four to be most prominent: sex and money—the issues of power and control—and parenting and in-laws—the issues of influence.

SEX

Efforts at attaining dominance in a relationship may be overt and explicit—one partner may demand that the other do or not do something —or covert and implicit—one silently withholds something of value to coerce the other into behaving in a certain way or to punish the other for a perceived or real injury. These efforts are often played out in the sexual lives of married people. One spouse will complain about the sex in the relationship—its frequency, timing, content, or location—and the other will be defensive. Very often one of these themes will be used by the complainer and another by the defender.

One husband complained about frequency: "I need sex at least once a day, while I'm sure my wife thinks once a month is too much." His wife defended herself by using timing: "I can't be expected to turn on a switch at 11 P.M. when the rest of the day has been hell. Why can't he ever approach me in the morning?" Sometimes the complaint is about content —the nature of the sexual activity each spouse is interested in. One wife said, "He has no interest in foreplay; he just wants to get in and out; slam, bam, thank you ma'am." Complaints about where sex takes place usually come up when one spouse is critical of the other's predictability. One man said, "She always wants it in bed, under *clean* sheets. I'd like to go outside or on the kitchen floor, or any place. She's never spontaneous." A typical defense involves bringing up aspects of the spouse that are not a part of sex: "How can I make love with a man who never takes a bath?" or "Who wants to be close to someone who has been such a shrew?"

It is safe to assume that the complainer is the sexual initiator and that the defensive one is the withholder. The therapist can then begin the assessment and intervention around initiation and withholding or lack of interest. The timing of intervention depends on the intensity and duration of the conflict. When a couple has been fighting bitterly about sex for twenty years, therapy directed at the sexual problem will fail unless a great deal of groundwork is first done to reduce the reactivity and bitterness. After that has been done, or where the conflict is less intense in the first place, a simple pursuer-distancer experiment may reveal more of the conflictual process, increase self-focus, and begin movement toward resolution.

The protocol for this type of experiment depends on whether there is a split between emotional pursuit and sexual pursuit (one spouse is the emotional pursuer and the other is the sexual initiator) or a convergence of both in one partner. In both cases the sexual pursuer is asked to put no sexual pressure on the spouse, and the sexual distancer is asked to take responsibility for the couple's sexual life. When the sexual pursuer is also the emotional distancer, he is asked to initiate nonsexual contacts with the spouse.

In the following example the husband was the emotional distancer and the sexual initiator, and the wife was the emotional pursuer and the sexual withholder. The goal of the experiment for the husband was to learn how to move toward his wife with affection, tenderness, interest, and caring, not just with sexual demands. The goal for the wife was to increase the responsibility she took for the sexual activity in the relationship and for her own sexual arousal and gratification as well.

Eric and Sylvia Rollins were in their late thirties and had been married for twelve years when they came for therapy, with sexual problems as the primary complaint. Eric, a lawyer, had been made a partner in his firm two years earlier, and Sylvia had been a homemaker for most of their married life. She had returned to work sixteen months before they came in. They had two children, a girl of ten and a boy of eight. In the course of the evaluation it became clear that Eric was an emotional distancer who had been physically absent a great deal of the time because of professional and civic commitments but that he was an intense sexual pursuer. Sylvia's pattern of withholding sex began shortly after they were married. Eric described her as "frigid" with an "abnormally low interest in sex." Sylvia defended herself by saying that it was impossible to be interested in sex with him because she was so angry about his lack of involvement with her and the children.

Prior to therapy Eric was initiating sex four or five times a week. Sex to him always meant intercourse and was always initiated quite late at night. Sylvia turned him down seventy-five percent of the time. When they did engage in intercourse, usually because she wanted to avoid an argument, he had no trouble reaching orgasm, but she had never had one in her life. Eric was very preoccupied with Sylvia's lack of arousal and would barrage her with questions during and after intercourse: "Does this feel good? Can you feel this? Are you getting excited? Where are you?" Both of them would end up frustrated, angry, and emotionally depleted.

The process was brought out during the evaluation, and the therapist had no trouble getting each of the partners to see that it was not working. He coached Eric to stop pursuing Sylvia, and although Eric understood that the kind of spotlight he put on her about sex was not helpful, he had a great deal of difficulty pulling back. In order to do so he had to understand the function that sex served for him. By asking questions like "What would happen if you could never have sex again?" the therapist brought out that sex served as a way to keep Eric's anxiety down, to reward him for staying in control all day in his work, and to keep him feeling connected to the human race. It was clear that if Eric were going to pull back from his sexual pursuit of Sylvia, he would need other ways to relax and to feel connected to people. Developing a range of options in both areas was an important part of his work in therapy. For example, the therapist encouraged him to move toward his children, taking more responsibility for their care and developing closer relationships with each of them. Together the therapist and Eric also considered ways that Eric could move toward Sylvia that were more loving than sexual.

One of the most difficult aspects of working with someone in Eric's position is that he will often comply in pulling back initially, but only as part of a strategy to get his wife over "her problem." If she does not move in sexually, he becomes impatient and angry and resumes his pursuit. We alert people to the probability that this will occur and then work with them through those periods to get their expectations in line with the reality of the situation.

In order to increase the amount of responsibility that sexual distancers take for their own sexuality, we try to awaken them to what they are missing and to the importance of approaching sex for themselves rather than for the relationship or for the partner. The work with Sylvia toward this goal had a threefold focus: sexual programming she had received from the extended family and the culture, her sexual awareness, and the relationship patterns in the marriage that were reinforcing her sexually distant behavior. It is important to note that a significant amount of work was done to decrease Sylvia's level of bitterness before she was encouraged to tackle the sexual issue.

The following dialogue is from a consultation with Sylvia as she was beginning to focus on her sexual awareness.

THERAPIST: If you were to imagine that your sex life was very satisfying and that you got a lot of pleasure out of it, what would it be like?

SYLVIA: Well, I guess spontaneity would be a part of it. I would like to be more spontaneous. I would like it to be something I didn't have to think so much about—just to be a normal part of life.

THERAPIST: Do you have a picture of what "normal" would mean? For instance, how frequently would you want sex?

SYLVIA: Well, I don't know. Maybe two or three times a week.

THERAPIST: Who would you want to do the initiating?

SYLVIA: It would be either, I guess. I guess it wouldn't always necessarily end up in intercourse, either.

THERAPIST: Which it does now?

SYLVIA: Yes. It would be a situation where if it didn't end in inter-course, that wouldn't be any big deal.

THERAPIST: Okay. So you would like it to be two or three times a week, taking turns with initiating it, and you want other options besides intercourse. Do you have some sense of the kind of sex you would want other than intercourse? Would you want part of it to be oral, for instance?

SYLVIA: Yes. And it would include having sex someplace other than the bed, the bedroom.

THERAPIST: So that would be a part of the spontaneity, too?

SYLVIA: Yes, definitely.

THERAPIST: You wouldn't always have to be in the same place. How about the timing? When would it happen?

SYLVIA: Well, it wouldn't always be 11 P.M. Sometimes when my kids are at school, if Eric were not working, or something like that. Or maybe on vacations, sometime other than late at night.

THERAPIST: And when you're actually involved in it, give me some sense of what you picture yourself doing.

SYLVIA: I would like a mixture of sometimes being aggressive and sometimes being passive.

THERAPIST: Okay, if all this were true, do you think you'd lack ideas, or do you see yourself as a creative person?

SYLVIA: Um, I think I could come up with a couple of ideas.

THERAPIST: Let's leave Eric out of this for a minute and talk about what else would be happening sexually if you didn't feel so shut down.

SYLVIA: I don't know. Maybe I'd read erotic books and watch X-rated movies.

THERAPIST: Is that something you've done before?

SYLVIA: I've never seen an X-rated movie, but I might be interested. I'd like to watch it alone sometimes, but I would want to feel comfortable enough with a partner to watch it together.

THERAPIST: Would masturbation be a part of your life in this picture you're creating?

SYLVIA: It isn't now, but it might be. I think it probably would be.

THERAPIST: How much would you like to see this picture become a reality?

SYLVIA: There are times when I've felt very disappointed and very cheated. Generally I would say I recognize it as a part of my life that is not going well, and I do want to see that change.

In this session they went on to explore Sylvia's inability to have orgasms, her hopes for her daughter's sexuality, her theories about her mother's, and the impact that her bitterness toward Eric had on her own sexuality. In the ongoing therapy the therapist continued to help her define the kind of sex life she wanted and supported her efforts to reach it, suggesting that she read *For Yourself,* by Lonnie Barbach (1975), which spells out a method for nonorgasmic women to learn to have orgasms. This book is an excellent resource for any woman who sets out to take more responsibility for her sexuality. We have also frequently suggested that men read it as well as Barbach's next book, *For Each Other* (1983), in order to increase their understanding of their partners and of themselves.

In the ideal outcome for a case like this one, where the conflict has been organized around sex, both partners would be (1) informed about sexuality in general and about their own sexuality in particular; (2) aware of how their culture and the extended family have programmed them regarding sex and of how that programming affects their performance and desire; (3) able to initiate sexual activity, willing to take responsibility for their own sexual arousal and gratification, and responsive to the desires of their partners within the limits of what they consider acceptable behavior; and (4) committed to weaving the ways that sex functions for them individually into a fabric that would be uniquely theirs and that would provide mutual gratification.

MONEY

The control of money is the other major power issue in the marital relationship. In some situations the same spouse is in control of both the money and the sex. This is not a fair deal, and most often it results in the other spouse becoming dysfunctional. The dysfunction then becomes that spouse's source of relationship power; this phenomenon is dealt with in chapter 5, in the discussion of the dysfunctional spouse. More commonly one spouse controls the money and the other controls sex.

The mutual management of financial assets is one of the primary objectives of the marital partnership. The issue becomes conflictual under four circumstances.

First, one spouse may attempt to leverage the relationship and enforce his or her way of doing things by withholding funds and distorting the financial picture. David Simpson was a successful forty-five-year-old attorney who earned all the money and made all the major financial decisions in the family. Barbara, his wife of twenty-two years, confined her interest and participation in financial affairs to signing the income tax forms once a year. After the last child left home for college, Barbara began taking courses at the local community college, and through meetings at the women's center on campus she came to feel that she should be a more active financial partner. Barbara began to demand to play a bigger part in the family's financial life. David promised to meet with her, but somehow the meeting never took place. A crisis erupted when Barbara received a notice of nonpayment of tuition from the college. David said the check must have been lost in the mail.

Second, one spouse may be irresponsible in keeping track of the couple's assets and spend beyond their means, at the same time criticizing the other for being too conservative financially. Kevin Leary was a forty-two-year-old bank executive and an effective money manager for many of his bank's clients. Within the family, however, he followed the protocol he had learned from his family of origin: every two weeks he handed his entire paycheck over to his wife, Kathleen. She kept the books, managed the checkbook, and made most of the major financial decisions. She tried to involve Kevin, but he was always busy and would break appointments made with her to discuss their personal finances. Kathleen, who did not work outside the home, willingly accepted the job of managing the money. She had always been good with figures and prided herself on her frugal ways. She was frustrated, however, with Kevin's liberal spending. When she would remind him that they could not afford to dine out again that week, he would fly into a rage and accuse her of mismanaging the money. Kathleen absorbed this abuse for a number of years, dutifully trying to find new ways of juggling the money. She would often jokingly refer to herself as a master of "Peter to Paul" economics. The couple ended up in therapy after Kevin, without consulting Kathleen, came home one evening with a new automobile. Kathleen promptly got the checkbook, handed it to Kevin, and resigned as family comptroller.

In a third scenario, new money is inherited or acquired after years of marriage; a wealthy relative dies, or a family business is bought out by a larger company, with a windfall to one spouse. Dick and Fran Anderson met and married three years after each of them had come through a bitter divorce. Dick was a successful corporate executive, and Fran was a junior partner in a local law firm. Five years into the marriage Fran's father died, leaving her a substantial inheritance, including a trust fund income equal to her salary from the law firm. Dick viewed this windfall as an opportunity to enjoy a more lavish life style. A significant part of his income went to the support of his first wife and their two children, who were now in college. Fran's daughter from her first marriage lived with Fran's former husband and was supported by him. Fran looked on the new money as hers. She decided to leave her job and go back to being an artist, a promising career she had left when financial troubles in her first marriage and then the divorce sent her in a more practical direction. Her father had paid her way through law school but had refused to support her beyond that. When

Fran told Dick what she intended to do, he protested loud and long. When she went ahead anyway, he stopped contributing any money to the household. At that point they entered therapy.

The fourth situation leading to conflict is a shift in earning patterns. Bill Elder was a forty-five-year-old fire captain who had retired after twenty-five years of service. He had expanded his house-painting business to make up the difference between his regular and his retirement income. Janet, his wife, had passed her exams as a stockbroker and was busy building a clientele. She had become quite successful in a short period of time and was earning in excess of $90,000 a year. Neither Bill nor Janet had anticipated her success; she was making more than twice his income. They entered therapy, with fights about money as their presenting problem.

In each of these cases money is an important conflictual issue, but it is also a catchall organizing point for numerous other problems that are often unrecognized. The marriage therapist must be knowledgeable about both financial matters and the relationship process that underlies the conflict. Just as one would not try to help a couple resolve sexual difficulties without having a knowledge of human sexuality, one ought to have the same kind of competence when the conflictual issue is money.

The following are guidelines we follow in assisting the resolution of money problems.

1. Money inherited or acquired by a person prior to marriage belongs to that person unless negotiated otherwise before the marriage.
2. Money earned by either spouse during the marriage belongs to both spouses equally unless negotiated otherwise prior to the marriage.
3. Money inherited during the course of a marriage belongs to the spouse who inherited it unless otherwise agreed upon at the time of the inheritance.
4. Children are the financial responsibility of the biological parents, even after divorce whenever possible, and even if one stepparent is quite wealthy.

These guidelines boil down to "what's mine is mine and what's ours is ours." The people involved need to separate the hard financial realities from the relationship problems intrinsic to the emotional process between them.

PARENTING

Couples manage their parenting tasks in different ways. Some are in agreement, sharing one fantasy for their children. These couples get into conflict around parenting only when the children fail to fulfill their dream; then their common effort deteriorates into mutual blaming. In another pattern we see frequently, one parent is overresponsible and overinvolved, and the other is underinvolved and underresponsible. Conflict over parenting in these marriages usually takes one of two forms, though both may occur together. In one, the overinvolved parent, usually the mother, is critical of her distant husband's lack of attention to their child. Her complaint often represents a displaced complaint that her husband is neglecting her. In the other, the underinvolved parent, usually the father, is critical of his child (usually a son) and blames his wife's parenting for the son's shortcomings.

Conflict over parenting in a marriage is best conceptualized as a child-centered triangle and managed clinically in this way. Child-centered triangles and their management are dealt with in detail in chapter 4.

IN-LAWS

The issue of the "in-laws" and the "out-laws" and other extended-family phenomena can be a part of marital conflict from the beginning of the marriage. From the invitation list and the choice of the wedding party to the acceptance or rejection of a new son- or daughter-in-law, family members are potential sources of conflict. The intricacies of these triangles are dealt with in chapter 4, in the section on in-law triangles.

Underlying in-law problems is the struggle for influence. This struggle usually plays itself out in one of three ways.

The extended families may vie for the position of influence over the couple. After two years of marriage, Jim and Ellen McGowan entered therapy with a presenting problem of marital conflict and Ellen's depression. Their initial visit occurred at the end of January, so the therapist inquired about the recent holidays and what involvement there had been with family. Ellen tearfully reported feeling torn between her husband and her mother. Her mother had insisted that they spend Christmas Day with her family at their condominium in southern Florida. Jim insisted that they spend some time with his family and therefore was unwilling to go to Florida. Ellen felt that their problem lay in Jim's inability to deal with his mother's demands that he be with his family every holiday. Jim thought that Ellen's mother was far too pushy and had altogether too much influence over Ellen. Ever since the struggle began in early December, Ellen had been having difficulty sleeping, was not concentrating at work, and often cried. Jim saw all this as manipulative behavior that Ellen had learned from her mother.

To dilute such attempts at influence, the husband and wife may establish substantial distance—often thousands of miles—from their extended families. Tom and Kathy Lynd presented to the clinic with intense marital conflict of two years' duration. They were both from Oregon and had met at the University of California at Berkeley. After graduation both of them sought and obtained employment in New York. They were married on a trip to Canada two years after graduation. They both sent their families postcards from Montreal, announcing the wedding and promising to come west on a visit soon. It was now five years later and they had not made the trip. They had telephone contact with their families on Thanksgiving and Christmas, and Kathy's father had spent the night with them while on a business trip to the East Coast.

Their conflict centered on Kathy's complaint that Tom was cold and distant, and although she had a number of good friends, she felt lonely, as though she didn't belong to anyone. Tom was resentful of Kathy's emotional demands and lack of understanding about his business commitments. During their courtship days he had been impressed by her "independence" and was disappointed that she had turned out to be just another "clingy female." Tom and Kathy are a good example of the marital cocoon, in which two people in flight from what they consider the malignant influence of their families join together to build a mutual refuge, which eventually crumbles under the weight of unrealistic expectations.

Finally, one of the members of the couple may flee from his or her family and join the family of the spouse. Here the channels of influence are clear. Steve and Ann Viner came to the clinic after Ann discovered her husband was having an affair. They had met when Steve was nineteen and Ann seventeen. They were married after Steve's graduation from law school. During their courtship Steve found the warmth and acceptance of Ann's family a welcome contrast to the cold, conflictual climate of his own. His mother's unhappiness and his father's passivity upset him, and he found comfort in the hours he spent with Ann and her family.

Ann was the elder of two girls and enjoyed her family, though perhaps not quite as much as Steve did. Steve became close to his father-in-law; both were sports addicts, and they shared season tickets to football, basketball, and hockey games. All went well until Ann's younger sister, Joan, married Harry. From the time of that wedding Steve had been resentful of the relationship between Harry and their father-in-law. Over time he felt more and more alienated from his wife's family, refused to attend family functions with Ann, and pressured her to stay home with him. Ann refused, and the conflict between them intensified. It wasn't long before

Steve began his affair with an attractive and intelligent coworker who was "more sensitive" to his needs.

In dealing with Steve and Ann, and with most other in-law problems, we follow two basic operating principles. First, each spouse takes responsibility for the relationship with his or her own biological family and works toward a functional connection with them. Second, neither spouse cuts off his or her own family and joins the other's family. To do so creates the risk of becoming "a man without a country," for an in-law child is rarely accepted to the same kind of membership in a family as that of the biological child.

In-laws and other family members as well as outsiders often become involved in triangular relationships with marital couples. In the next chapter, we turn to a consideration of the very important phenomenon of the triangle, inevitably found in cases of marital conflict.

3

Triangles

TRIANGLES and the emotional process that operates within them have long been considered central to marital conflict and are well documented in the family therapy literature (Bowen, 1966; Jackson, 1967; Guerin and Fogarty, 1972; Haley, 1973; Fogarty, 1975; Guerin and Guerin, 1976; Hoffman, 1981; Kerr, 1981; Nichols, 1984). The extramarital affair has been called "the eternal triangle," and triangular relationships have been recognized as significant clinical phenomena since the time of Freud.

Understanding triangles and triangulation in marital conflict is essential to identifying the dysfunctional process in marriage and mapping out appropriate intervention. In this chapter and the next, we will review the nature of triangles and triangulation, discuss how triangles contribute to marital conflict, and then consider a typology of the most common kinds of triangles that occur in marital conflict.

The Nature of Triangles and Triangulation

Our concept of the relationship triangle begins with Bowen's assumption that the emotional process in any dyad is unstable. Like Bowen (1966) and Fogarty (1975), we believe that this instability is tied to people's conflicting needs for autonomy and connectedness. Efforts to meet these two needs simultaneously result in alternating cycles of separation and incorporation anxiety (Bowen 1957). One or both members of the dyad then begin to experience internal discomfort, anxiety, and emotional arousal, and the tension escalates in the relationship itself. At this point the dyad is set up for the formation of one or more triangles as a means of stabilizing the relationship process.

We believe that two basic mechanisms operate in the formation of marital triangles. In the first, the spouse experiencing the most emotional discomfort moves away from the other and connects with a third person as a way of calming his or her upset or gaining an ally in a conflict. For example, a wife upset by her husband's distance may increase her involvement with the children or with one particular child. The second mechanism involves a third person (often a child) who is sensitized either to the intense conflict in the relationship or to anxiety in one spouse. This third person moves in to calm the upset or is caught up in the process and acts out in some way. For example, an older daughter may attempt to mediate intense marital conflict by talking individually to each parent or to calm the parent with whom she has the most influence. Meanwhile, her younger brother may absorb the tension of his parents and handle it by acting out in an antisocial way. The acting-out behavior also serves the function of pulling the parents together to try to solve the common problem of their son's acting out.

There is a distinction between triangles as a relationship structure and triangulation as a relationship process. A triangle is an abstract way of thinking about a structure in human relationships, and triangulation is the reactive emotional process that goes on within that triangle. In any relationship system, there are any number of potential triangles, and the emotional process of triangulation within them can be either dormant or active in varying degrees.

The clinical description of a triangle is the way the three-way relationship looks at a given moment or the pattern to which it regularly returns after temporary realignments. For example, at the time a couple presents for treatment, the triangle with their son may have become relatively fixed so that the mother and the son are overly close and the father is in the distant outsider position. This alignment may occasionally shift, so that there are times when either the mother or the son is in the outside position and the father has some closeness with his son or his wife, but then it shifts back to its usual structure.

Triangulation is the emotional process that goes on among the three people who make up the triangle. For example, in the triangle just described, the father might desire a connection with his son and resent his wife's monopoly of the boy's affections; the mother may be angry at the father's distance and compensate by substituting closeness with her son. The child in turn may resent his father's inattention and criticism and may move toward his mother but at the same time be anxious about his overly close relationship with her. As the emotional process of triangulation moves around the triangle, it can produce changes in the structure of the triangle. For example, the father may try to reduce his loneliness by moving toward his son or his wife, or the son may try to avoid fusion with his mother by distancing toward his peers, causing his parents to draw together in their concern for him.

Thus triangles can shift their structure at any time, and the process of triangulation always has the the potential for motion. As changes occur, demands are placed on the individuals and on the system to realign in a way that ensures the emotional comfort of the most powerful person and preserves the stability of the system. As Bowen (1978) points out, the most uncomfortable person in the triangle may try to lower his or her anxiety or emotional tension by moving toward a person or thing. If that effort is successful, another person becomes the uncomfortable one and will work to become more comfortable.

Triangles and Triangulation in Marital Conflict

The tension and upset of a conflictual marriage inevitably lead to triangulation. The function of the third person in the marital triangle is to allow stability without change, to dilute the tension between the couple, and to create a displaced issue around which the husband and wife can organize their conflict.

Triangles can either intensify marital conflict, organizing the conflict around an external issue or person, as in the classic case of the mother-in-law triangle, or stabilize or cover over marital conflict, as in the case of the extra marital affair before it is discovered. In either case, the triangle serves the function of externalizing the conflict. By fighting over the mother-in-law's interference, a couple may intensify their conflict, but the issues of their own relationship are obscured. By having an extramarital affair, a husband or wife satisfies a need for closeness or sexual satisfaction without dealing with the problems of emotional distance or sexual dysfunction in the marriage.

In clinical work with triangles, it is important first to identify the important triangles that surround the marriage and to assess the intensity of the triangulation in them. The following section and the next chapter present a typology of the triangles most commonly found in marital conflict.

Of the six main types of triangles, two—extramarital affairs and social network triangles—have one member outside the family. Four types occur within the multigenerational family: in-law triangles, triangles with children, stepfamily triangles, and the primary parental triangle, made up of one spouse and his or her parents. In the following section we will consider triangles that go beyond the family. Chapter 4 will deal with triangles within the family.

Triangles Extending Beyond the Family

It is worth noting that triangles that go beyond the family almost always represent externalization of a dysfunctional process going on within the family. The clinician who sees such a triangle can safely assume that it is connected to a triangle or an interlocking set of triangles within the family. The multigenerational family has been unable to contain the reactive emotional process in those internal triangles, and the result is that the process spills out and involves people from outside the system.

THE EXTRAMARITAL AFFAIR

A spouse who is uncomfortable may move toward an affair in an effort to reduce his or her level of discomfort and anxiety by externalizing the process. An affair can have any of several effects on the couple. It can calm the uncomfortable partner without disturbing the other spouse, thus stabilizing the marriage and covering over its dysfunction. But this effect is often temporary and usually ends when the other spouse finds out about the affair. Then the affair itself becomes the central issue between the spouses, again covering over the conflictual process in the marriage that triggered the affair in the first place.

When the affair is an open issue, it is especially important for the therapist to remember the distinction between being part of a relationship process and being responsible for one's own behavior. A spouse who is having an extramarital affair must take responsibility for his or her own behavior and not attempt to excuse it on the basis of preexisting problems in the relationship. On the other hand, both spouses must take responsibility for their parts in the relationship process that preceded the affair.

If the affair is not totally successful in covering over the couple's problems, the couple may present for treatment around other issues with the affair still a secret. The issue of confidentiality then arises if the therapist learns of the affair. An argument can be made for revealing the affair in a conjoint session, but in general we are against doing so. Informing the other spouse of the affair will raise the couple's anxiety at the very point in treatment when reducing anxiety is a major goal. The principal exception to this rule is the case in which that spouse, convinced that something is going on but confronted with constant denial, is becoming severely depressed or even psychotic.

The therapist who learns of an affair faces two important tasks in addition to making a clinical judgment about revealing it. The first is to make clear to the spouse having the affair that the affair must be terminated if progress is to be made in marital therapy. The second is to recognize and validate the pain and sense of loss that that person will experience. These tasks are done in sessions alone.

The extramarital affair raises some of the most interesting and challenging issues encountered in work with marital conflict. One of the authors faced the following situations within a one-year period in her practice. A married woman came alone for therapy to address the fact that unknown to her husband she had been having an affair for seven years. After several months of therapy, she died during emergency surgery, and following her death her distraught husband sought treatment to deal with his loss. His idealization of his wife and of the marriage was interfering with the grieving process and his return to good functioning. In another case the therapist knew that an eight-year-old daughter was the offspring of the wife's lover rather than of her husband. In a third case the therapist was working with two couples who were friends and learned that the wife of one was having an affair with the husband of the other.

Although these cases were particularly dramatic, our approach to treatment even in less dramatic cases is essentially the same. We focus on the following goals:

1. Systematizing the affair by bringing out the part each spouse plays in the underlying process
2. Shifting the behavior of each spouse, not only the one who is having or has had the affair, but also the other spouse
3. Reestablishing trust in the marital relationship.

Our clinical approach to these goals is illustrated in the treatment of Tony and Maria Lapomarda. Maria, a thirty-seven-year-old mother of two boys, aged ten and eight, stated the problem in a straightforward way when she called the Center one week after discovering a letter that Tony, her forty-year-old husband, had written to another woman: "I always thought our marriage was close to perfect. Now I find out he's been having an affair for a year. He's ruined everything." Maria felt that some drastic change had come over Tony, that the man she had been married to for eleven years could not have done this. She said that her husband was willing to come for therapy.

In the initial sessions, the therapist worked to lower Maria and Tony's reactivity by letting them know that she had had extensive experience working with people in their situation, that she was aware that it was a raw, painful time for both of them, and that it would take some time to sort out their problems. She told them she would be working with them in a combination of joint and separate sessions. She stressed that although she could give no guarantee about the way things would work out, they each had a better chance for minimizing the emotional impact of the affair if they made decisions based on a thorough understanding of the parts they each played in their marriage.

The discovery of an affair often sets off a crisis in which ordinary daily functioning suffers severely. By the time they came in, both Maria and Tony were in emotional states that were wreaking havoc with their daily lives. In the early sessions, therefore, the therapist worked to get them to take one day at a time and to make priorities of their daily responsibilities so that they could manage what was essential.

Systematizing the Affair

An immediate task for the therapist working with an extramarital affair is to figure out the current triangulation process. The process with Tony and Maria was fairly typical: she was pursuing Tony for the details of his relationship with his lover, Ellen, and Tony was distancing by moving toward Ellen. All of Maria's movement was toward him. She searched through his drawers, closets, clothes, and car looking for new evidence, and she barraged him with questions about his sexual and emotional relationship with Ellen. She asked him to compare herself and Ellen physically, mentally, and sexually. He would withhold information for a time and then angrily burst out in hurtful detail: "You want to know so badly, well, I'll tell you." After a fight with Maria he would move toward Ellen.

The therapist let them know that both of them would need to change the parts they were playing around the affair if they wanted the situation to improve. Maria would have to stop pursuing Tony for information that only served to deepen her wounds, and Tony would have to stop running from the struggle in his marriage toward his lover. He would have to decide which system he wanted to be in, because his attempt to remain in both was not working.

Once the current process has been brought out, the therapist moves to understand the function the affair is serving in the marriage and the process that led up to the affair. Understanding the affair in systems terms does not mean that people are not accountable for their behavior. Tony was the one having the affair; Maria was not. Yet both were responsible for the state of their marriage. In order to detoxify the affair, which is often seen as the unforgiveable sin, it is important for both spouses to put it in the larger context of their marriage.

An affair is usually a refuge from a relationship problem and from pain in one's personal life. According to Martin Bauman of the University of California Medical School, each partner has engaged in behavior that has removed affect from the relationship. Both partners need to recognize their parts. The "innocent" partner is usually unaware that he or she is involved in a counteraffair that drains the relationship of passion. The counteraffair usually includes excessive involvement in normal everyday activities such as child care, work, and contacts with the extended family, at the expense of time and energy for the relationship. If both parties can accept responsibility, then they can move toward changing the parts they played (Bauman, 1982).

In order to understand the function Tony's affair was serving in the marital relationship, the therapist focused on the state of their marriage prior to the affair. Three relevant factors emerged: Tony's dissatisfaction with his own life, a triangle with Maria's family, and a triangle with the children.

Tony had been dissatisfied and unhappy for about two years. He had begun to take stock of his life just before his thirty-eighth birthday and had not felt comfortable with any part of it. His work as the administrator of a small mental health clinic seemed like a dead end, although he had been given increased responsibilities during his six years there. Financial pressure at home had been building, and he felt that he and Maria never did more than scrape by. It was the first time since they had been married that he had not been taking graduate courses at night. He had always thought that life would be better after he completed his master's degree, that he would have more time with his family, and instead he found that completing school left a big gap. Maria thought that Tony had been somewhat irritable over the past year, but she had been unaware of his emotional state. He had made no real effort to discuss it with her, and she had been busy with the boys and with her part-time job as a computer programmer.

As the therapist explored the fact that Maria and Tony had become so distant over a two-year period that there was no communication around Tony's turmoil, two triangles that had been operative since the early days of their marriage emerged. The first included Tony, Maria, and the boys, with Maria in an overinvolved relationship with the children and Tony in a distant position from all of them. This process had started naturally enough. Tony and Maria were convinced that she had become pregnant on their wedding night. Although the pregnancy was unplanned and both of them were disappointed that they would have the added responsibility of a child so soon, they met the demands in a responsible fashion; for a while Tony worked at two jobs in addition to going to school, and Maria immersed herself in child care. They had a second child eighteen months after the first, and both of them doubled their efforts.

Tony and Maria decided early on to take an apartment in the same building as her parents, who were eager to help out. Five years later they moved into a house in the same neighborhood. This close proximity nurtured the second triangle, in which Maria was overly involved with her family of origin and Tony was on the outside.

The outside position in both these triangles had not been particularly uncomfortable for Tony as long as he was satisfied with his own life. When he became dissatisfied, the outside position was intolerable for him.

The following dialogue occurred in an early session, with both Tony and Maria present, and covered part of the exploration of the extended-family triangle. After some discussion of the triangle with Maria's family, the therapist turns to Tony's passivity in his marriage and challenges him on the amount of creativity he has invested in making it work. This sort of challenge is often helpful in engaging a distant husband in the work of therapy.

THERAPIST: How do you get any companionship or intimacy out of the relationship?

TONY: Well, we used to strain the time, like wringing a washcloth. It wasn't planned. We would just find time when we were alone because everyone was sleeping.

THERAPIST: Did you know what to do with that time?

TONY: We didn't talk. At least I didn't communicate, and now we find very little time for each other.

THERAPIST: Do you consider yourself a creative guy?

TONY: Creative? Yeah, I consider myself creative.

THERAPIST: Are you creative in your job?

TONY: Oh, yes, very much so.

THERAPIST: How much creativity have you invested in the relationship with Maria over the years?

TONY: Maybe 1 percent.

THERAPIST: How much of a yield do you get from 1 percent?

[Tony next describes what he thought his contribution to the marriage was supposed to be. The issue of effort is always important. If each spouse perceives the other as trying, the emotional climate surrounding the relationship is improved.]

TONY: Up until a few years ago I got quite a bit. I was getting more of a return. My idea of putting in, it wasn't deliberate avoidance, my idea of putting in is I was holding two jobs plus going to school, and Maria was working and had the kids.

THERAPIST: You didn't have any time to have a relationship.

TONY: No, we didn't.

THERAPIST: Which one of you made the most effort to try?

MARIA: I think I did. Occasionally sending the kids to my mother and trying to set up some time for us. Not often, though.

[Now the therapist brings out Maria's passivity in the relationship and challenges her explanation of the affair.]

THERAPIST: Did you miss the absence of closeness, the absence of the two of you having a real connection with each other, or did it just seem like that's the way a busy life is, and that's the way it ought to go?

MARIA: I never felt we weren't close, though. It never occurred to me.

THERAPIST: So it felt fine to you?

MARIA: Yeah.

THERAPIST: Are you somebody who needs a lot of intense connection?

MARIA: I feel I need a lot of physical affection, and I felt I was getting it . . . up until . . . There were differences in the way Tony expressed affection from the way my family did. In the morning and in the evening my parents kiss each other. When my father walks in the door, he kisses my mother.

THERAPIST: A ritual?

MARIA: No, meaning it. Tony never did that. At the beginning of the marriage I'd bring that up to him. "Don't I get a kiss goodnight?" All right, so I gave up on that one, too. I figured he has his ways.

THERAPIST: He doesn't send you Hallmark cards? He didn't kiss you?

MARIA: Only now he sends me roses.

THERAPIST: What do you think happened last year?

MARIA: In my view? I think all the stress built up around his job and money.

THERAPIST: But you know, it sounds like your relationship has been atrophying. It's been shrinking for a number of years. You've been kind of going along in a parallel way with one another, doing what you had to do because you're both responsible people, but the degree to which there was any real creativity and investment in the relationship with one another is just kind of . . . You weren't oiling and greasing it, so to speak. You know?

TONY: You know, I've never been the type of person to look back on anything. I never took these theories too seriously, even though I have a master's degree in psychology. I always held it off as something that happens on TV and doesn't happen to real people. And then when I began to have these problems . . . If my father were alive, I truly would have gone to him. And to show you to what extent . . . I'll never forget . . . When I woke up the morning I realized I was fed up, I went to the cemetery and I said, "Why did you die now? I need you now." Because I never really had the chance to relate to him as a man. It was always as a child. I thought in my mind, who would I go to? And I came up empty. I just didn't have anyone to go to.

In this segment, the interlocking extended family triangles that are feeding into the triangle of the affair are beginning to be defined. The mutual passivity of Tony and Maria and their lack of creative effort toward the marriage is spelled out. Finally, Tony's distress over his father's death surfaces.

In short, a significant amount of emotional distance had grown between Tony and Maria over the course of their marriage. They had been able to maintain a working partnership, but there was little companionship and even less intimacy. The affair represented an attempt to ameliorate the discomfort that Tony was experiencing in his outside position in two key triangles—with his children and with Maria's family. It was a solution that did not require the couple to face the inadequacies in their relationship or to struggle to overcome them. As long as the affair remained a secret, Tony could have some of his emotional needs met and

Maria was free to continue a life that was relatively satisfying to her. After the affair was discovered, the problems in their relationship came sharply into focus.

As the process in their marriage was explored during the early stage of therapy, the problem was redefined as one of distance in the relationship, and both Tony and Maria were able to see the ways in which they had contributed to it. They had an intellectual appreciation of this kind of thinking, but it was months before their understanding influenced their behavior in any significant way.

Shifting the Position of Each Spouse

As we have seen, a major goal of therapy in the case of the extramarital affair is to shift the position of the spouse who is having or has had the affair and the spouse who has not. In a session alone with Tony early in the treatment, the therapist helped him to clarify his position in the affair. Spouses who are having affairs have three alternatives: they can give up the affair, they can end the marriage, or they can sit on the fence by continuing the affair and making no decision about the marriage. Tony said he knew he should stop seeing his lover, as he had promised his wife he would, but he was not feeling confident of his ability to stay away from her. Nor was he ready to end the marriage. Yet he agreed with the therapist that it would be impossible to work on the marriage while the affair continued. When the therapist asked him to predict what would happen if he continued the affair, Tony said he thought Maria would decide to end the marriage.

When people are on the fence, our approach is to help them as they struggle to take a position. This process needs to have a time limit placed on it, because if it goes on too long the therapy may be helping to keep the person stuck. Coming to therapy gives the person the illusion of working on the problem when in fact his or her behavior has not changed. When someone is unable to give up the affair after a period of time in therapy, we suggest getting some time alone to sort out the confusion. Specifically, we encourage the person to take a room alone for up to six weeks, leaving both spouse and lover, and to come to therapy to talk about the experience of being alone. The therapist warns that it will be difficult to stay away from both spouse and lover and that people in this position frequently move toward the lover.

The therapist proposed to Tony that they begin by looking at what would be involved in giving up the affair. Dealing with the feelings of loss in giving up an affair is an important step in helping the person shift his or her part in the triangle. The therapist must first determine the nature of the attachment. How important is the lover to this person? How long has the affair been going on? How much contact has there been? Working with someone who has had thirty-five one-night stands in twenty years of marriage is different from working with the individual who is deeply involved in his or her first extramarital attachment.

Tony had known Ellen for four years. She was a speech therapist at the mental health clinic where he worked. They began their relationship as friends, spending an increasing amount of time talking with each other, first about their work and then gradually on more intimate terms. He had been surprised when his fondness for Ellen turned to passion and more surprised at himself for acting on those feelings. He was at times exhilarated at the reawakening of his feelings and at other times tormented about the effect it was having on his feelings for his wife. With Ellen he felt better than he had in many years—more alive sexually, more interesting, and more able to give in a relationship.

Once the nature of the attachment is clear, the therapist spends time dealing with its loss. If the affair was a significant emotional involvement that is already over, the person is probably experiencing feelings of sadness and loss that need to be heard and validated by the therapist—in our experience a step often neglected in treatment. If the individual is contemplating the end of the affair, then the therapist focuses on the predictable feelings of loss. In a session alone, the therapist asked Tony the ways in which he thought he would be more vulnerable with Ellen out of his life, and Tony said he thought he would be very lonely. It is often productive to help the person connect this feeling of loss with other periods of his life. Questions like "Have you ever felt this way before?" usually lead back to the family of origin.

Clues to ways of dealing with the loss frequently evolve out of this kind of discussion. Tony described a rather lonely and painful childhood. He had been part of an intense three-generational triangle in his family, acting as his weak mother's protector from her powerful mother, who lived with them. His father and younger sister played distant roles in the family script. Most of his interaction had been with women, and he had few male friendships. In therapy Tony explored his family and his social network to find people he could move toward, particularly men, as he experienced the loss from giving up the affair. The therapist took the position that the lack of a well-connected support system was one of the factors that went into making Ellen so important, and getting better connected with friends and family became a critical aspect of the treatment plan.

Tony moved slowly. For a time he led the therapist to believe that he had stopped seeing Ellen when in fact he had not, so that therapy replicated the process that was going on in his marriage. Therapists need to be sensitive to the signs. If someone claims to have given up what was clearly an important attachment, with no difficulty and no sign of turmoil, the affair is probably still going on.

Some people even feign the pain of separation; Tony was one of them. Tony had for weeks been describing the anguish he felt at not seeing Ellen when Maria tracked him down at Ellen's house and he admitted that he had not stopped seeing her. This deception presented a challenge for the therapist. In such a situation a therapist may fail to recognize the degree of difficulty a person is having ending an affair and become punitive. Or the therapist may join with the aggrieved spouse, taking satisfaction in watching "the bastard" squirm instead of seeing the affair as a process in which both are responsible for their parts.

The therapist again encouraged Tony to spend time alone, which he was able to do only in short spurts, and he eventually came to a firmer decision that he wanted to keep his marriage together. In part his decision was motivated by the loneliness he was beginning to feel even in the presence of his lover, which he attributed to missing his children and the sense of a home and family. He thought with horror about the possibility that his wife might remarry and that another man would be living with his two sons. He was also responding to Maria's firmer position that she could not continue to live with him unless he ended the affair.

Once Tony had given up the affair, he was encouraged to reinforce the shift in his position in the triangle in several ways. First, he was encouraged to work at developing closer relationships with each of his sons, including spending time with each one alone, without Maria. Second, he was urged to build a support system that included a social network, with an emphasis on male friends. Third, he was encouraged to become reconnected with his extended family, particularly his father's side, from which he had been cut off.

With Maria, the therapist's first task was to validate the emotional turmoil she was in without taking a victim/villain view of the situation. During their early sessions alone, the therapist encouraged her to describe the feelings she had been experiencing since her discovery of the affair, feelings that ranged from bitter rage to devastating panic.

She talked at length about her fear of losing Tony and of raising her two sons alone. In order to minimize the fear, the therapist encouraged her to talk about what would happen if he left. They came up with answers to the question "Would the children and I survive without Tony?"

Much of Maria's behavior at the outset of therapy added to the intensity of her emotional turmoil. Pursuing Tony for details and following him in the car only aggravated the wound and kept her away from more satisfying activities. She agreed that these approaches were not working for her, but she found it difficult to pull back.

The therapist encouraged Maria to move toward her fairly extensive support system, which she had not done because she had felt so humiliated. This is a tricky step, because when the "aggrieved" spouse begins to talk to friends and family, it is often to rage about the "wayward" spouse. All too often the listener falls in with the rage, supporting the picture of the other as villain and pumping up the reactivity. The therapist therefore talked to Maria about moving toward family and friends for positive connection and not just to attack Tony. Could she let them know she was having a difficult time without staying focused on Tony, or could she find activities she enjoyed doing with them? Choosing the right person is important. For example, moving toward someone who is fond of both spouses might be better than moving toward someone who is in the midst of a bitter divorce.

Maria's effort to stop pursuing Tony was complicated by the fact that his affair was not over. Once she discovered, several months into the therapy, that Tony was still seeing Ellen, they went through a revolving-door period, when Tony would stay home for several nights and then stay out for a night. The therapist encouraged Maria to take a position, and she decided that she could not go on living that way because it was too hurtful. Tony could stay in the house only if he gave up the affair.

A person who takes a position must be prepared for the consequences. If her husband's affair continues, will she be prepared to prevent him from coming back home? It is important for the therapist to do reality testing around the various possibilities, so that the person is ready to handle them. It was after she took a firm position that Tony made his decision to give up the affair. Maria at this point was not as fearful of taking the risk of ending the marriage, but she was experiencing a great deal of sadness.

Another method that we use to shift the position of an aggrieved spouse is to move him or her toward the lover. For example, if it is the husband who is having the affair, the wife may be encouraged to talk positively about the other woman, saying things like "She must be very special for you to care so much." And she may even be encouraged to make contact with her. The purpose of bringing the wife and the other woman together is to introduce some reality into the situation—to bring the other woman down to life-size—and to put the aggrieved spouse in a more active position.

This step, if it is to be helpful, must be planned carefully so that the spouse having the affair takes it with the least amount of reactivity possible. The move is suggested when (1) the affair is still going on, (2) the spouse having the affair is not participating in therapy in a meaningful way, and (3) the other spouse has enough emotional control and good judgment to function within the triangle while avoiding its emotional traps.

This last point is extremely important. It is useless for an aggrieved wife to meet the lover only to beg her to end the affair or to chastise her for being a home-wrecker. Instead, the wife prepares for the encounter by making herself emotionally neutral about the lover. In the meeting, the wife then uses such techniques as thanking the lover for taking care of her husband at a time when she could not, thanking her for pointing out the deficiencies in the marriage, and wishing the two of them happiness. Such a meeting, when handled well, often has dramatic results.

Maria was coached to take this step but initially thought it too difficult and not really relevant. After she learned that the affair was still going on, she changed her mind. She planned the move in detail with the therapist. She told her husband she was going to do it, but not when. Then she called Ellen and invited her for coffee, saying she knew how important Ellen was to her husband and that she very much wanted to talk. Ellen agreed, and Maria came to therapy after their meeting to describe her feelings and impressions. She was surprised to find that Ellen looked like her and more surprised to find that as they talked about Ellen's life, Maria felt compassion for her. Maria also felt more in control than she had since discovering her husband's affair. Tony later said that he had secretly admired his wife's courage, although his initial reaction was anger.

To reinforce Maria's shift, the therapist encouraged her to take a number of additional steps. She had become painfully aware of her prior dependence on Tony. For example, she rarely did anything for pleasure unless it involved them as a couple. She began to work on developing her own social life and to focus energy on some of the activities and interests she had given up when she had children. The therapist also coached her to reconnect with a branch of her family from which she had been cut off. Finally, she began to plan a direction for her career.

All this while, the therapist monitored the emotional tone and reactivity in the marital relationship. The following excerpt is from an individual session with Maria several months into therapy. The therapist first checks on Maria's present feelings about the affair. She attempts to connect her feelings to the underlying relationship process with such questions as "If I had been watching the two of you at home . . ." and "Have you moved

toward each other at all?" As the connection is made, the therapist begins
to suggest that Maria may at some point have to take the risk of being hurt
again.

THERAPIST: I remember that your initial reaction after you found out about
the affair was shock—and then you got very angry. Where are
you now emotionally?

MARIA: I don't have the same kind of feelings I used to have for Tony.
When I first came in here, I talked about always being in love
with him. No more, now I'm completely numb.

THERAPIST: You're turned off?

MARIA: Right, and he's aware of it. What I don't want is to feel hate.
I'm trying to prevent that. A few weeks ago we weren't even
talking. The boys were aware of it—it was pretty awful. So I
went to him and told him I thought we needed to talk. But it's
always me initiating the talking. I'm tired of it. If I were quiet
for weeks I probably wouldn't get a word out of him.

THERAPIST: So you're feeling numb and you're quiet until you can't stand
it anymore. If I had been watching the two of you at home,
what would it have looked like?

MARIA: On a social level we're fine, fairly friendly, and he's okay with
the boys. It would all look pretty civil until nighttime, because
then we'd go to separate rooms. I can't stand the idea of sleeping together as long as we're so cold with each other. So I
usually go to bed earlier, and then he falls asleep watching TV
and then goes to the guest room.

THERAPIST: In the last few weeks has there been any physical contact?
Have you moved toward each other at all?

MARIA: Yeah, I might touch him, but then I'd see him stiffen, so I
stopped.

THERAPIST: Let's go back to "numb." Does that mean you're not expecting
anything from him?

MARIA: I guess it means I'm scared—too scared to open up. I'm not
going to give myself to him and then be hurt again. It's not so
much that I worry about the affair or even a new affair. It's that
he's not really emotionally there. He comes home and goes
through the motions with me and the kids, but he's just not
really with us.

THERAPIST: What signs would you have to see to know he was back in
there emotionally?

MARIA: If I could see some pleasure in the kids—in me—if he looked a little happier—if I got the feeling he really wanted to be there —that it didn't just feel like the responsible thing to do.

THERAPIST: If you could see those signs from him, how hard would it be for you to get out of the numb position?

MARIA: I think it would be fairly easy. I really don't want to end up as a wife who constantly complains about her husband. But just because the affair is over, it doesn't mean everything is okay. I want my husband back, and he's still not back.

THERAPIST: Do you have a timetable? How long are you willing to wait?

MARIA: I don't know. I know these things take time.

THERAPIST: I think you're right. It will take time. One of the things we have to talk about is that the two of you are in a real standoff. You're waiting for signs from him before you take any risks, and I think he's over there doing the same thing.

Reestablishing Trust

Once both spouses understand the function the affair has served in their relationship and have shifted their positions in the triangle, the arduous task of reestablishing trust in the marriage begins. This is often the most difficult phase of treatment, and many couples, relieved that the crisis is over and hoping time will take care of the old wounds, drop out of therapy before achieving this goal.

Some couples move rapidly into a honeymoon period once the affair is over, and it is important to teach them to move slowly. More commonly, however, this is a painful period in which the aggrieved spouse, whose primary feeling during the crisis was panic, now begins to feel bitter about what he or she has been through. The spouse who has given up the affair may still be struggling with that decision and with feelings of loss and guilt. In this case, for example, it would have been too painful for Maria to see or hear the impact of this loss on Tony. It was therefore important to schedule individual sessions with Tony to help him deal with the loss, put it behind him, and to move back into the marriage if that was his choice. The following is an excerpt from such a session with Tony:

TONY: Things are still not so great with Maria. I'm doing pretty well with the boys. Since I've made the decision to stay with the marriage, we haven't been sleeping together. That's Maria's decision, and I understand it. Since this whole thing has happened she has erected walls—I guess I've helped her to do that.

She doesn't know when to lower them. I still am in turmoil. I've been trying to be friendly and to do the ordinary daily tasks that husbands and fathers do, but I'm not out of the woods yet.

THERAPIST: What's the turmoil about that you describe?

TONY: Am I making the right move by staying where I am? Am I causing Maria any unnecessary suffering by being there? Because I know the months that I was not at home Maria did make a life for herself. Now with me there, I don't know if I'm doing her any good because I'm not fully committed there yet. I'm not the way I used to be. I don't even know if I can be. I don't know what to do that would rectify what's going on.

THERAPIST: Are you emotionally disconnected from the other relationship, or does that still have a hold on you?

TONY: The emotional ties are still there, but I fight them—I try to turn away. The physical closeness is not there.

THERAPIST: So you've made an intellectual decision that the place you belong is with your wife and kids and that you're going to get yourself unhooked from the other relationship. Is doing the unhooking more difficult than you thought it would be?

TONY: No. I thought it would be this difficult. I don't feel very healthy emotionally. I feel inhibited toward Maria. I feel a lot of guilt about what I've done, but I can't say I didn't like what I did.

THERAPIST: Does that make the guilt worse?

TONY: Sometimes.

THERAPIST: Is the guilt in relation to Maria or to your moral code?

TONY: I can't shirk my value system—my training—all those years are a part of me. I also feel hurt for what I did to the other party —I tampered with something that should not have been tampered with. That's something I have to live with.

THERAPIST: Did you ever talk with her about that?

TONY: The other party? Yes.

THERAPIST: What does she say about that?

TONY: She's naturally extremely hurt. She's erected barriers just like Maria. She's got to protect herself, too.

THERAPIST: So that leaves you out in the cold on two fronts.

TONY: In a way, yes.

THERAPIST: Do you feel like you deserve to be out there, or do you feel deprived?

TONY: Both. I take responsibility—as much as Maria and Ellen have

erected barriers—I contributed to that in my inability to commit to either one, but I also feel deprived because I had something with Maria and something with Ellen. I can't have both,
and if I go to one then the other is shut off.

Tony and Maria were in a dilemma. She was numb and wary about
taking any risk that would put her in a more vulnerable position until she
saw some evidence that Tony was emotionally committed to her. He had
made an intellectual decision to commit to his marriage, but with his
emotions still in turmoil he did not trust the depth of his commitment
enough to give Maria any signs of encouragement about the future of their
relationship.

To reestablish trust with couples in Tony and Maria's position, we
focus the work in therapy on two main areas: the marriage itself and the
interlocking triangles. We teach people to move slowly as they move back
toward each other. If they are to regain the intimacy they have lost or
perhaps never had, it is going to take time. The one who has had the affair
has to handle the bitter feelings that are surfacing in his or her spouse, and
the aggrieved spouse will have to stand by while the other deals with
feelings of loss.

We coach people to start rebuilding their relationship through partnership. If their ability to conduct the business of their daily lives has been
damaged, as it often has been by an affair, that needs to be addressed first.
When that function is repaired, they can move to the area of companionship, simply doing things together that they both enjoy. They need that
kind of foundation in order to work directly on restoring intimacy. When
they are ready, the therapist encourages them to work on self-disclosure
and on their sexual relationship.

There are always triangles that interlock with the triangle that is
central in the therapy, and working on these others helps to reinforce the
changes each spouse is making. For example, Tony was in a triangle with
his mother and his wife that had bearing on the extramarital affair. Until
his marriage, he had been in an overly close relationship with his mother,
giving her an important decision-making role in his life and avoiding
developing positions on issues himself. After his marriage, Tony began to
distance from his mother and to give Maria responsibility for directing
their lives. The two women had a guarded relationship with each other,
in which mutual criticism was not far from the surface. Tony needed to
take back from Maria responsibility that was appropriately his and to
move toward his mother less reactively.

Tony discovered that the affair had in a way been a move away from two powerful women. He began to see it as a rebellion that he never went through as an adolescent. Now he needed to learn to relate to Maria as a wife and to his mother as the mother of an adult son. The work also took him to the triangle with his parents, in which he was close to his mother and distant from his father, who died a year before Tony was married. Tony regretted never knowing his father as an adult and longed for his advice about his current situation. He began to move toward the few remaining relatives on his father's side and to spend time at his father's grave.

The triangle that was most relevant for Maria was her triangle with her parents. She was much more attached to her mother and her mother's side of the family, which was predominantly female, and she recognized that she was relatively uncomfortable alone with male relatives. She began to seek out the men in her family, to learn more about their perspectives on life and to develop personal relationships with them, starting with her father.

The work of reestablishing trust is really unending. Therapy probably works best when people at this stage develop a plan and then go off and work on it themselves, returning when they are stuck or unclear about the direction they need to move in. Sessions should be geared to the couple's need for continued professional guidance. If they are on track, they should be encouraged to decrease the frequency of sessions.

In summary, our clinical experience has led us to believe that the couples who do best in dealing with the triangle of an extramarital affair are those who understand the process that led up to the affair and the part that each played in it, who shift their respective positions in the current process, who move slowly and thoughtfully toward a new kind of trust and intimacy in the marital relationship, and who understand the ways their families of origin have influenced them.

SOCIAL NETWORK TRIANGLES

Other triangles may involve people outside the family system as the third parties in marital conflict. Two common types are the *social network feminist triangle* and the *old friends chauvinist triangle.*

A common complaint from husbands is that their wives are involved with women friends who are "giving them the wrong ideas." Triangles are often a matter of influence, and this is especially true with a social network feminist triangle. A triangle may be described as a competition of influences. We strive for autonomy but often end up migrating back and forth between different sources of connectedness and influence.

It is obvious that this pattern of competing influences does not cease with marriage. For example, a wife begins at some point to turn her attention to personal self-fulfillment. Along the way she may form a relationship with a woman whose beliefs may be in conflict with those of her husband, and as she adopts those beliefs a very intense triangle is activated. If the husband has a conservative outlook, the conflict will be overt and the battle for dominance will be right on the surface.

If, on the other hand, the husband is more liberal, the conflict will be more subtle. The husband who is initially supportive of his wife's career, equality, and independence reacts to the loss he feels when part of his wife's attention and emotional investment is directed elsewhere. When the husband is an emotional distancer, as is often the case, it is simply his wife's not being where she is supposed to be that creates internal discomfort. Because he cannot intellectually accept being upset at his wife's movement or angry at the new influence on her, he often expresses the conflict in covert ways.

The wife in this situation is often tripped up by her expectations that her liberal husband and informed children will applaud her movement toward self-actualization. They do, of course, but within certain limits, and these limits are defined by their own levels of internal discomfort.

Both male and female therapists must be alert to the obvious and subtle triggers that are presented in dealing with this triangle. The male therapist must be in touch with his residual emotional reactions even when he is firmly committed to equality between the sexes. The female therapist must avoid viewing the husband as old-fashioned in his approach to life.

Younger couples who have come of age during the women's movement have more or less explicit understandings around these issues. How explicit they are depends in large measure on the couple's political philosophies, the characteristics of their social networks, and where in the country they live. The question of influence is important in all marriages, however, and the therapist must be diligent in looking for this triangle when dealing with marital conflict.

The old friends chauvinist triangle is a triangle with the husband's premarital friends. He stays connected with them after the marriage, and the connection can cause several difficulties: the wife may see them as infringing on the time the husband has for her and the children, she may resent their influence on her husband's decision making, and his friends may provide him with the ammunition to shoot down his wife's moves toward school or a job.

Connie and Dennis Henderson, both age twenty-three, presented for treatment with severe conflict in their brief marriage, which had followed a longstanding relationship. The number of triangles surrounding their marriage was very great, and the intensity of triangulation in most of them was extremely high. One of the hottest triangles was the triangle with Dennis's friends from high school. Connie complained bitterly about Dennis's frequent absences from home to be with them and about the fact that he appeared to care more about them than about her and their children. She was extremely critical of the character and immaturity of these friends, and she was not on speaking terms with several of them. Dennis pointed out that he hated his job and needed time and space to relax with his friends to release the tension he felt after work each day. The more Connie complained, the more time he spent with them.

In working with couples like this, we help them sort out the problems of influence, find an appropriate balance of individual versus couple and family time, and resolve the underlying difficulty, always present, of balancing closeness and distance. A full-length clinical example of the treatment of a social network triangle is presented in chapter 9.

4

Triangles Within the Family

THE most common triangles of marital conflict that occur within families are extended family triangles, triangles with the children, and stepfamily triangles. We will consider each of them in turn.

Extended Family Triangles

The extended family triangles that predominate clinically are in-law triangles and the primary parental triangle of each spouse. Both kinds of triangles involve primacy of attachment and influence and displacement of conflict.

Primacy of Attachment and Influence

The formation of the marital bond requires each partner to shift primary emotional attachment from his or her parents to his or her spouse. If this shift takes place in a functional way—that is, if the spouses adapt success-fully—the relationship with the parents remains intact, but the relation-ship with the marital partner becomes more important. As couples attempt this shift, a variety of problems develop that greatly influence the structure of extended family triangles.

Diane Rosen, a real estate broker in southern Westchester County, was married to John, an account executive with a New York City firm. As the eldest daughter in her family, she had a special relationship with her father. Her mother told her he had cried for three straight days after her wedding. Much of the adulation and affection that passed between the father and daughter was implicit, but the mutual idealization was clear to all who cared to look. Throughout her childhood and adolescence, and even into the early years of her marriage, Diane's thinking was greatly influenced by her father and by her desire for his approval. While growing up she had come to dislike what she saw as her mother's passivity and depression, and she had resolved not to be like her mother.

John, who had been very positive about his father-in-law during his courtship of Diane, came to resent the extent of his influence on Diane after the marriage. In his own family, he had since adolescence distanced himself from a "demanding and dominating" mother, who from his per-spective had castrated his father and criticized his sister until she moved three thousand miles away. In Diane's family he found the warmth and acceptance he longed for, so he made application and was accepted as an "adopted son."

After the wedding Diane's dominating behavior surfaced, along with the potentially negative aspects of her special relationship with her father. Meanwhile the attachment between John and his mother-in-law, a soft-spoken, nurturing woman who was an excellent cook, grew considerably. When John and Diane had children, the predictable happened: their son became Diane's special child, and their daughter became John's. The fam-ily was now divided into two camps.

As this couple tried to shift the primacy of their attachment from their families to each other, Diane had difficulty separating herself from her father's influence, and John was in flight from the dominance and emotion-ality of his mother. Intellectually, Diane wanted to make John number one in her life, but her emotions would lead her to do things in a way her father would approve. John would be hurt by her focus on her father and would chide her about being "Daddy's little girl." Diane would become angry and defend her relationship with her father. In the aftermath a struggle would ensue around sex or money. As Diane became more assertive, John, pre-sensitized by his relationship with his mother, would become angry and bury himself in his work.

From this scenario developed two in-law triangles. Although John was cut off from his mother, the ghost of his relationship with her fed the conflict with Diane, as he had never successfully learned to deal with dominance and emotional demands from a woman. Diane was caught between the influence of her father and that of her husband. Somewhere in that process she had to define herself as separate from the two of them.

In the clinical management of this situation, John was moved toward two projects. First, he was coached to decrease the distance in his relationship with his mother in order to experiment with desensitizing himself to her toxic behaviors. Second, he was asked to move toward his father-in-law, praising him for his influence on Diane and asking his advice on how to be more effective in the relationship with his daughter.

Diane was moved toward sorting out the influences of these two important men and figuring out what she herself stood for and believed. Her second project was to increase her relationship time with her mother in order to gain a better understanding of her mother's passivity and "depression" and achieve a better perspective on her triangle with her parents. All these interventions were directed toward getting both John and Diane to free themselves emotionally from their extended families and increase their primary attachment to one another.

The ideal developmental goal would be for each partner to be open to the influence of others they respect, while at the same time forming personal positions relatively free from emotional alignments. In practice, however, this is more the exception than the rule. It becomes important, therefore, to sort out the potential sources of influence and the ways in which these forces compete in the triangles of marital conflict. In John and Diane's case the influence of Diane's father was easy to see. Often the process is more subtle and can be difficult to ferret out. There are times in every marriage when this process becomes overt. Making wedding plans, choosing a place to live, buying a car, the birth of a baby, choosing a school —all are times when this struggle may become explicit. A classic example is the time of a birth, when the "battle of the grandmothers" may begin.

Displacement of Conflict

In the midst of problems with primacy of attachment and hierarchy of influence, a significant conflict may arise between a parent and his or her son- or daughter-in-law. Most often this represents unworked-out conflict between the parent and his or her offspring, which is displaced onto the offspring's spouse. For example, in the Rosens' case, John's mother was unable to accept the fact that her "very special" son put significant distance between them because he could not handle her dominance and emotionality. She therefore accused Diane of trying to capture John and absorb him into her family and became extremely critical of Diane and her family. The unworked-out problems between John and his mother were thus displaced into a conflict between his mother and his wife.

Another variant of this problem occurs when both spouses distance dramatically from conflictual or overcontrolling parents, seeking refuge from them and making the marriage a protective cocoon. In this situation, the emotional demands placed on the marriage are excessive, and the cocoon becomes oppressive. When a marriage such as this begins to fall apart, unless there has been an affair, both spouses inevitably migrate back toward their families of origin, which are then seen as refuges from a "bad marriage."

In the course of a marriage all of these factors may come into play at different times and in varying sequences. The shifts can go back and forth from the primary parental triangle to some variant of an in-law triangle to an attempt at "cocooning."

IN-LAW TRIANGLES

There are three subtypes of in-law triangles that we have observed to be particularly important in marital conflict: (1) the wedding gift triangle, (2) the loyalty alignment triangle, and (3) the dominant father-in-law triangle. It is important for the clinician to recognize which specific form of in-law triangle is active at the time the case presents for treatment. The therapist then works to help the couple identify and neutralize the triangle, eventually working back to the beginning of the process in the spouses' triangles with their own parents. The therapy focuses on these areas:

1. Demonstrating through process questions and the therapist's own personal stands the importance of each spouse's taking responsibility for dealing with his or her own family
2. Assisting the spouse least caught in an in-law triangle to experiment with maneuvers to detriangulate himself or herself
3. Working to increase the primacy of the marital bonding over that with parents.

The Wedding Gift Triangle

A culturally acceptable way for a man to avoid the pressure of a relationship with his mother without cutting her off is to hand her over to his wife, giving his wife the responsibility for keeping in touch with his mother, seeing that his children have a relationship with her, buying her gifts and birthday cards, and so on. In this triangle, the husband's primacy of attachment is blurred and difficult to assess. Most often he assumes a distant position in relation to both his mother and his wife. The mother and the wife have several options. They may both like the arrangement and join in an alliance either to shape up their distant son and husband or to bypass him, allowing him his distance and focusing their energies on bringing up the children or even on a joint business venture. In such a case, the wife is usually in flight from her family of origin, looking for a sense of belonging in a different clan.

When this triangle presents clinically as marital conflict, it usually takes the form of a dysfunction in the husband; for example, he may be involved in an affair or may be abusing alcohol. When the triangle is first set up, the husband is relieved at the connection between his wife and mother. As time passes, however, his tolerance for being on the outside looking in may be exceeded. Relief turns into feelings of rejection and lack of appreciation. When these feelings are joined to explicit attempts by both wife and mother to shape him up with abundant criticism and emotionality and he ends up absorbing their concern and anxiety, the husband's functioning declines. He may turn to alcohol abuse or seek refuge in an extramarital affair to calm his inner turmoil.

In managing this triangle clinically, the therapist first makes an adequate connection with the wife and then encourages her to experiment, one at a time, with the following moves: (1) separating herself from her overinvolvement with her mother-in-law, (2) decreasing her efforts at over functioning for her husband, (3) looking to her functioning as a wife rather than as a mother and a daughter-in-law, and (4) investigating the way her position in her triangle with her own parents played a part in setting her up for her present position in the in-law triangle. Not infrequently in this situation the wife has cut herself off from a triangle in which her father was a passive alcohol abuser and her mother dominant and controlling.

The husband meanwhile is coached to master his dysfunction. If it is alcohol abuse, he must join Alcoholics Anonymous; if it is an occupational dysfunction, he must work on getting a job. In time he will be encouraged to assume more responsibility for dealing with his own mother and for sorting out the emotional factors that have resulted in his extreme distance from his wife and his mother.

In a variant on this pattern, the wife is dysfunctional and her husband and her mother are united in criticism of her. The husband and his mother-in-law may not otherwise be close, and their only unity may be in their attempt to shape up their wife and daughter, but the closer their relationship is, the worse it is for the wife. The clinical management of this variation is similar to the first: the husband must disengage from his alliance with his mother-in-law and stop his criticism of his wife; the dysfunctional wife must manage her own dysfunction, whatever it is, and then take on her own parent. In general it is one of our basic premises that biological offspring maintain primary responsibility for tending the relationship to their own families of origin.

More common than either kind of alliance is the triangle in which the mother-in-law and daughter-in-law both rebel against the attempt to graft their relationship. In this situation, the unresolved emotional struggle between mother and son is displaced into a sometimes open, sometimes camouflaged conflict between his mother and his wife. The underlying issue is usually the question of who has more influence and control over the husband.

Mort and Judy Berger were married for six years when they presented to CFL's clinical service in severe marital conflict. Mort was Judy's third husband, she his second wife. His first wife had died of mysterious causes after years of depression and alcohol abuse. Mort had a daughter, Laura, who was six when her mother died.

After his first wife's death, Mort handed his daughter over to his mother to raise. This arrangement worked well: it kept his mother occupied and off his back, and his daughter loved her grandmother very much. Two years later Mort met and married Judy, who had no children from her two previous marriages. Judy wanted to reunite Laura and Mort and then attempt to have a child. Judy, like her mother-in-law, was an outgoing, powerful woman with a great affection for children. The conflict between Judy and her mother-in-law was instantaneous and should have been brought to the attention of a family therapist years before it was.

The treatment plan called for Judy to back off from the conflict with her mother-in-law, to stop being critical of her to her stepdaughter and husband, to attempt to assume an emotionally neutral position toward her mother-in-law, and to hand her back over to her son.

Mort was not happy with this plan, because his emotional intolerance of his mother went back a long way. The following is a transcript of a consultation in which the therapist attempts to get Mort to relieve Judy of responsibility for his mother.

THERAPIST: Do you get really paralyzed, with an upset mother on one side and an upset wife on the other? What does that do to you?

MORT: It disturbs me, and I tend to want to favor my wife as opposed to trying to satisfy my mother.

THERAPIST: If I hear Judy right, she isn't going to be satisfied and calm until your mother is neutralized.

MORT: My mother will never be neutralized. She's too old. The only way to do it is to shut her out. That's the only way I've had any success is to shut her out.

THERAPIST: What does she do when you shut her out?

MORT: She tries to find ways of breaking in; she gets more obstinate. When we tried to keep Laura from seeing her, she tried to get custody. She got a lawyer and everything.

THERAPIST: So when you pull that cutoff she gets real riled up. What I figure is she needs more Morton medicine.

MORT: No, what she needs is what my sister gives her, and that's placating her and letting her think she's getting her way.

THERAPIST: But your sister isn't her son, you know?

MORT: Yeah.

THERAPIST: You've been handling your mother since you were sixteen by running away, but what she needs to calm her down is some Morton medicine. How big a dose of Morton medicine would you have to give her for her to stop being critical of Judy?

MORT: I don't know what form it would have to take.

THERAPIST: Time. Time and connection. Telephone time, visiting time, tune-in time.

Because of Mort's difficulty in picking up responsibility for his relationship with his mother, and because of his mother's direct involvement in both the conflict and the raising of her granddaughter, it was decided that her participation in the therapy was mandatory. Mort, however, rejected this idea, saying that his marriage had improved dramatically in the therapy thus far and that he was afraid that his mother's participation would make it worse again. On this note, therapy was interrupted, perhaps to be continued at a future date when the marital conflict recycled or a problem with Laura developed.

The Loyalty Alignment Triangle

This triangle centers around primacy of attachment and hierarchy of influence. One spouse, perhaps the husband, is in an overly close relationship with his family of origin, and his wife is in the outside position, unable to obtain membership in her husband's family or the appropriate type of bonding with her spouse. When a conflictual issue arises, such as money, the husband's family, especially his mother, may continue to have the most influence over him. The influence of the extended family and attachment to it take precedence over the marital relationship.

Fred and Emily Morrison provided a good example of this triangle. Fred complained that Emily was constantly in contact with her mother, calling her several times a day and visiting her every day on her way home from work. In addition, whenever she and Fred had an argument and she walked out "to cool down," she went to her mother's house. Emily complained that Fred's behavior was "crazy" and drove her out of the house. What she did not see but the therapist was able to bring out was that Fred's angry outbursts and his feelings of depression were related to Emily's distance from him and her overly close link with her mother.

In a case like this, until the wife accepts responsibility for dealing with her mother and their relationship, and until the husband gives her the time to do it, the potential for problems in their relationship remains high. Clinically the situation can be dealt with by helping the wife accept her responsibility directly or by coaching the husband to lower his reactivity and to try indirectly and subtly to create a climate that will give the wife and her mother the best chance for a successful relationship.

The Dominant Father-in-Law Triangle

The wife and her idealized father may be united in implicit criticism of the husband, as in the case of John and Diane Rosen. This triangle can be significant in marital conflict even when the wife's father is dead. Madeline Valentine, who came to treatment alone because her husband refused to come, complained that her husband was a poor provider, was abusive, and drank too much. Her father had died ten years earlier, just one year after her marriage. In questioning Madeline the therapist learned that her father had never approved of Madeline's husband and that except for that issue Madeline and her father had always been very close. Madeline admitted that after her father's death she had begun to compare her husband unfavorably with her adored father, and when she was asked what she thought her father's advice would be in her present circumstances, she said without hesitation that he would insist she and the children leave her husband and "come home."

In this case the therapist led Madeline to an investigation of her relationship with her dead father and how that fit into her participation in her triangle with both her parents. Visits with her mother and with her father's sister revealed to her the degree to which she had idealized her father and assisted her in gaining a more objective view of him. She was able to make connections between her relationship with her idealized father and her expectations of her husband, Frank. When Frank failed to live up to her image of her father, Madeline had begun to pressure him and to overfunction for him in an attempt to make him into the "man she married." All these factors were feeding Frank's dysfunction. The next steps were for Madeline to decrease the pressure on Frank by lowering her expectations and, without disconnecting from him, to detach from her mission of changing him by working to give up her pattern of overfunctioning.

The Clinical Management of In-Law Triangles

The goals in working with in-law triangles are

(1)   starting with the most obvious symptomatic triangle, to work through eventually to each spouse's primary parental triangle;

(2)   to increase the primacy of the marital bond without damaging the relationships the spouses have with their parents;

(3)   to assist the spouses in developing an ability to sort out the sources of influence on them and to be able to arrive at their own positions and courses of action without alienating important others; and

(4)   to shift displaced conflict and bitterness to the relationship in which it arose and to deal with it there.

A clinical case may help to pull together the process of dealing with these interlocking triangles. It is the rule rather than the exception that several subtypes of the in-law triangle occur together. Gerald Hanrahan, a surgeon, was married to Marie, a teacher. Both were in their forties, and they had three children. Their marital conflict was organized around the parenting of their oldest son, John. It was complicated by the direct involvement of Gerald's mother, who specialized in criticism of John. She always asked lovingly about the younger children, but when she spoke of the eldest son, she said things like "How's the case?" (referring to the fact that this son had been in therapy).

Gerald was very successful and competent, but as an only child he was locked tightly into the triangle with his parents. Thus, when he and his wife were married, both at age twenty-eight, Marie robbed the cradle and "stole the prince." The senior Hanrahans were retired real estate entrepreneurs from whom Gerald kept his distance. When he visited them at their retirement home in Arizona, they wanted to show off their son the doctor and their two favorite grandsons. Gerald tried to give his mother to Marie, but after years of battling, Marie banished her in-laws from visiting her home. Now on their trips east the senior Hanrahans stayed at a local motel. Gerald always felt caught between his mother and his wife, as well as angry at his eldest son for being a failure.

Marie never went home, because her father died three years ago and she felt that the link to her family had been broken. Her mother always idealized her younger brother Frank, alternating between Marie and her father as the objects of her intense criticism.

This family demonstrates the multiplicity of interlocking triangles that surround and impinge upon a marriage. In order to deal successfully with the problems in their marriage, the Hanrahans would have to deal with the triangle with their son John and the interlocking triangle with Gerald's mother. This step would automatically lead to the other relevant triangles in the system and directly into the marital relationship.

For example, Gerald was coached to stop distancing from his mother and to spend more time alone with her. He was instructed to leave his wife and children at home and to monitor his feelings so that he could gradually identify and disarm the mechanisms that triggered his reactions. He was helped to increase little by little the amount of time he could spend with his mother without his insides churning. The eventual goal would be to open up with her the issue of his son John.

In addition, Gerald was encouraged to observe the relationship patterns that developed when he visited his parents. One pattern of which Gerald became aware was his parents' constant negativity about everything in the universe. As an experiment he began to preempt their negativity by bringing them his negative feelings about his own life and problems. Usually Gerald was on the receiving end of their negative ideas, and this was an attempt to reverse the process, to neutralize it, and to move the communication to more fruitful areas.

Gerald was also encouraged to try to neutralize the triangle with his mother and wife simply by reporting to each of them fabricated positive input from the other. In addition, he was coached to take the problem back into his triangle with his parents by broaching with his father his problems with his mother, his wife, and his son John (who just happened to be named after the senior Mr. Hanrahan).

On the wife's side, it was important to help Marie recognize that her in-laws' feelings and behavior toward her were based to a large extent on displacement: the parents' feelings come from their upset at their son for leaving them and for continuing to be distant. Their behavior had little to do with her personally, and if she could understand that and accept it, she might be able to feel less injured by her mother-in-law's criticism and to establish a more neutral position in relation to her.

She also had to take a look at her own expectations about membership in her husband's family. Marie was in fact disappointed and angry about never really having been initiated into full membership. No one ever achieves full membership in a spouse's family, and it often helps people if they can come to grips with that fact.

Finally, Marie had to learn a way of dealing more actively with her in-laws instead of just swallowing her feelings about their behavior. One possibility might be to respond, when they called her eldest son a "case," "Well, all us Lanzas (her maiden name) are crazy, everybody knows that." Such a response would give her a way of dealing with her own upset and a sense of greater competence in dealing with them. It might even increase her in-laws' respect for her, for finding an effective way of dealing with them. In addition, Marie could eventually be coached to deal with the emotional cutoff from her own family of origin.

THE PRIMARY PARENTAL TRIANGLE OF EACH SPOUSE

The place each spouse has occupied in his or her family of origin always has significant impact on the marital conflict. The triangle consisting of the spouse with his or her parents is of particular importance. That triangle is the basic training ground for each spouse's emotional maturity. We would go so far as to say that the emotional maturity of a person can be measured by his or her ability to operate within that triangle with relatively low anxiety. That measure in turn determines how much is emotionally available for bonding in the marital relationship.

For example, the more energy a husband like Mort Berger expends fending off the emotional demands of his mother, the less he has available for his wife, Judy. Furthermore, if he cuts off from his mother, he repeats the problems with her in his relationship with his wife.

The reactive process in the triangle with one's parents also influences the marital relationship in at least two other ways. First, it presensitizes one to certain stimuli that set off automatic emotional responses. A spouse who comes from a family in which alcohol has been abused, for example, will be sensitized to alcohol as an issue and often to a particular form of drunken comportment as well.

Second, it sets up patterns of compliance and adaptiveness or of rebellion that are reproduced in the marriage. This phenomenon can be demonstrated by varying the scenario in the case of John and Diane Rosen. Remember that Diane had a special relationship with her father, a prominent and successful man. If Diane's mother had responded to this special relationship by pressuring and criticizing Diane, then Diane, given an appropriate individual temperament, might rebel openly against her mother with the strength gained from her relationship with her father and even, perhaps, with his covert support. She would then be more likely to approach a conflict with John by openly challenging him and threatening rebellion if he did not accept her terms or stop his undesirable behavior.

If we change the scenario again just a little, making Diane's father only marginally successful and adaptive to his wife in their relationship, then the mother's pressure and criticism might produce adaptive, compliant behavior from Diane. In her marriage to John, when he and her mother joined forces to change her, she would be more likely to become adaptive and subsequently dysfunctional. In this case her dysfunction would become her only source of leverage in the system.

There are three goals in working in the primary parental triangle of one or both spouses: (1) discovering and bringing out how the primary parental triangle of each spouse relates to the emotional process in the marriage; (2) coaching both spouses to increase their ability to operate nonreactively within their triangles with their parents; and (3) helping each spouse sort out his or her bitterness, differentiating between the bitterness that truly comes from the marriage and that which comes from the primary parental triangle.

Triangles with the Children

A couple's children are ready-made for a triangle. It would be difficult to imagine a more convenient way of confusing issues or diluting tension between husband and wife than by triangulating with one or more of their children. In fact, the two major functions served by such triangles are to cover over the marital conflict and to let parenting become the issue around which marital conflict is organized. Families create innumerable variations of this type of triangle, but three major subtypes are the most common; all three are dealt with extensively in Guerin and Gordon (1984).

THE CHILD-AS-REFUGE TRIANGLE

In one version of the triangle with the children, one parent is overly close to and overinvolved with one or more of the children and the other parent is in the distant position. A wife who is an emotional pursuer, frustrated by her husband's distance, may turn to pursuing her children. One child, sensitive to the mother's upset, accepts the triangle and cooperates in an overly close relationship with her. The mother's distress over the marriage is alleviated by her closeness with the child, and the marital conflict is thus covered over. The husband's resentment of this triangle, especially if it involves a son, may underlie much of his bitterness about the marriage.

The fact that the relationship with the mother is very close does not always mean that it is a calm emotional connection. As the mother's anxiety about the marriage increases, the anxiety may be transmitted to the child and the child may become symptomatic. The child-as-refuge triangle may then turn into the target child triangle.

THE TARGET CHILD TRIANGLE

A child who is special to one parent may become the target child of the parent in the outside position in the triangle. This parent's anger may be directed at the target child because the child possesses qualities that resemble those of the other parent or that parent's family, or just because of the child's specialness to the other spouse.

Target children feel caught between their parents. They often incorporate a version of both parents, who wage war inside them. To relieve their emotional stress they behave self-destructively, forcing their parents to join in an artificial coalition to deal with them. The parents unite in their concern for the troublesome child, and the marital conflict is at least temporarily covered over.

Roger and Barbara Corrado provided a classic example of this pattern. A couple in their early forties, they presented with a thirteen-year-old son who was doing poorly in school and who a year earlier had had several seizures and was now on anticonvulsant medication. As usual with this type of triangle, the family came to us because of the child's problem, not because of their marital conflict. These families see the child's problem as primary and want it solved before anything else is brought up. In fact, in the case of Roger and Barbara, when the child's problem was "solved," therapy was terminated.

THE TUG-OF-WAR TRIANGLE

In the third common kind of triangle with the children, both parents are attempting to be closer to and more influential with the child. Rosalie and Harry Blumenfeld fought incessantly about how their children should be brought up. Harry was Jewish and Rosalie was Catholic, although neither had practiced any religion for years. They had agreed when they were married that their children would not be brought up in either religion. When their first son turned twelve, Harry changed his mind about this agreement, and the dispute rang from the rafters day in and day out. There was marital conflict aplenty in this case, but it was about parenting, and this became the issue around which the conflict was organized.

Triangles with the children can take these and many other forms, and they must be treated carefully by the therapist. When the marital conflict is not the presenting problem, the therapist must avoid the temptation to raise it prematurely.

A full-length clinical example of treating a triangle with children in marital conflict is presented in chapter 9.

A Family Triangle: The Randalls

In-law triangles, triangles with parents, and triangles with the children are all triangles within the family. We have already pointed out that the emotional process in these relationships forms a set of interlocking triangles. The Randalls are a good example of how such triangles are linked together and create marital conflict.

Frank Randall was devastated because his wife, Edith, had kicked him out and had begun divorce proceedings. In the first interview, Frank admitted to a history of infidelity and alcohol abuse and an intimidating, controlling posture toward Edith. He also admitted that the same things had led his first wife to leave him. After many years of taking this treatment, Edith had rebelled. She had first gone through a phase of pursuing Frank about these problems, trying to get him to go for therapy, and then had tried to ignore him while she worked on her own life and interests. She finally got to the point of saying, in effect, "Frank, you're out."

When he came for therapy, therefore, Frank was an emotional distancer with his emotions out of control. His wife's decision had blown open the inner compartments in which his emotions had been contained. He was obsessed by his wife and determined to win her back at all costs, and he had no other options for relationships either in his family or in his social network. The initial treatment plan was to calm his emotionality by making a connection with him and to help him get better connected with his children, his social network, and his extended family. In doing these things the therapist would also directly and indirectly be getting him to moderate his pursuit of Edith and moving the treatment toward Frank's extended family.

FRANK'S TRIANGLES

During the early part of the treatment, when Frank was coming alone, a major goal of therapy was to connect Frank with his children, in part with the hope of warming the emotional climate with Edith. When a bitter wife sees her husband really making an effort to be a father, her feelings about him sometimes moderate. In addition, one does not divorce one's children, and Frank had already been through one divorce that had resulted in a near cutoff from his son by that marriage, Franky.

In the triangle with the children, Edith was in an overly close position with their two children, especially with their son, Ted, and Frank was on the outside. Working this triangle was important for Frank's relationship with his children, and also for deflecting his pursuit of Edith. The therapist presented Frank with all these reasons for working on his relationship with his children, but Frank's reaction made it clear that the reason he found most compelling was the chance that it might soften Edith toward him.

Frank needed quite explicit coaching on how to reconnect with his children. He was encouraged to call them regularly on the phone, but when Edith answered he would engage her in long conversations. This behavior was clearly more pursuit of her, and he was coached simply to ask to speak to the children. The therapist also kept track of when Frank went to see the children and what he did with them. As might have been predicted, he often stayed around the house during his visits, and his attention was directed largely toward Edith. He was therefore urged to take the children out or to his apartment.

Frank's difficulties in sustaining a move toward his son and daughter enabled the therapist to surface his own primary parental triangle, linking the process across the generations, as the following excerpt illustrates.

THERAPIST: Did you want to be a different type of father from your own father?

FRANK: Yeah. I think a lot of it has to do with the relationships in my family, what I saw, and how my father treated us kids, and how his father, as he tells it, treated him. And that to me is a life script that's very difficult to break. For instance, my father never took me to a ball game, never took me out to a restaurant, basically never did anything with me. Absolutely nothing.

THERAPIST: Work. Didn't you work together?

FRANK: Yes. We worked. That was it. Work, work, work. We got up in the morning, and . . .

THERAPIST: Was that with him, or did he send you off to work by yourself?

FRANK: We would work for him, it was never really with him. That's the reason we got food on our plates, because we were going to bust our chops every day doing whatever we had to do to get done. I think I have a lot of anger at my dad over that whole thing. For instance, when the other kids could take dance lessons at school, I couldn't take dance lessons because I had to get home and feed the cows and the pigs. To this day I'm a lousy dancer, and it makes me very self-conscious about things. But I'm sure a lot of that has to do with my inability to get close to the children, especially Ted and Franky. It's a little easier with Susan. It's just that I have difficulty knowing how to go about getting close to them.

Frank described his relationship with his extended family as having no open affection. What he got from his father was an insistence on work. His mother was "always there" and took care of the family, but she was not affectionate. His relationship over time with all of them was distant. His first wife had become quite close to them and taken over responsibility for that side of the family. Edith did not care for them and refused to fill the role that Frank's first wife had filled, that of devoted daughter-in-law.

Work was done on reconnecting Frank with his mother without Edith or the children as buffers. He did phone and write to his mother extensively during this period and even made one trip to Oregon to see her. He was gratified by his mother's response to him, although it was colored by some suspicion. Frank now had assumed responsibility for dealing with her, rather than expecting it of his wife.

Frank worked well in therapy for six months. He spent more time with his children, reconnected with his extended family, and stopped the kind of sexual and alcoholic behavior that had been a dysfunctional feature of his life. These changes enabled him to decrease his pursuit of Edith and his attempts to control her.

Toward the end of the six months, Frank reported that Edith seemed to be having second thoughts about the divorce. Those reports were confirmed when Frank and Edith came to a session together one day and announced that they were going to make another try at their marriage. Edith at this point entered therapy (she had come twice before, at the therapist's request, to give him "her view of Frank").

EDITH'S TRIANGLES

Edith's entry into therapy marked her tentative move off her "island of invulnerability" and her willingness to experiment with having feelings again. As might be expected, those feelings included a lot of bitterness, and it was obvious that work on this bitterness would be an essential element in her work in therapy. It was a question, however, whether that work could be done with the therapist who had been seeing Frank virtually alone for six months. The therapist raised this issue with Frank and Edith and offered to refer them to another therapist. After a discussion in which Frank and Edith resisted strongly the idea of "starting all over again" with a new therapist, it was decided that Edith would try working with the original therapist.

The most obvious extended family triangles for this couple were Edith's triangle with her parents and the in-law triangle with Edith's mother.

Edith's Primary Parental Triangle

Edith reported that her mother had brought her into the world just to have someone who would take care of her. She had already had three sons, and she kept the third in dresses and curls until Edith was born. Edith's mother, who had come to the United States from Ireland alone, apparently was determined never to be alone again.

Edith and her father had a close relationship. Edith was special to her father, and she idealized him. Both the specialness and the idealization were implicit, but Edith felt it and still remembered it. This relationship did not provide a counterweight to Edith's negative relationship with her mother, however, because her father died when Edith was seven. Less than a year after her father's death, her mother made Edith kneel in front of her and swear that she would never leave and would always take care of her. Edith kept this promise until age twenty-four, when she moved out into an apartment of her own. She continued to see and help support her mother, however, and her mother continued to make demands on Edith for her help and her company, at the same time criticizing her for having moved out. Edith continued to idealize her dead father and dealt with her mother by giving in to her while keeping secret as much of her life as she could. Her brothers signed the family house over to Edith, but the price they extracted was that they were not to be bothered with any aspect of their mother's care.

The In-Law Triangle with Edith's Mother

By moving into an apartment and not telling her mother everything about her life, Edith managed to preserve enough of a life outside her relationship with her mother to be available for relationships with men and ultimately to marry. She expected to find someone to take care of her without the restrictiveness and controls that her mother had exercised. Her reactivity to her mother and the unresolved issues with her, however, made it almost inevitable that Edith would repeat the pattern and end up in a triangle with two people who, though negative toward each other, would join in controlling her and making demands on her.

It was her marriage to Frank at age twenty-seven that enabled Edith finally to loosen the entanglement with her mother just a bit. Even this took time, however. At first Edith and Frank lived in Frank's apartment and made frequent visits to her mother. When their first child was born, they moved into her mother's house. It was ten years after they were married before an appropriate physical separation was attained. At that time Edith and Frank bought a house in Connecticut. Edith told one of her brothers that their mother would have to stay with him while they were moving in and getting settled and that she would pick the mother up in two weeks. Once she had moved, she cut off contact with her mother and brothers, leaving her mother in her brothers' care. The brothers promptly put their mother in a nursing home. The mother's initial reaction was to refuse to have anything to do with Edith, but later their relationship improved at the mother's initiation.

When Edith and Frank were first married, and later when they moved into Edith's mother's house, the mother avoided Frank. She did not particularly like him, thought he was "ugly," and made it very clear that she did not approve of the marriage. When Frank was home, the mother usually insisted that Edith bring her meals to her room, because she did not want to eat with Frank.

Both Frank and her mother made continual demands on Edith, who tried to satisfy both of them. Frank's demands seemed to come from his anxiety about the lack of intimacy in his life from childhood on, and Edith's mother's demands seemed to come from her anxiety about being alone, and especially about dying alone. Edith found herself unable to assert herself with either one of them and felt caught between the demands they made for her service and loyalty. The triangle with Edith's mother had Edith and her mother very overinvolved, leaving Frank on the outside. Edith regularly moved toward Frank to lessen the intensity of her relationship with her mother, however, so the triangle was always moving and shifting.

Eventually Edith went into open rebellion. First she rebelled against her mother, by giving her to Edith's brothers without leaving a forwarding address. Four months after her mother died, Edith went into open rebellion against Frank and threw him out.

Working the Triangles

The fact that Edith's mother and father were both dead made working in these extended family triangles particularly difficult. Her brothers were the key to working through some of these issues in her triangle with her parents, but Edith was full of excuses for not working on her relationship with her brothers.

Edith's bitterness was closely tied to her extended family triangles. By dying, her father abandoned her to a demanding, controlling mother, who tried to claim her life. Her brothers allowed her mother's domination of her and even abetted it. When she met and married Frank, she was caught in a battle for control between Frank and her mother. The first step in working these triangles was to help Edith get in touch with the intensity of the bitterness inside her and its potentially negative effect on her well-being. The therapist offered the idea that bitterness eats away at a person's perspective and sense of self. Next, an attempt was made to connect the bitterness with its various sources. This was difficult since, as in any case of intense marital conflict, much of the bitterness acquired in her extended family experience had been displaced into the marriage. Sorting out what belonged in the relationship with Frank and what belonged in the relationship with her mother was the key task.

The following excerpt from an ongoing therapy session shows the therapist labeling the bitterness and exploring its effects on Edith. What emerges here as well is a clear description of bitterness that has been "capped"—sealed off and forgotten until some event, behavior, or interactional pattern causes a leak.

THERAPIST: How are things going?

EDITH: I got real hostile a few weeks ago, but I guess it's under control. When things are going all right, I don't dwell on all this bitterness crap, but when things aren't going all right, everything comes into a different perspective.

THERAPIST: The bitterness leaks out then, and . . .

EDITH: It all comes crashing in on me, like everything I forgot I suddenly remember.

THERAPIST: The memories hurt?

EDITH: I put them on a shelf and leave them there and I don't live with it day to day until something happens, and then all of a sudden it starts hitting me from different angles, like I remember all this stuff from before, all the same feelings and aggravation and everything. It's like going back in a time capsule.

THERAPIST: What does it do to your insides when this happens?

EDITH: It makes me furious, frustrated, angry. There is rage about people trying to control me, and I can't control it, I can't get out of it, the only way out is to leave.

THERAPIST: Do you mean get away?

EDITH: Yes.

THERAPIST: What importance does all this have for your day-to-day life?

EDITH: I function, but I'm miserable. Most people don't realize that I'm angry. I cover it well with an Irish smile.

THERAPIST: Do you experience this as destructive?

EDITH: Yes.

THERAPIST: When it's happening, what do you see as the solution?

EDITH: That's when I think about leaving and getting away by myself, thinking that I shouldn't live with someone who makes me feel that they've got strings and they can get me crazy by pulling them . . . It feels like a dog on a chain, that I've got to break away from that chain before it chokes me to death.

THERAPIST: When you say get away by yourself, do you mean just away from Frank, or really alone by yourself?

EDITH: No, just away from Frank, not away from the kids. They never bother me.

Edith gives a vivid description of what many of our patients experience in the turmoil of long-term marital conflict. It is important to bring this bitterness out into the open, connect it to the relationships that have formed it, and make explicit the ways it affects behavior in the marriage.

In the next segment, the therapist explores the way Edith's bitterness finds its way into her interaction with Frank.

EDITH: He wants a clean slate. I'm supposed to forget everything and just take him and love him, and everything that has gone on in the past is over; that's how he wants it.

FRANK: I don't know how to verbalize it exactly, except that its ramifications are that if I get out of line for whatever reason, then the marriage is over and boom, it's kaput, and I accept that and I've been pretty good about it. I've been excellent about it, as a matter of fact.

EDITH: Oh, come on. There have been some major setbacks.

FRANK: Okay, but I quit drinking again.

EDITH: Again! Two weeks ago, Frank.

FRANK: It happens to be the eighth of December. It's longer than two weeks.

EDITH: It's not a lifetime.

FRANK: Fine, but I quit drinking anyway, so let's throw that out. But stepping out of line in terms of having an opinion that may upset Edith, may hurt Edith a little bit, Edith closes the door and all of a sudden I'm banging on the door to say I'm sorry and I won't do it again, and that sort of thing, and I'm almost to the point where if I stay in line, if I'm a good boy and if I don't do anything wrong, then I get rewarded by Edith not going and closing her isolation booth, and then maybe if I do this for a number of years, then maybe someday Edith will say "I love you" again. That's my feeling.

· ·

EDITH: One thing I find intolerable is when he says "if I'm a good little boy," because that's what he said for fourteen goddam fucking years. If I don't go drinking, and if I don't smoke pot, and if I'm a good little boy, will you sleep with other men. What the hell does that mean, "if I'm a good little boy"? That makes me want to throw up, that phrase is . . . you might as well take a knife and stick it in me, I can't tolerate it. He's not a little boy. He is forty-one years old, and I am not his fucking mother.

This demonstration of how Edith's bitterness leaks into her relationship with Frank points to the necessity of sorting out the various sources of bitterness. In addition to labeling and tracking Edith's bitterness, therefore, efforts were made to sort out how much of the bitterness was really attributable to Frank and how much of it came from other sources—from her father, who died when she was young, from her brothers, who dumped her mother on her, and mostly from her mother. The following excerpt illustrates one attempt to do that.

EDITH: I think Frank is basically the same personality as my mother. Not that that's such a bad thing, but I'm probably more comfortable with him and his bizarreness because that's what I've been used to. But when I got away from my mother, I realized how nice it could be.

THERAPIST: What do you mean, it was nice?

EDITH: Not to have those feelings of being pulled around by a chain.

THERAPIST: You still have them.

EDITH: I do, yes.

THERAPIST: So you really didn't get away from it.

EDITH: Well, sometimes when he's not pulling me around I don't feel that way. But sometimes it's bizarre: here I am married to someone who's playing the same games, and I guess I must be playing the same games, too.

A CONSULTATION

At the end of this period, the therapist requested a consultation with a colleague. Edith had continued to come to therapy regularly, sometimes alone and sometimes with Frank, for the next four months. During that time she had made some progress in achieving self-focus and in recognizing that some of her bitterness came from her experience with her mother and her brothers. However, she insisted that her bitterness from her relationship with her mother, though once strong, had been dissipated even before her mother died. She was reluctant to bring these issues back into her cut-off relationship with her brothers and continued to nurture her anger at Frank. Frank continued to try to make a pretzel out of himself in order to get back into her good graces. The goals of the consultation were (1) to assess Frank's efforts at change and the impact these efforts were having on the relationship, and (2) to focus on Edith's progress in neutralizing her bitterness by distributing it more accurately and then dealing with it in the context of those relationships where it belonged.

The consultation had two parts. In the first, the consulting therapist focused on Frank and how much of his effort at changing had been directed at influencing Edith to change her mind about leaving him. In the second, he looked at whether Edith had attained self-focus and was motivated to work on herself and her own part in her dilemma. He placed her bitterness in the context of the triangle consisting of Frank, her mother, and herself.

In the following segments, the therapist moves in to get Frank focused on his own problems with intimacy rather than complaining about Edith's. He then presses Frank about how much his efforts at change have been a fabrication aimed at getting Edith back rather than at really changing himself.

THERAPIST: Were you kind of presenting the worst side of yourself to Edith for a long time?

EDITH: Yes.

FRANK: Yes, I probably think so.

EDITH: Want the laundry list?

THERAPIST: Edith has the list over there and she's going to run it up.

FRANK: Oh, yeah.

THERAPIST: If you want to get intimacy you have to prepare yourself. One of the ways is learning to talk about yourself.

FRANK: I would think that the worst part of me is the manner in which I have tried to control Edith's life.

THERAPIST: Let me tell you what I'm driving at. I get a picture of you, for whatever reason—anxious, or depressed, or whatever state you were in—presenting to Edith a kind of obnoxious Frank, or the worst side of Frank. This was doing damage to you and to the relationship. Now, with Edith threatening to leave you, you've kind of had shock therapy and it made you realize what you almost lost, and that served the purpose of getting you to do something. Now, if you're going to do something about it, you've got a choice. You can manufacture a Frank that fits Edith's criteria, and try to do some kind of a dance that will fit those criteria, or you can find the Frank that is valuable and the positive person to be with, and begin to be able to lead with that and become more of that person than this fabricated Frank that you might manufacture to fit what you think Edith wants so you can hold onto her. The fabricated Frank won't work.

FRANK: Yeah, and I don't want to fabricate myself on the basis of keeping Edith and that sort of thing. I really want to change myself, to be able to be happier.

THERAPIST: So how are you doing with that?

FRANK: Well, tonight I start bridge lessons.

THERAPIST: That sounds like the fabricated Frank. Come on now, tell me about the real Frank—you know, the positive parts of Frank, your natural resources. That's mainly what I'm talking about.

FRANK: I feel that I've gotten to the point where I can relate much better to our children.

THERAPIST: So Frank the father has been improving. What parts of you have come to the fore in that improvement? How are you different now from the way you were?

FRANK: Well, I talk to them, I relate to them a little better.

THERAPIST: What are the assets that you bring to those kids, that they can benefit from?

FRANK: Experience, having gone through growing up. Shelter and comfort in terms of when they hurt for whatever reasons. To listen to them and try to get more involved in activities that they are interested in and concerned about, and just in fact doing more things with them.

THERAPIST: Is that the real Frank or the fabricated Frank?

FRANK: I think it's the real Frank.

THERAPIST: Now Edith doesn't mind that you go off and do this with your kids and with Franky?

FRANK: No, she enjoys the fact that once in a while I can take the kids and do something and leave her to herself.

THERAPIST: Take the pressure off.

FRANK: Yes, and she doesn't mind at all.

THERAPIST: How else is the real Frank coming to the fore?

FRANK: Well, in my job, I think I'm starting to get the respect, knowledge, and ability in the areas that I'm working in and starting to accomplish things at work. They say I'm getting a promotion now, which is the first promotion I've had in years.

THERAPIST: So your natural resource as a professional has improved.

FRANK: I'm also in the process of getting a professional engineer's license. That's another goal I have this year.

THERAPIST: It's beginning to look like you don't have enough time to be outrageous any more.

.   .   .   .

THERAPIST: Over the years have you seen Edith as more easily and naturally comfortable with intimacy than you have been?

FRANK: Yes, I think so.

THERAPIST: Have you ever allowed her to teach you ways of getting in touch with yourself that might increase your skill?

FRANK: We've never really pursued that element of it.

THERAPIST: Do you have trust in Edith's ability to be a good mentor?

FRANK: I don't know, I'd have to see. I think I would; on the surface I think so, but I don't really know.

[At this point, the consulting therapist turns his attention to Edith, to assess her self-focus and to evaluate the extent to which she has succeeded in sorting out her bitterness and distributing it appropriately. The following excerpts illustrate the work and bring into sharp focus the triangles with Edith's mother.]

THERAPIST: What are you thinking sitting there, Edith?

EDITH: I was thinking of all the years I was trying to teach him and he didn't want to hear it or talk about it.

THERAPIST: Well, do you think he's more available now?

EDITH: Certainly he's more available, but he wouldn't let me teach him how to relate to people. He's never listened that closely.

THERAPIST: Do you think he's ready to listen to you yet?

EDITH: I don't think it's a question of ready; I don't know if he's capable.

THERAPIST: So that's still your question—whether there is any potential there. You must have thought that the potential was there some time ago, or you wouldn't have married him.

EDITH: Yeah, I guess, but I guess over time I found eventually that there was sort of a vacuum in him when it comes to intimacy. When I left him I thought it was totally a vacuum. Now I'm thinking that there's maybe more potential there.

THERAPIST: Would you be a good mentor if he let you be?

EDITH: I think if he let me I'd probably be good, if he really listened and believed in me.

THERAPIST: Would he be afraid that you'd try to control him, even though you've never done it for fifteen years?

EDITH: I don't think he'd be afraid that I'm trying to control him. I wouldn't tell him how to be.

THERAPIST: Because you don't want a fabricated Frank?

EDITH: No, I don't. That really sickens me.

THERAPIST: How would you judge his progress? How much has been fabricated Frank, how much has been an evolution of the really positive him that was hidden behind all that crap for so long?

EDITH: I don't know. I think there is some positive Frank, but I think that some of it is fabricated only on the basis that sometimes he squeaks out these statements that make me feel that it is a fabrication, using terms like "if I behave in such a way" or "I'm afraid to do this because if I do that you'll get angry."

FRANK: Well, it's true.

THERAPIST: It's like even if he gets the more lovable Frank to the surface, that other Frank is still going to be back there someplace. I mean, it ain't gonna go away.

EDITH: I don't think so.

THERAPIST: Now are you sitting there just kind of waiting for him to somehow prove himself, or are you working on you, too?

EDITH: I think I'm working on me.

THERAPIST: What are you working on?

EDITH: I'm working on my bitter bank. [Laughter] No, I'm really working on myself as an individual to pull my life together with or without Frank. It's a lot more interesting.

THERAPIST: Part of that entails working on your bitterness and resentment and stuff like that.

EDITH: No, holding, keeping the bitterness. Our therapist is under the impression that we should investigate our bitterness and throw it away, and I've decided in the last week or two that it's a very important thing for me to hold onto.

THERAPIST: Tell me about that.

EDITH: Well, because I'm very easygoing, and unless I have something to hold onto, I'm going to get stepped on all over again. Some people have a natural instinct to protect themselves and that's good and I want my kids to have that, but some of us don't, really. I have to have my bitter bank to say, well, there is another part of everybody that has to be strong and not be a patsy.

THERAPIST: I think that's valid. Would you have an eventual goal to be able to do it without going for the elixir of bitterness to fortify yourself?

EDITH: Yes, absolutely, that would be the ideal. It's like the feeling with a person who's really sweet and nice to you, and forgetting that that person can turn around and stab you in the back, but if you have that knowledge up front and you hold onto that knowledge, you're not going to be stabbed in the back quite as easily.

THERAPIST: But when you get to the point that you don't need the elixir, you'll still have to take the risk of being hurt again in the relationship.

EDITH: True.

THERAPIST: That's a tall order.

EDITH: I think so, especially in a short time.

THERAPIST: I agree. Do you think that with your therapist you've been able to divide up that bitterness in terms of what belongs to Frank and what belongs to other relationships in your life? Or is it 99.9 percent organized around Frank?

EDITH: There is some bitterness I have that doesn't belong to Frank, but I don't think I mix them up. I think his bitterness is all his.

THERAPIST: How do you know that you're not overloading it, how can you be sure? Maybe you're accurate, I just wondered how you make the distinction.

EDITH: Well, I think the bitterness he's talking about is from my previous relationship with my mother, and I finally came to terms with her and dealt with it and told her about it before she died. Then she came to me and said I was right, so I think a lot of that bitterness has been diffused or it's gone. Unfortunately, the bitterness with Frank is like I recreated another situation that is very similar. His trying to control is my mother all over again, and actually Frank is a lot easier going than my mother was.

THERAPIST: Your mother was quite a lady, huh?

EDITH: You got it. But I think he built his own mess.

THERAPIST: So you are presensitized to some of his stuff from your mother, but Frank also had a big part in it himself, apart from your mother.

EDITH: Right.

THERAPIST: Tell me about how you resolved it with your mother.

EDITH: Well, I just put her in a rest home. I divorced myself from her in that I cut her out of my life by putting her in a position where I was no longer involved with her daily care.

THERAPIST: I think your therapist told me about that. That was the thing where you handed her off to your brothers and said, "Enough."

EDITH: Yeah, enough is enough, and she said that she never wanted to see me again, and I said fine, that's very good, I agree with you, and it was she who came back to me and said she was absolutely wrong in her dealing with me and she apologized for it. So I think because she said it before she died, a lot of that bitterness is gone. If she didn't I would probably carry it around with me a lot now.

THERAPIST: So you and she worked everything out before she died?

EDITH: As it turned out when she did die, she told me she was going to say good-bye now. Was I okay? If I was okay she was going to sleep and not wake up. If I wasn't okay she would hang in there, but she couldn't hang in much longer. So she actually willed the day she was going to die.

THERAPIST: Did she do it?

EDITH: Yes.

THERAPIST: That's a lady with real control. She wasn't faking it.

EDITH: No. But she waited until I was there and then said to me, "I can't hang on anymore. Can I go now? Are you okay?" And I said, "Uh-huh," and she said, "I'm going to sleep now and not wake up again." And she did.

THERAPIST: Was she looking for forgiveness?

EDITH: No, she's not the type. She did ask me for forgiveness, but her statement was that she was sorry, that's the end of it. She forgave herself.

THERAPIST: Did the two of you ever get into the specifics of the stuff

between you? I mean the kinds of ways you think she damaged you, that she felt that you hadn't been enough of a
daughter?

EDITH: Yes, absolutely. Oh, she never felt I wasn't enough of a daughter; she just felt she owned me until she died and I should
make my life taking care of her. In fact, I should never have
gotten married, I should have waited until she died. A pretty
old bride. She actually had me so I could take care of her. That
was her whole idea, and Frank's idea was he had married me
to take care of him. Neither of them really gave a damn about
what I needed.

THERAPIST: What do you need?

EDITH: Space, to be myself.

THERAPIST: What does that mean?

EDITH: Being able to come into the house without explaining why I'm
five minutes late or ten minutes or an hour late.

THERAPIST: Did both of them do that—did your mother used to quiz you
like that, too?

EDITH: Basically, they liked to know I was around, I think then they
knew where I was.

THERAPIST: Do you see much of your brothers?

EDITH: No.

THERAPIST: You're still angry with them?

EDITH: No, not really.

THERAPIST: Suppose I told you that every time Frank set off feelings of
upset and resentment in you, I wanted you to call one of your
brothers and talk to him about your mother. You know, resur-
rect her for a few minutes.

EDITH: Why would I want to do a thing like that?

THERAPIST: At least your brothers never tried to control you. Maybe they
dumped their responsibility, but they were deprived of knowing your mother the way you did. Only you can do something
about their deprivation.

EDITH: Just what I need, a few more grown boys to mother. Anyway,
how would I do it?

THERAPIST: Do you still dream about your mother?

EDITH: Yes.

THERAPIST: Tell them about your dreams.

The consultant's attempt to move Edith toward her brothers and to
deal with her bitterness about her mother and about their leaving the

mother with her is a key move. Unless she reconnects with her brothers and deals with the unresolved extended family issues with them, she will continue to place all her bitterness in her marriage.

As a result of the consultation, which was done in the presence of all the members of the Marital Project at CFL, a treatment plan was decided on. First, the theme of the "fabricated Frank" was to be pursued in sessions with Frank. He was to be confronted again and again with how much his efforts at change were directed at Edith rather than at himself. He was to increase his work at developing his relationships with his children and with his extended family. He was to allow Edith to be his intimacy mentor when she said she was ready. For Edith, the treatment plan was for her to work on her triangle with her parents by reconnecting with her brothers.

The consultation revealed the fact that their therapist had a problem in establishing a connection with Edith. This problem was complicated by the length of time he had worked alone with Frank before he began to see Edith; in Edith's eyes, that made him Frank's therapist. The team recommended that the therapist bring up this problem with Edith and see if it could be worked out. If not, the couple would have to be referred to another member of the Marital Project who could establish a more equitable relationship with each of them.

Stepfamily Triangles

A final group of triangles within the family are those that occur in stepfamilies. As in all the other triangles we have mentioned, stepfamily triangles allow for the avoidance of issues between husband and wife. Often entwined in the marital issues are pieces of unfinished business from the spouses' previous marriages. At the heart of the triangulation are questions of loyalty in relationships. The biological tie to children and the historical and financial tie to previous spouses present a multitude of opportunities for the stepfamily marriage to fall into conflict. Often the honeymoon is over before the wedding takes place, as the family systems involved begin reverberating in response to the impending marriage. Added to this already complicated picture is the potential for triangles with four sets of in-laws and former in-laws, including worried grandparents who fear that a remarriage will disrupt their relationships with grandchildren.

TYPES OF STEPFAMILY TRIANGLES

Remarried couples present clinically with one or more of the following triangles:

1. *The wicked-stepparent triangle.* In this triangle there is open warfare between stepchildren and stepparent, and the natural parent is pulled back and forth between children and new spouse. The stepparent is usually critical of the stepchild, and the stepchild, often an adolescent, is enraged at being criticized by this interloper: "Who does he think he is?" "You're not my dad." The biological parent often feels torn by the need to defend one or both parties in the conflict. It is seen as a no-win situation.

2. *The perfect-stepparent triangle.* The stepparent may treat the stepchild as his or her own, often in response to an implicit demand from the spouse. In this triangle the stepparent operates as the rescuer, moving toward the stepchild to "straighten out" the child or perhaps to make up to the child for the past. The biological parent is in a distant, more comfortable position, initially delighted at the relationship between the child and the new spouse. Trouble arises when the stepparent inevitably fails in some respect and the biological parent becomes critical. The stepchild also becomes reactive as the stepparent attempts to fill in the distance between the biological parent and the child. This triangle is most commonly seen with an overly close stepmother and a distant biological father or with a stepfather trying to make it up to a stepchild for the absence of a biological father because of death or divorce.

3. *The ghost-of-the-former-spouse triangle.* In this triangle, the wife or husband is reactive to the partner's relationship with a former spouse, usually the mother of the stepchildren. Issues of alimony and child support as well as the nature and frequency of contact with the former wife can create open conflict between the marital partners.

4. *The grandparent triangle.* This triangle is especially pertinent if the grandparents are forced to deal with a former son- or daughter-in-law with whom there was a good deal of reactivity prior to the divorce. For example, if a husband feels that his mother-in-law was too interfering and influential with his former wife, he may have trouble allowing her a grandmother role after divorce and remarriage. This can also happen when the custodial parent has not remarried, but it is more likely and perhaps more intense when there has been a remarriage.

TREATMENT GOALS

After the therapist identifies the most relevant stepfamily triangle and the process is brought out, he or she tries to shift the relationships so that they reflect the real and functional picture of the role of each member of the stepfamily. For example, stepparents who attempt to act as though they are the biological parents frequently run into difficulty. A stepparent who is seen as "good" or "wicked" may be moving too quickly or attempting to cross biological boundaries; he or she should carve out a more appropriate role and develop it over time with the child. Remarried parents need to have realistic expectations of each other as stepparents. The ghosts of former spouses must be made explicit and dealt with openly. The couple must accept the fact that the bonding between former spouses is never broken when the marriage has produced offspring but lives on for generations to come.

The second goal in dealing with the stepfamily triangle is to address the interlocking triangles that are affecting the central triangle. In the case of a remarriage, the first marriage and the relationships with biological children may have been pushed to the background by the new relationship, and the hurts and anger attached to these relationships become displaced onto the stepfamily. A father cut off from his own children may be moving in on his stepchildren to shape them up or make them his, without regard for the loss he has suffered by not having a relationship with his own children. When met with a rebuff from his stepchildren, his reactivity can be intense.

Residual bitterness from the previous marriage is inevitably exposed as people move from their position in the triangle and begin to understand that movement. Unfinished business, mainly the buried bitterness from the previous relationship, needs to be explored. This is the third goal in treating stepfamily triangles.

A STEPFAMILY TRIANGLE: THE ADAMSES

The following case is an example of a remarriage that immediately fell into conflict. Three stepfamily triangles were active at the time the couple sought treatment.

Joseph and Mary Ellen Adams, fifty-nine and forty-two respectively, had been married a little less than six months when they decided to see a therapist. Although both their families had seemed happy with the idea of the marriage, Joseph was running into a good deal of conflict with his two stepsons, and Mary Ellen was critical of his manner of dealing with them. Moreover, Joseph's daughter Liz was becoming an irritation to Mary Ellen by dropping in unannounced on the weekend, bringing her boyfriend and hanging around. Ruth, Joseph's former wife, was phoning Joseph asking for rides to her various medical appointments. She did not drive, and Joseph would often fit her trips into his schedule. Mary Ellen was furious at Joseph for accommodating Ruth. By the time the therapist saw them at evaluation, Joseph was talking about leaving Mary Ellen, because he felt like a stranger in the house. Mary Ellen saw the problem in Joseph: his temper with her children and his inability to face the consequences of standing up to his former wife.

Both Joseph and Mary Ellen had been married to alcoholics when they met in Al-Anon several years before their marriage. Joseph had been married to Ruth for twenty-five years, and prior to their divorce she had spent many years in and out of alcohol treatment centers. She had also been admitted to psychiatric hospitals many times for suicide attempts and depression. Since the divorce Ruth had been going to AA meetings. Though she was having occasional slips, by and large she was doing better than she had in years.

Joseph had a twenty-three-year-old daughter, Liz, who shared an apartment with her boyfriend. As an adolescent Liz had been in and out of trouble; she was arrested several times for shoplifting and suspended from school for drinking. At the time of Joseph's marriage to Mary Ellen, Liz had a job at the local pub and was attending school at night. She never saw her mother, and although Joseph had been physically abusive to Liz earlier in their relationship, both reported that over the last few years their relationship had been pleasant.

Mary Ellen and Robert had been married fifteen years when he committed suicide during a drinking binge, hanging himself in a motel near his home. He had threatened suicide several times in the past, but he had never actually made an attempt. The couple had three children: Rick, now seventeen, Robert, Jr., fifteen, and Suzy, ten. At the time of Robert's suicide Mary Ellen took the children to a mental health clinic for treatment so that the impact of the suicide could be minimized. As far as Mary Ellen was concerned, her Al-Anon program had adequately helped her deal with Robert's death.

Mary Ellen had always been a career woman, and after her husband's death she worked more intensively to make up for the lack of money. Being the eldest child in a family of many children had taught her how to take responsibility for others even when she was somewhat shaken. Her greatest fear was that her children would somehow be marked, not only by Robert's death but also by his dependency on alcohol. As they entered adolescence, Rick and Robert, Jr., swore to their mother that they would never touch alcohol—or smoke, for that matter. So far they had managed to stick to their pledge, but as they went through high school they were both feeling more and more apart from the local teenage social life. At home, all three children were constantly bickering with one another and also with their mother and stepfather.

The therapist chose to address the triangle that seemed to be creating the most obvious pressure on the family. The wicked-stepparent triangle in which Joseph was in battle with Rick and Robert, Jr., and at times with Mary Ellen, was easy to pick out. In the first session in which all members of the household were included, the children eagerly told the therapist how Joseph, who had moved into their house, was now trying to boss them around.

RICK: He [referring to Joseph] is unreal. He comes storming into the den demanding that we clean up the dishes and start dinner. I told him to chill out. . . . I didn't eat today. [Robert, Jr., and Suzy start to laugh and begin talking at once, voicing their complaints about Joseph.]

THERAPIST: Hold on, guys. I hear that you're having trouble with Joseph, but I need to ask him a question. Joseph, how did you get to be the wicked stepfather?

JOSEPH: It took hard work . . . [He laughs.] Mary Ellen works long hours, and these kids are spoiled; wouldn't think of picking up a dish or starting a meal. Even Suzy is picking up their bad habits. I made a chart—one for the kitchen chores and one for the laundry—with everyone on it. It works for one day, and then we're back to square zero.

MARY ELLEN: Last night was so bad that Joseph and Rick got into a physical fight. I've had it with all this fighting. I end up screaming at everyone.

THERAPIST: Joseph, I need to go back to the question of how you got into this position.

JOSEPH: I can't stand to see all this chaos and mess. I can't work in a kitchen . . .

THERAPIST: But how is it you are shaping up the kids, instead of their mother doing it?

JOSEPH: I think she's been too lenient, and also they have had no father around to keep them in line.

The remainder of this session dealt with Joseph's and Mary Ellen's expectations of themselves as stepfather and mother and with their expectations of each other. The children's resentment was partially in reaction to their previous relationship with Joseph; prior to the marriage Joseph had been seen as friend and companion, especially by Rick. Since he had married Mary Ellen, he had become a "shape-up" stepparent. They had lost a friend.

Mary Ellen had had problems with the boys and their lack of responsibility long before Joseph entered the picture. She admitted that she handled them in an inconsistent manner, mainly by blowing up and yelling when she was frustrated and ignoring the problem the rest of the time. The therapist put Mary Ellen in charge of handling the kitchen and laundry detail with her children. This move confronted her discomfort with being firm and consistent, especially with her boys. As she began to work through her discomfort, the interlocking triangle with her first husband and the children began to emerge. Mary Ellen's grief for her fatherless children undercut any attempt on her part to establish authority and firmness: "After all, hadn't they been through enough, living with an alcoholic father and then his suicide?" Being tough felt to her like being punitive. Mary Ellen began to see that she had not allowed herself to admit that she too had "gone through enough."

As Mary Ellen became more focused on her expectations of Joseph, she began to link her dreams for her second marriage to her disappointments in her marriage to Robert. She presented herself as a woman who had been through a great deal but with no ill effects emotionally. As the therapy progressed, it became clear that Mary Ellen had several islands of sensitivity that had developed in her marriage to Robert.

THERAPIST: Mary Ellen, you seem to have spent a good deal of time sorting out Robert's suicide.

MARY ELLEN: Oh, I have. He had threatened a few times before. This time he was out on a two-week binge. He called me and was drunk. I had told him if he didn't stop drinking and get some help I was going to end the marriage. I don't feel guilty. He had said several times he would kill himself if I left him, but I'm not responsible. Thank God for Al-Anon. It saved my life.

THERAPIST: Does anyone ever commit suicide without leaving walking wounded behind?

MARY ELLEN: My kids are wounded [she begins to fill up], but not me.

THERAPIST: Maybe angry.

MARY ELLEN: Oh, you bet. I carried that man around for years, even supported him, but he always kept me hanging . . . waiting . . . always waiting.

THERAPIST: For what?

MARY ELLEN: You name it. For him to come home, to pay bills, to be drunk, to talk. I can't stand waiting for anything, even today.

THERAPIST: How does your hating to wait affect how you handle the kids and Joseph?

MARY ELLEN: I don't know. Well . . . maybe I can't wait for the kids to do what I tell them. I start hollering, and Joseph and I get very uptight when he is not working on getting a job. Here I am waiting on a man again.

THERAPIST: I hear that both the kids and Joseph get to you, but how do you know how much of your upset is attached to them and how much is left over from Robert?

The presence of Robert's ghost and its impact on Mary Ellen as she dealt with both her children and Joseph became clearer as the therapy progressed. The triangle with Mary Ellen, Robert, and Joseph was particularly explicit in the session in which Mary Ellen presented the therapist with one of their many battles. The conflict was over what Mary Ellen called Joseph's messiness and "pack-ratting." Joseph wanted to have a desk in their bedroom and Mary Ellen refused, claiming that Joseph never cleaned off the top of a desk and insisted on piling old *New York Times Book Reviews* on any flat surface. Joseph was angry that again Mary Ellen was considering the house her house and the bedroom her bedroom. Mary Ellen had a solution to which Joseph objected vehemently:

MARY ELLEN: It's really so simple. I told Joseph that he can have Robert's desk, which is in my office in the basement. I kept the desk in case the kids want it one day. It's filled with old junk, but I told Joseph that I would even clean it out for him.

JOSEPH: I have to say that I take it very personally that Mary Ellen describes me as messy. I only wish you could see the pile of clothes Mary Ellen has in the bedroom on her chair. [Mary Ellen starts to jump to her own defense, explaining why she has clothes piled up, and the therapist motions her to be quiet.] Moreover [Joseph raises his voice and becomes tight-lipped] I do not appreciate being relegated to the basement, especially when she puts her crap all over *our* bedroom.

MARY ELLEN: Now wait a minute!

THERAPIST: Hold on, folks. How did we get from Robert's desk to World War III, Joseph?

JOSEPH: First of all, I can't use that man's desk. How would his kids feel, and honestly I would feel very uncomfortable. It is a symbol of Robert. I never could think of it as mine.

THERAPIST: You mean it seems to you as though Robert is still there—sort of his ghost, or something?

JOSEPH: That's it exactly. His kids, his desk, his house, sometimes even his wife. I can't explain it, it's almost spooky. Mary Ellen wants me to just fit into the house and her life . . . not make waves . . . I don't feel as if anything is mine or ours.

THERAPIST: Mary Ellen, Joseph speaks of Robert as though he's still living in the house.

MARY ELLEN: I think Joseph has more trouble with Robert than I do.

THERAPIST: Do you have a theory about that?

MARY ELLEN: I guess I'm still pretty angry at Robert, and although I'm not glad he's dead, I'm glad he's gone. Joseph seems almost sympathetic toward him.

THERAPIST: What do you think of Mary Ellen's idea, Joseph?

JOSEPH: I am sympathetic toward him. I knew him, and he was a nice guy . . . except an alcoholic . . . A rotten disease. [His eyes fill with tears.] It was so sad, his death, especially for the children.

THERAPIST: What makes you sad for the children?

JOSEPH: I guess the same thing that makes me sad for my daughter, for Ruth, for Mary Ellen, for myself . . . all of us affected by alcoholism. Such a waste!

THERAPIST: You struggled with Ruth's suicide threats for years.

JOSEPH: Oh, yes. [He fills up again.] I never will get over that dread, that feeling when I'd walk into the house—maybe she's done it, I hope Liz hasn't found her on the floor. [He heaves a sigh, wipes his eyes, reaches for Mary Ellen's hand; she looks very somber.] Enough of that, those days are behind us.

THERAPIST: I know, according to the calendar they are, but apparently not according to your insides. Sometimes it takes a long time to process the kinds of experience you have both been through, and it takes a long time to grieve over lost hopes and dreams.

Both Mary Ellen and Joseph had unfinished business with their first spouses. It was only in making a connection to their hurt and disappointment and sadness in their first marriages that they were able to make any progress in calming the conflict in the relationship with each other.

In this chapter and the previous one we have dealt at length with what we consider to be the most important element in marital conflict: the triangle. Marital conflict always involves triangles, usually several at once and always fairly intense. Triangles can organize the marital conflict, providing a focus for it, and often they cover up the dysfunctional process in the marriage itself. Triangles outside the family usually are activated because the system cannot deal with one or more of the triangles within the family. The formation of triangles and the process of triangulation are closely related to the well being and level of functioning of the two people who make up the marital couple. We turn now to a consideration of the dimensions of the individual that affect the marriage.

5

Dimensions of the Individual in Marital Conflict

EACH PARTNER comes to a marriage with a temperament and operating style that have been shaped and honed in the family of origin. In that family the person has experienced an emotional process that is inevitably carried over to the marriage. The extended family experience, combined with the cultural and social context of the time, forms in each spouse both a set of expectations about marriage and a set of personal characteristics that together determine to a large extent how he or she will function in the marital relationship.

In our model, the individual in the marital couple is considered from five perspectives:

1. Differentiation and the adaptive level of functioning
2. Behavioral operating styles
3. Projection versus self-focus and the relationship position

4. Expectation-to-alienation progression
5. Dysfunctional Spouse.

Differentiation and the Adaptive Level of Functioning

As we have seen, in assessing the multigenerational family system, we first determine the premorbid state of the family prior to the onset of symptoms. Similarly, in considering an individual member of the family, we attempt to establish his or her basic level of emotional maturity and ability to function autonomously. The concepts of *differention of self* and *adaptive level of functioning* are most useful in this regard.

DIFFERENTIATION OF SELF

According to Bowen, "the level of differentiation is the degree to which one self fuses or merges into another self in a close emotional relationship" (1978, p. 200). In pure form, it is the absence of fusion. Bowen has attempted to objectify his concept of differentiation by placing it on a scale from 0 to 100, 0 representing the lowest level of emotional functioning or complete fusing with another, as in schizophrenia, and 100 the highest level of functioning, a theoretical level that would be found only in some biological and psychological being yet to be discovered. Bowen developed the concept while doing research on schizophrenia and then attempted to refine it working with people from the opposite end of the scale, the "high functioners."

In the Bowen schema the scale serves at least two functions: it can be used to predict the chances for change after clinical intervention, and it can serve to measure change over long periods of time. The scale is Bowen's least clearly developed and his least well understood concept; its focus on individual family members clearly defines the Bowen principle that a change in one member of a family system will eventually result in a change in the entire system.

In our model, differentiation is defined as the process of partially freeing oneself from the emotional entrapment of one's family. Being caught in the family emotional process makes human robots out of most of us, and being freed from it, even to a small degree, represents an increase in differentiation.

Ninety per cent of the time we know that we are caught only by the symptoms: defensive and reactive behaviors that are accompanied by significant projection. We all have triggers that set off emotional reactivity in us, people or events that we are especially vulnerable to.

How does one get uncaught? It is best, obviously, not to get caught in the first place, but to do that one would have to settle for not being born. The fact that one is dealt one's family of origin has a significant impact on one's potential level of differentiation. On the one hand this reality may produce envy toward those dealt "better" families, but on the other hand it may also serve to provide a reality base for one's expectations. The more one knows about the state of one's family system prior to one's birth, the better understanding one will have of the emotional system one is a part of.

The opposite of being caught is getting free. Getting free calls for analyzing one's own role as an active participant in one's relationship system, instead of analyzing the characters of the important people in one's life. Pigeonholing other people serves only to foster and support an automatic projection process. Rather, those people must be seen as just other members of the same system responding to the same anxiety that one is reacting to oneself. To get free one must take responsibility for one's anxiety and for the reactive feelings and behaviors that go along with it. In short, one must stop blaming others and look to oneself.

The concept of differentiation, then, serves two major purposes. First, it is a good measure of an individual's or a family's baseline level of functioning. Second, it provides a justification for extended family work, whether that work is done to relieve pressure from the marriage or as reinforcement of a positive therapy response. At any rate, change in one's level of differentiation is a long-term goal. As a marker of progress in therapy or of short-term improvement in functioning, it is of limited usefulness even in its originator's terms. Differentiation of self is therefore best used as an indicator of one's long-term psychological functioning—as a baseline measure of a person's strengths over time, resilience in the face of significant stress, and accessibility to therapeutic intervention.

ADAPTIVE LEVEL OF FUNCTIONING

Because differentiation is difficult to understand and measure and at best can be evaluated only over time, there would seem to be a need for a concept of self that is more easily measured in the short term and that can be incorporated with the concept of differentiation into a method for evaluating an individual's short-term and long-term functioning within the family. The concept of the *adaptive level of functioning* meets that need.

Like differentiation, adaptive level of functioning can be a fuzzy concept. We use the term to mean the relative ability to maintain functioning in the areas of productivity, relationships, and physical and emotional well-being in the face of significant amounts of stress.

For example, a person faced with a certain amount of stress may have a high enough level of differentiation so that he suffers little emotional distress and therefore requires little conscious effort to maintain a certain level of functioning. Given a greater level of stress, however, one that does create emotional distress, that person might need a significant amount of conscious effort to maintain functioning. The adaptive level of functioning consists of the ability to make that conscious effort. Thus, at a given level of differentiation a person might automatically handle x amount of stress without the production of symptoms. An increase in his level of differentiation would enable him to handle automatically $x + y$ amount of stress. But that same person might also be able to handle $x + y$ amount of stress without an increase in differentiation by consciously mobilizing the coping forces at his disposal—in other words, by increasing his adaptive level of functioning.

Since 1979 Guerin has used a Personal Functioning Index as a measure of a person's adaptive level of functioning at a given time. It is important to note that this index is a measure of present functioning rather than a categorization of psychopathology or character structure. Its categories are similar to those in DSM III's Axis V and include productivity, relationships, and personal well-being.

Productivity refers to the level at which a person is functioning in whatever job he or she has to do—as a physician, a housewife, a student, or whatever. The amount of energy available for work, the satisfaction obtained, and the efficiency and creativity expressed should all be evaluated.

Relationships refers to a person's connections with important others. How much attention and creativity are invested in nurturing relationships? It is often useful to compare that investment with the time and creativity invested in productivity.

Personal well-being refers to the amount of attention and creativity invested in taking care of one's own physical and emotional needs.

Very few people do well in all three areas at the same time. High functioning in two out of three areas at any given time is the best that most of us can expect to achieve. The life cycle can create shifts in the areas in which one functions well and those in which one functions poorly. For example, in the early stages of one's work life one may focus primarily on productivity, allowing relationships to suffer somewhat, and later, after certain occupational or professional goals have been attained, turn one's attention to relationships.

Marriage may allow a person to neglect one area because the spouse is functioning highly in that area. For example, a husband may feel he can neglect the relationship area because his wife is taking care of that, while his wife may neglect productivity because she feels that is her husband's job.

It is important clinically to reinforce the areas of strength and use energy from those areas to improve the less functional ones. It is also helpful for people to be aware of the order in which they allow these areas to decline under stress. For example, in one person, productivity may be the first to go and the last to return during periods of increased stress, whereas someone else may stop exercising and put on weight as the initial response to an increase in stress.

An example of the difference between differentiation and adaptive level of functioning is provided by George Conrad, a fifty-year-old physician who first entered therapy at the age of thirty-six. After three or four months of couple therapy, both he and his wife Kay were able to obtain a workable amount of self-focus and experiment with their marital struggle in more effective ways. At that point George elected to continue therapy in order to work on his relationships with his extended family. His decision was prompted by two things. One was his sense that the relationship with his parents was, if anything, overly close and that it impinged on his marriage. The other was what he believed to be an inappropriate fear that one or both of his parents would die. In therapy he talked about how this fear was present from childhood and may in some remote way have been connected to the fact that both his maternal grandparents had been orphans.

George also speculated that his choice of medicine as a career might have been prompted partly by his attempt to master his fear. He joked about how he had been intrigued by psychiatry when he was in medical school but had decided it did not offer enough opportunity to be a hero. The fear that his parents would die reached its peak when as an intern in a Manhattan hospital he would experience flash fantasies of being called to the emergency room to treat an injured or acutely ill patient, only to find one of his parents dead on a stretcher. Eventually he handled those fantasies by doing his medical residency three hundred miles from New York City.

When George began therapy, those flash fantasies were several years behind him, but even then an unexpected call from his brother would unnerve him. If one of his parents became even moderately ill, he would overreact, cancelling days of office hours to fly home and check the situation at first hand. In monthly sessions for two years, he and the therapist worked on lowering his anxiety and on decreasing his excessive sense of responsibility and power. He opened up the issue of his grandparents' deaths with his mother and her siblings and worked on bridging the cutoffs in his mother's sibling subsystem. He also began to talk to his father about his fears about his mother.

The outcome of this work was quite positive. George was able to visit home with much less anxiety and to take the unexpected phone calls and his parents' illnesses more in stride. He consciously overrode the impulse to fly home and gave up an appropriate amount of responsibility to his quite competent brother.

Seven years after terminating therapy, George called and asked for an appointment to discuss the impact on him of his father's terminal illness. He and the therapist worked off and on for eighteen months as he saw his father through the illness to his grave. Considering the cohesiveness and relatively low level of differentiation in this family, he managed himself and his relationship with his father and other extended family members in a highly functional way. His productivity slipped somewhat, but only at those times when it was appropriate for him to be away from work and more available to his father and mother.

After his father died, George took up the work of closing the hole in the system by working on the relationship with his mother, his siblings, and his children. During this time there was a reactivation of the marital conflict, triggered by what he considered a lack of emotional support from his wife. They reentered couple therapy for two months, with significant improvement.

In nine years, then, there had been approximately thirty months of therapy with a total of thirty-eight visits. A question arises as to whether George's response to therapy represents an increase in his level of differentiation or simply an increase in his adaptive level of functioning. Probably it represents the latter. His ability to maintain his level of functioning was not accompanied by a significant decrease in his internal emotional distress. Rather, he limited his loss of functioning by skillfully managing high levels of emotional distress.

Four years later George returned to therapy, this time concerned about his fifteen-year-old son, who was mildly depressed and doing poorly in school. George had been struggling with the problem for over a year without success and found himself almost as phobic about his son's well-being as he had been years earlier about his parents'. Flash fantasies of automobile accidents involving his son had replaced the old ones about his parents, reinforcing the conclusion that therapy had produced an increase in adaptive level of functioning rather than an increase in basic level of differentiation. To say this is in no way to minimize this man's accomplishments or to denigrate increases in adaptive level of functioning. Rather, it is meant to keep a therapist grounded in what is possible in therapy in the short term and in what is predictable over the long term.

Behavioral Operating Styles

The phrase *behavioral operating styles,* as we saw in chapter 2, refers to the various ways people behave in relationships: how they manage and express their feelings, whether they are oriented to relationships or to objects and productivity, how open or closed their personal boundaries are, what emotional rhythms and time orientation they have, and whether by nature and in times of stress they move toward or away from other people. In our model, behavioral operating styles take the place of the notion of personality or character type, and temperament is included as one of the components of a person's operating style.

The concept of behavioral operating styles developed from our clinical experience, out of frustration with the limited usefulness of the more traditional personality and character descriptions. During the 1950s and 1960s, studies of the marital relationship often focused on the interaction between the personality types and character structures of the spouses. The classic psychoanalytic formulation was the combination of the obsessive male and the hysterical female. Therapy based on these constructs often attempted to elicit the psychogenetic factors in the coming together of these personality types and to deal with the "naturally occurring" transferential material in the couple's relationship.

Although these methods were based on valid observations of the connection between the relationship with one's parents and the subsequent relationship with one's spouse, they left us with two major dilemmas. The first was that the vast majority of marriages analyzed in terms of these constructs could be labeled as neurotic or existing largely to meet the neurotic needs of the individual spouses. The second was that these constructs represented fixed structures and left little room for interventions that might modify the interaction in the marital relationship.

In struggling with the second dilemma, Fogarty (1979b) introduced the idea of studying the movement patterns of the spouses toward and away from each other in response to stressful stimuli. He organized these ideas into the concepts of *the emotional pursuer* and the *emotional distancer.* He observed that in times of stress and conflict the emotional pursuer, usually the wife, moves toward her husband, who in response to the stress and the pursuing movement of his wife distances from her, usually moving toward involvement with an object.

In working with this idea clinically, Guerin has attempted to expand the concept to include a more detailed description of the emotional pursuer and the emotional distancer as well as a stepwise, predictable pattern that occurs in the relationship—the *interactional sequence,* described in chapter 2. Behavioral operating styles are seen as determined both constitutionally and in the context of specific relationships, in which they provide the balance necessary to long-term relationships. The characteristics of these complementary behavioral operating styles are spelled out in table 5-1.

Emotional pursuers tend to take the lion's share of responsibility for maintaining relationships. They have an internal and interpersonal rhythm that runs on two speeds: either full speed or dead stop. They are either doing everything at once, frantically keeping all life's balls in the air, or they are doing nothing at all and are oblivious to everyone and everything around them. Emotional pursuers value free access across boundaries into their own and others' emotional space. They enthusiastically undertake new tasks and adventures, taking more than reasonable risks with unbridled optimism. Their errors are errors of commission. Apology and making things explicit come easy, while endings and good-byes come hard.

Emotional distancers, on the other hand, are concerned mostly with productivity and have little interest in communicating personal thoughts and feelings. Their rhythm is steady and predictable. They would prefer that one not cross into their personal space, and they will gladly return the

TABLE 5–1

Characteristics of Emotional Pursuers and Emotional Distancers

Characteristic	Emotional pursuer	Emotional distancer
Expression of affect	Expresses emotions freely	Impassive, conceals and compartmentalizes emotions
Communicativeness	Open and frank in communicating personal thoughts and feelings	Uncommunicative with regard to personal thoughts and feelings
Orientation	Relationship-oriented	Object-oriented
Rhythm	Full speed or dead stop	Slow and steady
Temperament	Optimistic	Pessimistic
	Takes risks	Cautious
	Makes things explicit	Leaves things implicit
	Dislikes good-byes and endings	Less pain about good-byes and endings

favor by not crossing into anyone else's. Temperamentally they approach new tasks and adventures cautiously and with a "healthy" seasoning of pessimism. Errors are usually errors of omission. Apologies come especially hard, while leaving things implicit is easy, and ending and separating appear to cause little upset and emotional pain.

When the emotional climate is right, transition times are minimal, and stress is low, these two operating styles complement each other beautifully and bring out the best in both. Under stressful conditions, however, the very factors that provide the balance and the synchrony become a problem.

It should be noted that although people seem to operate with the same behavioral style in the majority of their relationships, there are always a few circumstances and relationships in which the tables are turned. A woman who is an emotional pursuer, for example, may more than meet her match and in response find herself operating with some of the characteristics of an emotional distancer. Similarly a man who is usually an emotional distancer can sometimes find himself operating as an emotional pursuer. Thus although personal factors are important in determining one's operating style, contextual factors are also highly influential.

Let us postulate a pursuer-distancer spectrum, ranging from 1 to 10, that measures people's constitutional tendencies to emotional pursuit or distance, with 1 referring to an extreme distancer and 10 referring to an extreme pursuer. Let us further imagine a husband who is a 5. If he is married to woman who is at 6 or above on the spectrum, he will over time become the distancer in their marriage. If he is married to a woman who is at 4 or below on the spectrum, he will over time become the pursuer in their relationship. Thus constitutional makeup and context combine to make members of a couple become either pursuers or distancers in their interaction with each other.

Real people are not pure types. The labels of pursuer and distancer describe general trends in a person, not the total person. There is a distancer in every pursuer, and a pursuer in every distancer. A person's opposite tendency can come out under any of several conditions: (1) in a relationship with someone who is at a more extreme point on the pursuer-distancer spectrum, (2) around certain issues (as in the case of the emotionally distant husband who is the sexual pursuer in a marriage), or (3) in response to changes in the other's actions (as in the case of the pursuing wife who distances when her husband finally moves toward her emotionally). Nevertheless, in spite of the qualifications, it is valid to speak of a complementary relationship between pursuer and distancer in most marriages.

Projection and Self-Focus

The therapist must reinforce the ability of each spouse to recognize projection for what it is—blaming the other for one's own limitations—and to understand his or her own role in the conflict. In reaction to emotional pain or upset, we all have an automatic emotional reflex that places the cause of that pain or upset outside ourselves. The more intense this projection becomes, the more it produces an experience of victimization and a tendency to hold others responsible for the way we feel and act. It demands that others change, instead of allowing us to take responsibility for our own behavior and emotional reactions.

The opposite of projection is self-focus, the ability to see one's own part in an emotional process. Instead of "you made me angry," which is a projective response, a person with self-focus is able to say: "You behaved thus, and so I responded by getting angry and going away." In the self-focus response, there is an acceptance of responsibility for one's own emotional response and subsequent behavior.

Self-focus involves maintaining enough *detachment* to be able to see the variety of responses that we may use in any given interaction. It is important to note, however, that detaching carries with it the potential pitfall of emotional disconnection, which is just a cover for projection. This phenomenon often occurs in a system with alcohol abuse. The alcoholic's spouse attempts detachment but in the process disconnects, with significant amounts of covert anger. The implicit message here is, "The problem is yours; I have no part in its maintenance." This response is projective, unlike a detachment that allows one to focus on one's own part in a relationship process that produces dysfunctions as a by-product.

Relationship Positions

Projection and self-focus may be used as the measuring rods of the three basic relationship positions that spouses may assume in a marriage: reactive, experimental, and functional. Projection keeps people in the reactive position, and some degree of self-focus is necessary for the experimental and functional positions.

THE REACTIVE POSITION

In the reactive position, the individual reacts to the behaviors of others. The husband who becomes quiet and withdrawn and spends more time at work in response to his wife's overflowing emotionality is in a reactive relationship position. That same husband exploding in anger when he can't take one more ounce of criticism is also in the reactive mode, as he is when he maintains a distant critical posture toward his wife's favorite male offspring. The wife who moves away in anger after years of unmet demands for relationship time or emotional connectedness is also in a position of reactive distance.

The reactive position works against the balanced functioning of the individual and the attainment of intimacy in the relationship. The form one's behavior takes in the reactive position is linked to one's operating style. For example, the emotional pursuer in the reactive position will either offer a "helpful" program for change or deliver abundant amounts of criticism. The emotional distancer will withdraw and become almost totally preoccupied with things or projects, limiting suggestions for the relationship to paths the emotional pursuer might take to get help with his or her problems. In this way the distancer tries to relieve the pressure of explicit emotional demands or the implicit demands from the pursuer's dysfunction.

The reactive position contains an abundance of projection and very little self-focus. The following transcript from a consultation with a severe marital conflict demonstrates an intensively reactive position full of projection. The therapist attempts to move the husband toward self-focus.

JOHN: This is very difficult, but I'll try. I think that without trying to sound like I'm trying to put the blame on you, which I'm not, you can jump in whenever you care to.

THERAPIST: She already grunted.

JOHN: Well, I anticipate the grunts. It just really came to a crisis point.

THERAPIST: What's that mean?

JOHN: She just runs wild.

THERAPIST: What's that mean?

JOHN: It's chaotic, no structure, no discipline.

THERAPIST: You mean you don't know where she's going to be? Or if she's going to be there?

SUE: I drink usually.

JOHN: That I don't know, because she doesn't drink in front of me. Because I would not tolerate that.

THERAPIST: What is most difficult for you to deal with about Sue when she gets upset?

JOHN: The fact is that I can't do anything for her. This is her problem, and it's an internal struggle that she has to work out herself. I feel that it's really just kind of hopeless now.

THERAPIST: How does it affect your insides when she really gets upset, like yesterday?

JOHN: I feel, you know, impotent, helpless. Not sexually, just impotent. You know, as a man I can't do anything, I can't relate to her. I love her, I can't help her. I can't do anything; there's nothing I can do.

THERAPIST: So you get feeling so helpless that you behave how?

JOHN: I either withdraw or else become hostile.

THERAPIST: When you withdraw you go where?

JOHN: To myself.

THERAPIST: You mean you pull into yourself. You might be there physically, but you're not there.

JOHN: Right.

THERAPIST: Do you fall asleep or just talk?

JOHN: I just kind of talk in quick sentences—kind of preach to her my doctrine of life, which is struggle, hard work, maintain discipline, get a job, function, because that's the only thing I know. This is I think getting into another area of the problem —that Sue is not functioning, she's not functioning. I mean she has no responsibilities, no responsibilities day to day. She does not take care of the house, she does not take care of her child, she does not work, she is twenty-six years old. Now that's not functioning, as far as I'm concerned, and I would think it's important and necessary and crucial that everyone functions, no matter what he or she does.

THE ADAPTIVE POSITION

A variant of the reactive position is the adaptive position, in which a person gives up one's own program and knuckles under to intense relationship pressure to behave in a certain way or to go along with someone else's program. This position may be a way of avoiding the consequences of behaving in ways different from those prescribed by the other in a relationship. It is closely tied to the reciprocal process in which one person in the relationship overfunctions and the other, the adaptive one, under-functions.

In the following segment, John's wife relates the onset of her adaptive position within her marriage. Even in the adaptive position there is, as this segment shows, a pseudo–self-focus with a great deal of projection underneath.

SUE: I used to be very healthy all my life, until I guess about three or four years ago. I used to be very sporty. I used to not smoke cigarettes. I used to eat the right foods and really take care of my health and my looks and everything—take care of myself physically. Then I found when I married John it all fell apart. He couldn't relate to my child as a child; he always sort of acted like the child was much older and could understand John intellectually.

THERAPIST: What does John think of your mothering?

SUE: He thinks I'm totally incapable of taking care of a child or having a family. He gives me the impression that he thinks that I'm completely incapable as a human being.

THERAPIST: How does that affect you?

SUE: I can't deal with it.

THERAPIST: So you go helpless and can't deal with John when he gets angry with you and becomes an expert about what's wrong with you and what your problems are?

SUE: Exactly. I used to fight it for a long time, screaming, fights, then I guess I just kind of accepted it and destroyed myself.

All of us spend a considerable time in the reactive position in our relationships. In work with the individual spouses in a case of marital conflict, it is useful to help them define the position they occupy, to delineate the process that leads to that position, and to get them to explore other positions that will enable them to establish a more functional relationship. These other positions are the experimental and the functional positions.

THE EXPERIMENTAL POSITION

In therapy an experimental position may be devised as a strategy for individual and relationship change. The strategy can be either a modification of behavior within the marital couple, as in the "planned distance," or the alteration of the behavioral process in a relationship through a key triangle surrounding the marriage. The wife who moves away with anger in an effort to shift the dysfunctional equilibrium in the relationship is in a reactive position; when the move is done consciously as a strategy, minus the anger, it is a planned distance. The wife has assumed an experimental position. The impact that the experimental relationship position can have can be seen in the distancer whose repressed emotions are blown into the open by his wife's planned distance. He talks to anyone who will listen, and the emotions come pouring out.

Another experimental position is the "I-position." An I-position is a nonreactive statement of where one stands on some issue, with a willingness to accept the consequences of that stand and a firmness about it even in the face of opposition or disapproval. Theresa and Jack illustrate this concept. Theresa, thirty-four years old, and the mother of two boys, aged seven and fourteen, sought consultation when her husband Jack, a very successful bond broker who had been abusing alcohol for the past two years, left to live with his mistress of eight months.

After a thorough evaluation of the clinical situation, Theresa was encouraged to take an "I-position" with Jack the next time he wandered home to express his ambivalence about his present living situation. The position would be that she was already going for help and had started attending Al-Anon meetings and that he could return home when he was ready to give up alcohol and his mistress, start an AA program, and go for marital therapy with her.

THE FUNCTIONAL POSITION

In the functional position, one is emotionally and physically available to one's spouse. Communication is open, and one does not assume responsibility for the other's well-being. One is able to join in such mutual tasks as child-rearing and managing finances, and is flexible about the amount and type of relationship time spent together. A person in the functional position is open to negotiating differences of opinion, able to take a strong "I-position" when necessary, and willing to allow the other to take the lead in areas where the other is more competent. One can both take control and relinquish control as circumstances warrant.

Recognizing the characteristics of these four relationship positions will assist the therapist and the individual spouse in formulating a direction for functional change. At any given moment, however, the relationship positions of the individuals in a marriage may change. The therapist must keep this fact in mind while weaving the threads of the therapy experience.

The Expectation-to-Alienation Progression

The expectation-to-alienation progression is a theoretical construct that attempts to provide the therapist and the individual spouse a way to track the development of negative feelings within the individual in response to relationship stimuli. The progression begins with the expectations with which a person entered a marriage and traces what has happened to those expectations through years of disappointment and conflict to a state of emotional alienation. In the process it provides a pathway for processing and eventually neutralizing the negative feelings.

In our clinical work we have found that most people enter marriage expecting the positive experiences in the family of origin to be duplicated in marriage, and the negative experiences to be replaced by more positive ones. The expectations of each spouse can be linked to the behavioral operating styles of the emotional pursuer and the emotional distancer. Pursuers usually expect an intense emotional connection or attachment, and distancers usually expect above all acceptance of themselves as they are, including their need for detachment. These notions place an excessive load of expectation on the marital relationship.

Fogarty has developed a progression of responses to unmet expectations. In brief, he hypothesizes that a person responds to unmet expectations first with disappointment, then with hurt or anger or both. If the anger is sustained by a lack of resolution in the relationship or further disappointment, it results in the development of resentment and eventually bitterness.

To this progression, Guerin (1982) has added two additional steps, which follow a prolonged state of bitterness. They occur when one spouse decides that he or she can no longer afford to remain vulnerable to the relationship. "It just hurts too much." At this point that spouse moves across a symbolic bridge to an "island of invulnerability": a place where he or she cannot be hurt or even reached emotionally. All hope for the future of the relationship is then abandoned, and alienation sets in.

Thus Guerin, working on the interactional sequence in the couple, and Fogarty, working on the steps that go on within the individual in response to disappointment, hurt, and anger, both arrived at the importance of bitterness.

As Fogarty worked with couples around pursuit and distance and around the progression from expectations to bitterness, he became intrigued with the inability of apparently well-motivated emotional pursuers to live with their feelings—to accept them and not attempt to run away from them. He believed that this inability fed their tendency to pursue and eventually led to a recycling of the pattern of marital conflict. To counter this tendency he began to experiment with having emotional pursuers imagine that they were lowering themselves into the pit they felt in their insides, at the same time attempting to hold a planned distance from the spouse. From this experimentation Fogarty developed his existential concept of *emptiness* and began to try to map the individual's emotional makeup in a way that would discover the "inner system."

Fogarty defines emptiness as a state "made up of many feelings," including loneliness, a feeling of nothingness, confusion, hopelessness and helplessness, not belonging, sadness, feeling uncared for, shame, failure, paranoia, and emotional death (1976b, pp. 4–5). He sees people avoiding their emptiness in a number of ways. Some just muddle around in their emptiness; others focus on the problems of others. One can avoid emptiness by avoiding closeness, by being depressed and focusing on the depression rather than on the emptiness of which it is an expression. One can fill one's emptiness with other people or things or with activity, and one can avoid it by "skipping over and skittering out" of it (pp. 6–7).

Fogarty advocates the "voluntary depression" as a way to deal with emptiness. People, he says, "must learn to take certain actions, fully aware that they are precipitating their own feelings of emptiness. This is the only way that they can avoid running from their feelings and believe that they can survive the experience" (1976b, p. 7).

Guerin developed three ideas to explain the same dilemma of recycling marital conflict and deal with it clinically. First, as we have seen, he added the "island of invulnerability" and alienation to Fogarty's progression of expectation to bitterness. Second, he hypothesized the need to focus on the triangles surrounding the marital relationship instead of operating directly on the marital couple in severe conflict. This idea ultimately led to the concept of the four stages of marital conflict.

Third, Guerin assumed, in agreement with Fogarty, that individuals in therapy were successfully modifying their behavior in the marriage but were not dealing with their internal emotional distress. He focused on bitterness. He assumed that a person's bitterness derived from many relationships but that the blame for the bitterness was placed almost entirely on the marriage.

In the course of treating severe marital conflict, we work with one or both spouses individually to detoxify their bitterness. The path we take entails several steps:

1. *Exploring the content and organizing issues that make up the bitterness.* For example, the wife may be bitter about what she perceives to be years of indifference to her loneliness and other emotional needs.

2. *Linking the bitterness to the expectations with which the person entered the marriage.* How much investment in changing the partner was there from the beginning? How much idealization made the spouse into someone he or she was not, in order to meet unmet needs in a fantasy? This step can be difficult, because the long-term conflict and bitterness may have so altered the perception of the spouse that a realistic appraisal of early expectations is elusive.

3. *Tracking the unmet expectations through the disappointment to the hurt, anger, resentment, and bitterness.* This step is especially important when the conflict is filled with expressions of intense anger by one or both partners. In this situation, one or both of them must be put in touch with their hurt and assisted in expressing hurt rather than anger. This step must be accomplished without invalidating the appropriateness of the anger that is tied to certain repetitive patterns in the relationship.

4. *Working with the link between the content of the bitterness* (for example, the spouse's indifference to one's loneliness) *and the premarital expectations in a way that weaves them into the extended family experience.* This step assists greatly in eventually dividing the bitterness and redistributing portions of it to the relationships and triangles that predated the marriage, relieving the marriage of bitterness that belongs elsewhere. Such efforts are best begun with and reinforced by extended family work, either through involving family members directly in the sessions or through coaching the marital partners in explorations of their extended families.

5. *Encouraging the individual to take the risk of leaving the island of invulnerability and becoming immersed in the interactive process of the marriage.* If this step is not accomplished, the marital relationship is doomed either to chronic unresolved conflict or to eventual dissolution. In assisting people with this step, the therapist must carefully prepare them for the inevitable disappointment, hurt, and anger that accompany taking the risk. The resolution of the conflict must be worth the effort and the emotional cost.

The Dysfunctional Spouse

In the treatment of marital conflict, the clinician is often faced with a specific psychiatric dysfunction in one or both spouses. The symptoms of this dysfunction may be overt and may be the primary presenting problem, or they may be covert, camouflaged at first by intense marital conflict. The dysfunctions seen run the gamut of severity from schizophrenia and major affective disorder to addictions and anxiety disorders. In each instance this primary dysfunction must be tended to first and the marital therapy worked into the therapeutic program after the symptoms of the primary disorder are under control.

While the symptomatic spouse is struggling to regulate his or her internal distress and gain control of the symptoms, the asymptomatic spouse can be worked with in a way that can facilitate the recovery and lay the foundation for the work on the marital relationship. It is best to begin by lowering the asymptomatic spouse's reactivity to the symptoms. What often surfaces at this point is the asymptomatic spouse's difficulty with the emotional demands the symptoms place on him or her. Further exploration often brings out a preexisting pattern in the relationship in which emotional demands went unmet and emotional upset was invalidated.

The asymptomatic spouse is instructed to work on relating to the partner without talking about the symptoms (asking how they are, for example). An effort is thereby begun to bypass the symptoms and make a connection based on something else. In addition, the asymptomatic spouse is instructed to begin communicating about his or her own vulnerability, in order to restore some sense of balance to the relationship. This step in turn provides the symptomatic one with psychic energy to be invested in symptom recovery.

The following session segment illustrates this procedure.

THERAPIST: Are you vulnerable, John?

JOHN: Of course.

THERAPIST: Tell Sue how you're vulnerable. Give her some instances.

JOHN: Well, I'm subject to a lot of pressures, a lot of frustration, a certain amount of dissatisfaction about my job and my career and where I'm going. All my energies and talent have been devoted to keeping this thing alive. I just told her when I came here, I have no more personal business days, no more sick leave, no more vacation time. I mean, they have my number at work. I've used it up.

THERAPIST: So you sort of want to return to the straight life, or something like that?

JOHN: Yeah.

THERAPIST: Are you vulnerable personally with people, as opposed to the big world?

SUE: Not so much.

JOHN: What do you mean by vulnerable?

THERAPIST: Tell him, Sue.

SUE: Are people your friends, do they really hurt you, do you get despair because of people hurting you, you know, like your friends or your mother.

JOHN: I don't really feel that I need anybody else. In other words I want a nice relationship with my old lady, the person I'm with, my woman.

THERAPIST: It's like you can do it alone, but to have a full life you'd like to have a close relationship with your old lady.

JOHN: I know that if Sue left and got a divorce or whatever, I'd just go on, I've done it before. It's like a man suffering cardiac arrest, if you get through the first one you know what to expect, you know the danger signals, it strengthens you in some way. It's like the guy who's had one shoe drop. He's waiting for the second one. That's the way I feel. In other words, there hasn't been a strong foundation of trust.

THERAPIST: So you've never been hurt, John?

JOHN: That's not true; that's not true at all.

THERAPIST: Did you ever talk to Sue about when you'd been hurt in your life?

SUE: He told me when I first met him about how his father had hurt him. And how he had this turmoil. But then he changed; all of a sudden he told me that he loves his father more than anything and that he admires his father more than anything, and that his father had been really a great father.

JOHN: That's true in a sense. I've always respected my father and I admire him. Yes, but being involved, all of a sudden having a child . . . I really understood my father, and I am thirty years old.

THERAPIST: Relating to David really helped you understand your dad?

JOHN: Absolutely.

THERAPIST: How?

JOHN: I saw the conflict that my father must have had in his relationship with my mother.

SUE: I remember the first time we were going to meet his parents. We were in a hotel room. We were lying in bed and he called Switzerland, where his parents lived, and he said, "Hi, Mom and Dad," and they said something on the phone, and then he was very disappointed and hurt. I said, "What's the matter?" and he said, "Well, they have each other, they really don't need me." He said he was very disappointed, he hadn't seen them for one and a half years, and it's kind of like a neighbor that would drop in any time. And it was like—we'll see you tomorrow. And it wasn't a warm kind of thing—"Oh, we're so happy you're here." That all of a sudden changed when he got in a relationship with David. He would tell me before that he thought he was intruding on his mother and father's love.

This segment demonstrates an attempt at restoring balance to the relationship by focusing on John's vulnerability. In the twofold approach John is first coached to bypass Sue's dysfunction, forming a connection with her organized around something else, and second is helped to get in touch with his own vulnerability and to talk to Sue about it.

This segment also demonstrates the importance of triangulation to this process. It has been our experience that the dysfunctional spouse is caught in a triangle that includes his or her emotionally most important parent as well as the marital partner. In this case the triangle consisted of John, Sue, and her mother. The goal of the initial intervention with this triangle was for John to stop trying to shape up Sue, put distance between himself and his mother-in-law, and let the conflict between the two of them surface where the therapist could assist Sue in dealing with it.

These first five chapters have presented our overview of marital conflict. We turn now to the more specifically clinical considerations of how marital conflict is evaluated and treated.

PART TWO

Evaluating and Treating the Four Stages of Marital Conflict

6

Identifying the Stage
of Marital Conflict

EVALUATING marital conflict is a two-step procedure in our model of marital therapy. First, the therapist gathers information about the multi-generational family system by means of a *genogram,* a kind of family tree that allows the therapist to assess the state of the family over time and the amount of stress the family is undergoing at the moment. Second, the therapist considers the individual spouses, the marital couple, and the surrounding triangles in the light of various criteria to determine the severity of the conflict and to devise an effective treatment plan.

During this two-step procedure, it is important that the therapist successfully connect with each spouse, engaging them in the therapy process. The therapist must keep down his or her own anxiety, remain relevant to the couple's view of the problem, listen to both spouses, and validate each of them without taking sides. These measures, combined with appropriately timed and relevant feedback to the couple, create the safe climate that is essential to successful engagement.

In this chapter we will describe how the therapist assesses the stage of marital conflict using the genogram and will illustrate the process with a case history.

Criteria for the Stages of Marital Conflict

The four stages of marital conflict correspond to the four groups discussed in the Introduction. In order to assign a couple to a particular stage, we evaluate the overall family system, the marital relationship itself, including the triangles surrounding it, and the functioning and emotional well-being of each spouse. Some of the criteria are difficult to define and to measure with precision, but an awareness of each is essential to the evaluation and treatment of marital conflict.

FAMILY SYSTEM FACTORS

The most important family system factors are the premorbid state of the family—that is, how well or poorly individual members were functioning and how cut off they were from each other—and transition times and cluster stress. The family's premorbid state, as we saw in chapter 1, is the result of long-term stress throughout the family's history and a source of chronic stress in the present. The more problematic it is, the more intense will be the marital conflict. For example, consider a couple in which the husband's father is an alcoholic and his mother has chronic, severe rheumatoid arthritis and is cut off from all her siblings, while on the wife's side her father committed suicide and her younger sister is schizophrenic. This couple has more to contend with and fewer supports than a couple with fewer family problems. It is our contention that chronic extended family stress has both a direct and an indirect impact on a developing marital relationship.

Transition times, as we also saw in chapter 1, are times of vulnerability for any system. Marriage, the birth of a child, adolescence, mid-life, retirement, and the death of a family member are some of the significant transition times that can produce a sense of loss of control. All are stressful and raise the family's level of anxiety and the level of emotional arousal in individual members. In every family there are periods in which several transition times occur within a short interval, producing cluster stress. It is in these times that emotional and physical symptoms in individuals or conflict in relationships are most likely to surface. As a general rule couples

in stages III and IV of marital conflict are feeling the impact of a significantly higher index of transition times and cluster stress than those in the
less severe conflicts of stages I and II.

MARITAL DYAD FACTORS

The conflictual process in the marital relationship itself is evaluated
on the basis of the emotional climate, the ways in which the couple
maintain the relationship, and the degree of fusion in the marriage.

As we saw in chapter 2, the emotional climate of a marriage is a
combination of temperature, ranging from frigid cold to intense heat;
turbulence versus stability; and safety, the degree of risk entailed in approaching the other for connection or support. Unless the therapist reads
the emotional climate accurately and acts to make it stable and safe, any
intervention will inevitably fail.

A set of simple questions can assist in evaluating the emotional climate. For example, the therapist may ask, "Is it safe to be vulnerable in
this marriage?" and "Can you tell if she is upset when you first come into
the house, before you've even seen her or spoken to her?" Asking such
questions of both spouses will provide the therapist not only with a reading on the emotional climate but information about how sensitive each
spouse is to the emotional climate. Chapter 2 discusses in more detail the
ways in which the therapist evaluates and works with the emotional
climate.

As chapter 2 pointed out, the two areas that are critical for nurturing
and maintaining the marital relationship are communication and relationship time and activity together. Important to communication are both its
content—not only the exchange of simple information but more personal
self-disclosure—and its character—the levels of criticism and credibility.
Relationship time and activity together are measures of the investment in
the relationship by both spouses.

Table 6–1 shows how these two areas relate to the stages of marital
conflict. The table makes clear that as the conflict becomes more severe,
communication becomes more compromised, reactive, and critical, with a
loss of credibility, while relationship time and activity together decline.

Marital fusion, as we showed in chapter 2, can be plotted in a series
of steps called the interactional sequence. We have found that step 1
(pursuit and distance in response to stress) and step 2 (intensified pursuit
and distance) are almost always associated with stage II marital conflict;
step 3 (the pursuer in reactive distance and the distancer in reactive pursuit) can be present with either stage II or stage III conflict; and step 4

TABLE 6–1

Stages of Marital Conflict and Means of Maintaining the Relationship

	Stage			
	I	II	III	IV
Communication	Open, some conflict	Open, with conflict	Closed, with conflict	Closed
Information exchange	Excellent	Good	Compromised	Poor
Self-disclosure	Good to excellent	Adequate	Reactive	Absent
Criticism	Low	Moderate	High	Very high
Credibility	Very high	High	Moderate	Low
Relationship time and activity together	Excellent	Good	Compromised	Minimal

(attack and counterattack) and step 5 (fixed distance) are good markers for stage III conflict.

TRIANGLE FACTORS

An assessment of the triangles surrounding the marital relationship is essential to an accurate evaluation of the conflict. Triangulation can intensify marital conflict, as in the classic mother-in-law triangle, or stabilize or cover over conflict, as in the equally classic extramarital affair. The activity and intensity of triangulation escalate considerably in stages III and IV; they are less prominent in less severe conflict. The more fixed and polarized the relationships in a triangle, the more intense will be the marital conflict. Relationship triangles and the process of triangulation are dealt with in detail in chapters 3 and 4.

INDIVIDUAL FACTORS

Any treatment of marital conflict must include evaluations of the emotional state of each of the spouses. In chapter 5 we cited three criteria as essential: the degree of projection and self-focus, position on the expectation-to-alienation progression, and the adaptive level of functioning.

Finding out how much self-focus each spouse has in viewing the marital conflict is an important index of the severity of the conflict, as well as one prognostic sign of outcome. The higher the projection, the higher the intensity of the conflict. One way to assess the degree of self-focus is to ask each spouse to draw up, without help from the other, a list of his or her own limitations that are getting in the way of the relationship.

The position of each individual spouse on the expectation-to-aliena-tion progression is closely related to the severity of the conflict. In stages I and II, the position varies from disappointment to hurt and anger. Resent-ment and bitterness are found in abundance in stage III, and alienation is present in late stage III and in stage IV.

The three measures of adaptive level of functioning are productivity, relationships, and personal well-being. The various ways in which the adaptive level of functioning of individual spouses can present clinically are extremely complicated, but in general lower levels of functioning in at least one and more often both spouses are found in more severe marital conflict. In stage I or II, both spouses may be doing rather well on two of the three measures and not severely compromised on the third. In stage III or IV, both spouses may be functioning well on only one measure and significantly compromised on the other two.

The Stages of Marital Conflict

STAGE I

The couples in stage I are at a low level of conflict. The family system surrounding the marital relationship in this stage is relatively healthy, and the emotional climate is safe, warm, and nonturbulent. The number of transition times and the amount of cluster stress are minimal. The level of anxiety and emotional arousal are well within the ability of the relation-ship to contain them. The behavioral operating styles of the spouses are either in balance or easily restored to balance. Reactivity and criticism are at low levels, while credibility is high. Communication in the marriage is open, and there is minimal polarization of power.

The individual spouses are mostly self-focused, with occasional bursts of projection. Their productivity and personal well-being are high, and the negative response to unmet expectations has progressed only as far as disappointment.

Our experience is that stage I is in fact a limited reality. It occurs mostly in the early years of marriage when both spouses come from well-functioning families that have endured only minimal amounts of stress. This stable beginning allows for a smoother course of separation from the families of origin and an emotional climate conducive to the development of secure marital bonding.

To help these couples maintain this level of functioning and to reinforce the strength of their relationship in preparation for the inevitable transition times and cluster stress, the Center for Family Learning offers an education and prevention program called Family Systems Training (FST). FST is a six-week course that teaches how family systems work. The course attempts to give a perspective of people not just as individuals but as members of a complex multigenerational network of relationships called the family. Participants are taught about normal stresses that alter the family system in predictable ways, in the hope that if these events are understood stress may be minimized, change may become possible, and crises can be avoided. This protocol will be presented in detail in the next chapter.

STAGE II

The couples in stage II are experiencing significant marital conflict that they define as a problem. The emotional climate has cooled, and there is more turbulence and less safety. Transition times and corresponding cluster stress have begun to build up. Anxiety and emotional arousal are sufficient to override the relationship's ability to contain them, so that explicit symptoms have been produced in the form of active marital conflict.

Communication remains open in stage II, however, with adequate exchange of both general and personal information. There is still ease in doing things together. Criticism is on the increase, but credibility remains high. There is little power polarization, and the struggle for control is more playful than deadly. Each spouse is in a projective mode and unable to restore self-focus alone. The expectation-to-alienation progression has reached the level of hurt and anger, with a degree of resentment beginning to build. The couple is at step 1 or 2 in the interactional sequence: pursuing and distancing in response to stress, or intense pursuit and distance. Step 3, the pursuer in reactive distance, is sometimes seen, but later steps will usually not be observed in stage II conflict.

In stage II therapy, the therapist provides a structure for the couple by moving in directly on the marital conflict, working either on ways of maintaining the relationship, on fusion, or on both. This structure lowers emotional arousal and anxiety and helps the spouses reestablish self-focus. It is in the treatment of stage II that the close tie between the ways of maintaining the relationship and fusion in the marriage is most easily seen. For example, an experiment can be set up in which the emotional distancer is given responsibility for initiating the exchange of information and the planning of some of the relationship time and activity together, and the emotional pursuer is instructed to create the verbal and emotional distance necessary for the distancer to do so and to refrain from critical comment on how it is done. This experiment gives both spouses the experience of behaving in opposition to their own inclinations and observing what goes on within themselves and in the relationship when they do it.

Experiments like this can help people understand how much their behavior serves the purpose of inner calm and how much they depend on their spouses to fill in the deficits in their own functioning. This experience helps each spouse to take the other's behavior less personally and to regain some degree of self-focus. It is important, however, to present such tasks as therapy experiments rather than as solutions.

Obviously there are many variants to the strategy just presented. A husband who is the emotional distancer may be skilled at general information exchange and at planning activities but rarely indulge in self-disclosure. He can be given the task of talking to his wife about himself as a son, a father, and a husband. Or a wife who is the emotional pursuer may be sexually distant and withholding; she can be put in charge of increasing the quality and frequency of their sexual relationship. After successfully completing tasks like these, as self-focus returns each spouse can be coached to enlist his or her creativity in developing new ways of dealing with the other's toxic behaviors. This activity reinforces self-focus and taking responsibility for one's own emotional and behavioral responses.

A full discussion of the treatment of stage II will be presented in chapter 8.

STAGE III

In stage III the number of transition times and the level of cluster stress are significantly elevated. The emotional climate is marked by sudden and dramatic changes in temperature and by turbulence. The level of anxiety and emotional arousal is high, as are the intensity and polarization of the surrounding triangles, although these may not be immediately visible.

Both spouses have an impaired ability to exchange information on either the general or the personal level. Self-disclosure is either an uncontrolled release of pent-up emotions or is misheard as criticism or complaint, and it further increases the upset. The level of criticism is high, and credibility is often fading. Activity together often resembles parallel play, with considerable distance and without engagement. The pursuer-distancer balance is disturbed to the point where behavioral characteristics formerly seen as assets to the relationship are now experienced as problematic. The therapist may have difficulty identifying who is the pursuer and who the distancer. The power struggle has lost most of its playfulness, and there is a "life-or-death" quality to much of the couple's interaction. In the interactional sequence, the couple is at step 3 (the pursuer in reactive distance) or more likely at step 4 (attack and counterattack) or step 5 (fixed distance).

Self-focus is fleeting in both partners, and the projection process is rampant. One or both spouses are marinating in their bitterness, and one or both may have passed over to the "island of invulnerability."

In the treatment of stage III a direct move on the couple's interactional process will either create confusion or even escalate the conflict. The therapist can take steps to avoid falling into this trap and at the same time foster more positive therapeutic movement. In split and conjoint sessions, the first two orders of business are to define the sources of cluster stress, making them explicit, and to work on improving the emotional climate. The former allows the spouses to view their marriage as suffering from stress rather than as intrinsically bad. The latter sets the necessary environment for further clinical experimentation.

One useful technique for altering the climate is to move the husband, especially if he is in a distant critical position, toward the children. This maneuver demonstrates his willingness to make an effort and often softens the climate surrounding the marital relationship. The husband can be motivated simply by being told that if the marriage fails the children will still be his and he will want a relationship with them.

Detoxifying issues related to the extended family may also be helpful in improving the emotional climate and relieving pressure on the marriage. For example, if the husband has not spoken for years to a brother because of a dispute about an inheritance, and if that issue is never brought up between husband and wife, the therapist can normalize the problem for the couple simply by asking many calm, nonjudgmental questions about the facts in the case.

When these two steps have been taken, the therapist can begin to focus directly on the marital couple. He or she can instruct them to confine their information exchange to topics of general interest, dropping discussions of any toxic issues and any attempts at heart-to-heart talks. Both spouses can be encouraged to diminish both their implicit and explicit criticism of one another. Their togetherness activity ought also to be kept light.

Meanwhile in the individual sessions the therapist can work to decrease projection and increase self-focus. Focusing on the expectation-to-alienation progression often helps here. Usually each spouse is experiencing significant resentment and bitterness. If these negative feelings have progressed to the point where one or both spouses have moved to an island of invulnerability, it is essential to move them back. The therapist initially explores with each of them the risks of becoming vulnerable again. The inevitability of being hurt again if the risk is taken and the question of whether or not the emotional pain is worth the risk are given slow-paced, lengthy consideration. If this approach is successful, the path to detoxification of the bitterness and resentment is then open. The therapist walks each spouse backwards through the expectation-to-alienation progression, getting them in touch with their anger and hurt, their disappointment, and finally their own expectations. If these interventions are effective, direct access to the interactional patterns in the marital couple becomes possible and they can be addressed clinically with significantly better chances of success.

The treatment of stage III will be fully discussed in chapter 9.

STAGE IV

Stage IV is marked by the extremes in all the criteria used for evaluating marital conflict. The definitive marker for this stage, however, is the engagement of an attorney by one or both spouses. In the vast majority of cases this move closes the door on conciliation and places the marriage in an adversarial context. It is the attorney's job to foster doubt and suspicion concerning the credibility of the other spouse, now an adversary, in order to protect the client's bargaining position.

When a couple has reached this stage, therapy is most profitably invested in helping each spouse with the internal emotional experience and with a successful disengagement from the relationship. In addition it is important to try to minimize the emotional damage to everyone involved, especially the children and the spouses' parents. A detailed presentation of the treatment of stage IV can be found in chapter 10.

The Genogram

Determining the stage of a marital conflict and choosing an appropriate treatment plan depend on a careful and thorough evaluation. Our evaluation consists of taking a *genogram* and assessing the couple in terms of the criteria described earlier in this chapter.

The genogram is a clinical variant of the family tree used by genealogists and the "family diagram" introduced by Bowen. A simple but thorough road map of the ongoing life of a family across three generations, it

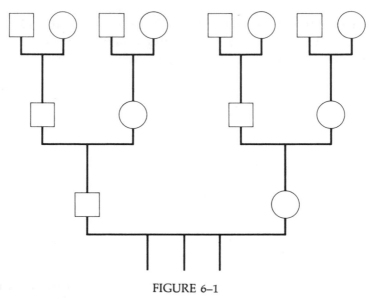

FIGURE 6–1

The Basic Genogram

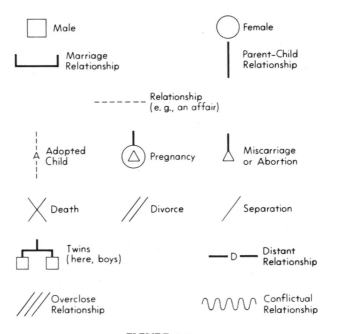

FIGURE 6–2

Genogram Symbols

Source: E. Pendagast and C. O. Sherman. A Guide to the Genogram Family Systems Training. *The Family* 5 (1977):4.

is a structural framework, developed by Guerin (1972), that permits a vast amount of information about a family to be stored on a relatively simple one-page diagram, shown in figure 6–1. A series of symbols standing for persons, events, and relationships accounts for the simplicity and completeness of the genogram. The symbols are shown in figure 6–2. Fuller explanations can be found in Guerin and Pendagast (1976) and Pendagast and Sherman (1977).

In preparing a genogram for a couple in marital conflict, the therapist develops all the basic facts of the three- or four-generational family system, just as for any other kind of presenting problem. In marital conflict, however, the therapist is especially concerned with the premorbid state of the family and the acute stress the couple is currently experiencing. The premorbid state of the family includes significant physical or emotional dysfunction in family members, significant conflict within the family, and any cutoffs, complete or ritualized, between family members. The presence of acute stress is indicated by transition times and cluster stress in the family system and by changes in the family system such as a wife's going back to school or starting a job). While taking this information, the therapist monitors the emotional climate, both in the marital relationship and as it is described throughout the family system.

The case of Victor and Anna Selig will illustrate our use of this tool. Anna, a pretty twenty-eight-year-old woman, came in a few minutes late for the first appointment, looking hurried and anxious. Her husband, Vic, a boyish twenty-seven, seemed extremely tense. The therapist began the session by asking Anna whether it had been a problem to find someone to look after their son. They chatted for a few moments about the difficulties of getting to· places on time when a thirteen-month-old is involved. The therapist then turned to Vic to find out whether it had been a problem for him to take time off from work for this daytime appointment.

The therapist explained that she was eager to hear about the problem that had brought them to therapy and let them know that in the first three or four sessions she would need to gather a great deal of information in order to understand their situation. She showed the couple the genogram form (Figure 6–1) and said that much of that information would go directly on that sheet: "I'll use this as a map of your family, and as I get to know you, this page will be completely covered. It's my way of trying to organize what I learn, and it has been very helpful with other families."

The therapist listened carefully to the couple's descriptions of the problem. Vic said that they had been separated for two months and that they had agreed to therapy as a condition of their separation. "Anna

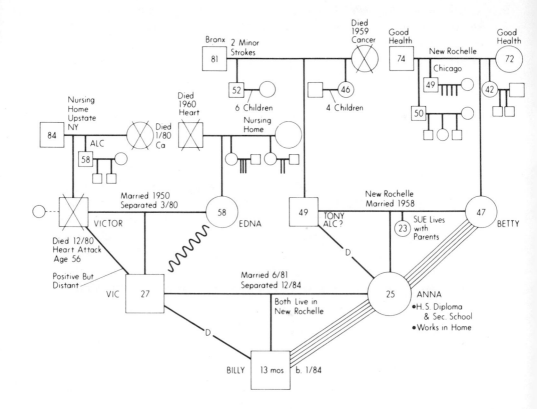

FIGURE 6–3

The Selig Genogram

wanted me to leave, and she was right. I had been a monster during our marriage, and I am 150 percent to blame. I love her. I love my son, and I'll do anything to get back together."

Anna said, "He's right. It is all his fault. I tried everything to make things work when we were together, and there was no changing him. He was cold and moody, and it got much worse after the baby was born. He didn't care about either one of us. He's been trying to change since we split up, but I don't know if I can ever start loving him again." She added that she was willing to come to therapy because she thought that avoiding divorce would be better for their son.

By the end of the first two sessions, the therapist had constructed the genogram that appears in figure 6–3. In taking the genograms the therapist looks for the following information:

1. *Names, ages, and state of health* of everyone who is or has been a member of the family system, including the couple themselves, their children, their parents and siblings, their grandparents, aunts and uncles, and any former spouses.

2. *Dates* of births, deaths, marriages, divorces and separations, serious illnesses, and rites of passage such as leaving for college or moving to a new home. These are all transition times and inevitably are sources of stress. It is important for the therapist to notice which, if any, of the transition times have occurred within the six months preceding the onset or exacerbation of the marital conflict.

   In the Seligs' case, the therapist noted that there was a clustering of transition times shortly before Vic and Anna married. His paternal grandmother died of cancer in March 1980, and his parents separated two months later. His father then died quite suddenly in August of that same year. Vic and Anna were married ten months later.

3. *Physical location and patterns of cohesion.* By noting where the significant members of the family system live, and by asking how often they visit or have contact and how, the therapist can get some idea of whether the family system is physically close and overinvolved, completely cut off, or ritually cut off.

   The therapist learned that Anna's family was very cohesive and that with the exception of one uncle in Chicago, her grandparents, aunts, uncles, and cousins lived in close proximity. Anna had been in contact with her parents about once a week before the separation and about twice a week since Vic had left. Vic's family was much more fragmented. He had no contact with anyone on his father's side of the family. His one living uncle and grandfather lived several hundred miles away. He kept contact with his mother to a minimum.

4. *Sibling positions* of everyone in the system. If the genogram is taken correctly, this information will come out naturally. Its importance is documented by Toman's classic work (1976). Information on siblings is important to have in assessing marital conflict, for several reasons. Siblings can trigger upset in the spouses; they can be a source of conflict; and they can also be a source of connection and support.

5. *Emotional cutoffs.* In asking how often, when, and how people in the system have contact with each other, the therapist is likely to discover that one or more important relationships in the system are cut off: mother and daughter are not speaking, for example, or two siblings have not had any contact for years. It is very important for

the therapist to note these for later exploration, for cutoffs always involve a very high degree of emotional reactivity. Indeed, a cutoff is a manifestation of intense fusion: it is the other side of enmeshment.

Four emotional cutoffs in the Selig family emerged during the first two sessions. Vic was cut off not only from all relatives on his father's side, whom he described as losers, but from his two aunts on his mother's side, whose feelings had been hurt over his wedding arrangements. His relationship with his mother can be described as a ritualized cutoff, in that he saw her only at times like holidays and without personal interaction or communication. The fourth cutoff involved Anna and Vic's mother and aunts. Anna felt that she had tried with them, but after a series of slights she had given up and stopped speaking to them. She also wanted to protect her son, Billy, from their influence.

6. *The education, occupations, and occupational history* of both spouses and of their parents. This information is important for a number of reasons, especially for insight into how specific members of the system have fared in relation to other members. For example, offspring who have experienced upward social mobility in relation to their parents have one view of themselves, while those who are equal in status to their parents have had a different experience. Offspring who have lost socioeconomic status have still other problems, as have people who have not done as well as their brothers and sisters.

There were no great differences in the socioeconomic or educational backgrounds of Anna's and Vic's families, but both spouses considered Anna's family to be a higher class of people.

8. *The ethnicity and religious background* of each spouse. Differences in ethnicity and religion, like those in social class, not infrequently become the basis of conflict. Anna reported that her Italian family had accepted Vic with open arms. The therapist suspected, however, that membership in that family might not be as easy as it appeared.

Applying the Criteria

After the genogram has been taken and the marriage has thus been placed in the larger context of the multigenerational family system, the therapist assesses the couple on the basis of the criteria for the four stages of marital conflict.

FAMILY SYSTEM FACTORS

The genogram provides the basic data from which the therapist assesses the premorbid state of the family and acute stress. In addition, the existence of triangles surrounding the marital relationship also begins to emerge during the taking of the genogram.

Vic's father had been involved in a long-term extramarital affair. When his own mother died, he left Vic's mother under the pretext of going to take care of his widowed father. As a result, Vic's father was cut off from the entire family, with the exception of Vic. Vic's father's brother was a chronic schizophrenic, having been diagnosed at age twenty-nine. In addition, Vic's mother was in a constant state of conflict with her siblings, often being cut off from them for long periods.

Anna presented her family as without tension or conflict and with no evidence of severe dysfunction. Such idealization did not hold up during the course of therapy. In this case, it turned out that Anna's father had a severe drinking problem and that her parents had gone through periods of intense conflict and one separation.

The evidence from the evaluation and genogram for the premorbid state of this family is consistent with stage III conflict. The chronic level of stress represented by conflict, cutoff, and dysfunction is greater than would be expected in stages I or II. The major transition time the couple was experiencing was that of Anna's pregnancy and the birth of their first child. Vic's father's death five years earlier and two years before their marriage, and the death of Vic's grandmother that same year, were by now factors in the premorbid state rather than acute stressors. The level of acute stress and the number of transition times is therefore less than might be expected in a stage III marital conflict. However, the intense reactivity in the marriage and in the extended system to Anna's pregnancy and to the baby are very much in keeping with stage III; Vic had been hostile and negative about the pregnancy, and Vic's mother was refusing to see the child. In stage II one would be more likely to see such symptoms as the husband's upset over the wife's distancing into a relationship with the baby and milder upset from a grandparent about the choice of a name.

INFORMATION ABOUT THE COUPLE

At least one session should have as its primary focus the assessment of the couple in terms of their communication, including credibility and the amount of criticism as well as their ability to exchange information and personal thoughts and feelings, their relationship time and activity, and their location in the interactional sequence.

The Seligs' communication was deficient in both the exchange of information and personal disclosure. Vic had lost his credibility with Anna, and all his pledges to reform were "too little, too late" as far as she was concerned. She criticized him continually, and his criticism of her had been converted to total self-effacement in his attempt to persuade her to stay in the marriage. Their relationship time and activity together were significantly compromised, as the following segment of a session shows:

THERAPIST: Anna, when did you and Vic stop enjoying each other's company?

ANNA: He took all the fun out of life. He never wanted to do anything that included other people. He didn't really want to go out—just stay home and watch TV. It got so I hated TV.

THERAPIST: Was it always that way?

ANNA: When we were first going out, it wasn't that way at all. Then after we got married he started to get that way gradually. After I got pregnant, forget it. He would never do anything.

THERAPIST: How did you handle that?

ANNA: For a long time I begged and pleaded with him. Sometimes I'd be crying. At first he would give in, but it wouldn't really be worth it because he was so awful once we got where we were going. He wouldn't talk; he was really rude. I would be so embarrassed. Toward the end I gave up trying.

THERAPIST: Did you ever go out and leave him home?

ANNA: Sometimes. But then I would have to explain and answer a million questions. I got tired of making excuses for him, so we stayed home a lot, which I resent because I like to be with people.

THERAPIST: Did you have a theory about that change in Vic?

ANNA: I could never figure it out. I think maybe the real him came out, and what I saw before we got married was just his best behavior.

A review of this couple's ways of maintaining their relationship, then, is consistent with a stage III conflict (see table 6–1).

Vic agreed with Anna's point of view consistently as the assessment progressed. He explained his earlier behavior by saying, "I was so selfish. I just wanted things my way, but I know I can change." An analysis of the pursuer-distancer balance and the interactional sequence clearly showed Vic in desperate reactive pursuit. He was offering, and indeed trying, to change drastically his manner of operating in order to win a second chance.

In therapy it would be important to work on the inevitability that this attempt at personality change, fabricated to the spouse's specifications, would fail.

Anna was in a phase of determined reactive distance. No longer was she attempting to get through to Vic, to get him to listen to her feelings. As far as she was concerned, all his protestations were suspect. He wasn't there when she needed him, and at this point he could "go to hell." Thus we see clearly a step 3 to step 4 progression in the interactional sequence, mixed with periods of fixed distance (step 5) when Vic got tired of rejection and retreated to tend his wounds.

ASSESSMENT OF TRIANGLES

The number of triangles operating around a marriage, and the intensity and polarization of the emotional process within them, are essential markers of the intensity of marital conflict. The existence of these triangles begins to be clear during the taking of the genogram, and the therapist reviews their intensity and polarization at the point of assessing the stage of the conflict.

The triangles surrounding the Seligs' marriage were numerous and intense. Vic's triangle with his parents was dramatically polarized by his maintaining a relationship with his father in the face of his father's extramarital affair and his mother's accusations of disloyalty. Anna's triangle with her parents was presented as dormant and nonreactive during the evaluation, but the process of therapy later demonstrated that it continued to have an impact on Anna. Vic and his mother and Anna were caught in a third triangle, intense and highly polarized, with Vic's mother refusing contact with Anna and clearly aligning with Vic emotionally, although maintaining physical distance from him. Vic floated back and forth between his wife and his mother, who remained in a negatively polarized fixed distance from one another.

This in-law triangle clearly interlocked with and fed into another triangle, involving Vic's mother, Anna, and the baby, Billy. Vic's mother had designated Billy as Anna's child and, at least for the present, had refused to see him and placed his picture face down on the mantel. This triangle in turn was linked with the process in Vic's nuclear family, in which Vic was much more distant from Billy than was Anna. The following transcript segment demonstrates some of the process in that triangle.

THERAPIST: Tell me about your relationship with your son.

VIC: He's fantastic.

THERAPIST: Do you like him?

VIC: I love him.

THERAPIST: How much time do you spend with him?

VIC: Not enough.

THERAPIST: How much?

VIC: A half hour here and there. Lately there has only been one day I spent the whole day.

THERAPIST: What keeps you from spending four hours on a Sunday with Billy?

VIC: My days off are varied. I'm not always off on Sunday, and I don't always know until that week. By the time I let Anna know she might already have made plans, like to go visit her mother.

THERAPIST: Is Anna blocking your spending the amount of time you would want to with Billy, or are you?

VIC: Sometimes I get that impression, sometimes I don't.

THERAPIST: Are you really making an effort to try to make sure you get some time with him? You know, a half hour is a lot different from three hours.

VIC: I have been feeling like I want to spend time with Billy whether Anna is there or not. But it's just making waves that I don't need. That she doesn't need. I don't know. It's a confusing time right now. [He looks questioningly at Anna.] I want to spend time with Billy very much, but I want to spend time with my family—Anna and Billy. I don't just want to spend time with Billy. I love him, but I have destroyed my wife's feeling of what a family should be like.

THERAPIST: I know that, but you know, if the Mets don't take the Cardinals tonight and tomorrow night, and they get their eyes on October first, they're in trouble. What I'm saying is that if you get your eyes on the World Series before you play out the rest of season, you may not get there. And part of your season is that you've got to establish credibility with your wife around your son. Anna, do you have trouble letting Vic have time with Billy?

ANNA: I don't really mind when Vic is with Billy. I just miss him. He's on my mind a lot—most of the time. I've been with him every day since he's born, just about. A couple of days here and there my mother's had him.

THERAPIST: You're really into being a mother, huh?

ANNA: He's the most important thing in my life.

THERAPIST: Would you say you've been more mother than wife?

ANNA: For a long time I was all wife, and that got me nowhere.

THERAPIST: Does your anger at Vic ever get in the way of giving him time with Billy?

ANNA: I don't think so.

THERAPIST: Can you be sure of something like that?

ANNA: I don't keep him from having time with him, but sometimes it's hard for me emotionally. Maybe because I still resent a lot of what he put me through when I was pregnant. I guess that's a part of it.

THERAPIST: What are you going to do with all that resentment?

ANNA: I don't know. Maybe eventually it will disappear.

In this dialogue the process in the triangle emerges. Anna is overly involved with her son and very distant from and angry at her husband. Vic feels positively about his son but spends almost no time with him; instead he is pursuing Anna and is heavily invested in trying not to upset her.

Thus four interlocking triangles surrounded Vic and Anna's marriage (see figure 6–4). The first two were triangles with their parents. Vic described himself as having been caught in the middle between his mother and his father since his early teens. Anna idealized her parents, and her relationship with them had become ritualized; she had no sense of them as real people. The third triangle was the in-law triangle consisting of Vic, Anna, and Vic's mother; both spouses were reactive to and distant from his mother. The fourth triangle consisted of Vic, Anna, and their son, with Anna overinvolved with Billy and Vic pursuing Anna and under involved with his son.

The intensity of the process in triangles is a function of the degree to which their structure is fixed and polarized. In the Selig family these four triangles were fixed and polarized, and their intensity is clearly consistent with stage III conflict.

INDIVIDUAL ASSESSMENT

We recommend that each spouse be seen separately at least once during the evaluation period. Such individual sessions allow the therapist to assess each one's level of functioning and allow each one to communicate to the therapist anything he or she may feel is important but may be unable to discuss in front of the other spouse. During this part of the evaluation, we assess each spouse's productivity, personal well-being, and

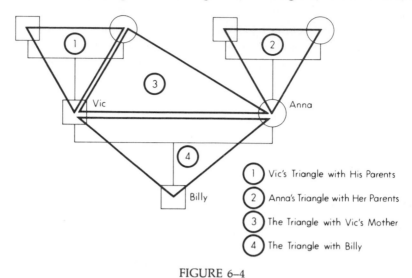

FIGURE 6–4

Interlocking Triangles in the Selig Family

relationships; his or her location on the expectation-to-alienation progression; and his or her degree of projection or self-focus.

Anna clearly projected the whole problem in their marriage onto Vic and his "crazy" family. At the time of the evaluation, she had almost no ability to see limitations in herself or in her family that might be contributing to the conflict.

Vic on the other hand had substituted total self-effacement for his previous blaming posture. His was a pseudo–self-focus, in which all effort to change was based on what he assumed Anna wanted in order to give him a second chance. When these desperate efforts on Vic's part failed, as they surely would, the underlying projection would surface and Vic's blaming would reappear.

Anna had clearly moved to an island of invulnerability, with a great deal of bitterness, especially with regard to Vic's pressure on her during the pregnancy. Vic's position on the expectation-to-alienation progression was clouded by his self-effacement and his attempts to win Anna's favor. As he tired of this and became frustrated by her intransigence, however, his bitterness, especially about his second-class citizenship in her family and her caring more about their son than about him, would readily surface.

The adaptive level of functioning was compromised in both Vic and Anna, although more clearly in Vic, at least on the surface. Vic's productivity was poor; he was making no headway in a dead-end job. His relationships with his wife, his son, his wife's family, and his own were in a shambles. He took reasonably good care of himself physically and made an acceptable appearance. Anna initially appeared to be doing better than in fact she was. Her productivity was suspect, and her relationships were difficult to evaluate because her whole focus was on Vic's victimization of her. A ritualized cohesive pattern appeared to be characteristic of her extended family. She also took good care of her health and made a good appearance.

As individuals, then, both Vic and Anna were compromised on two out of three measures of adaptive level of functioning; they were highly projective; and they were both well into bitterness on the expectation-to-alienation progression. All these findings are consistent with stage III conflict.

The following dialogue is a segment from the individual assessment that was done with Vic. It illustrates both an attempt to measure the degree of his self-focus and his adaptive level of functioning.

THERAPIST: What are your goals for yourself? Right now?

VIC: To start a new career.

THERAPIST: What have you been doing?

VIC: Right now I'm a store manager. And I'm going to go into the sales field—product manager.

THERAPIST: This job change—is it because you want more money?

VIC: Because I want the potential to make more money. I want a future, security, benefits.

THERAPIST: Is this because that's what Anna wants, or is this something that Vic wants?

VIC: This is something that Anna wanted and it is something that Vic wants now. Vic wants it because he understands it is the right thing to do. Because he did get good advice back when and didn't listen to it.

THERAPIST: What other goals have you got for you?

VIC: Gaining weight. It's part of the overall picture. I'd like to gain weight the right way: work out.

THERAPIST: What else?

VIC: To do the right thing.

THERAPIST: What does that mean?

VIC: Be considerate, be understanding, be the right type of person, have a basic human congeniality toward whatever comes up.

THERAPIST: Is that something you've had trouble with before? Are you kind of moody?

VIC: On the outside, I guess to people other than family or loved ones, I was happy and friendly with everyone; but as soon as

it dealt with a family member or a loved one, I became very
moody, very selfish, very sullen.

THERAPIST: So you think that's what got you into the jam that you're in,
and you want to change it?

VIC: Yes, I do.

Later in the session, the therapist asked about Vic's relationship with
his parents.

VIC: I don't know what my mother is really honest about. I don't
know if she's saying it just for the sake of hearing herself talk or
if she means it. And that's the way it's always been. And I think
that's one reason why I was doing a lotta, lotta thinking when
Anna told me, "Hey, pal, you're losing me." I really didn't take
it seriously. Ever since I can remember I was always being
threatened—my mother's going to do this, my mother's going
to do that, she's going to throw me out, she's going to kill me.
And I think that's one of the big reasons why I never took my
wife seriously, because it was that threatening all over again.
And when my wife decided to talk to me, try to get things out of
me, it was like my mother—it was like a lecture.

Later the therapist asked about his father.

THERAPIST: You father died about four years ago? Are you over that yet?

VIC: If I think about it, no. If I don't think about it, yes.

THERAPIST: You've got it locked away someplace. When it comes up you
still get emotional?

VIC: Yes.

THERAPIST: How often does it come up?

VIC: Lately, about three or four times a week.

THERAPIST: Since the difficulty with Anna?

VIC: Yes. It has to do with a lot of things.

THERAPIST: Like what else?

VIC: Prayer.

THERAPIST: You've been praying.

VIC: Oh, yeah. Praying is part of it. And I think about Billy. I think
about how my father really loved kids, and sometimes I just
say, I wish, if I could have something in life, I would like to
have seen my father see his grandchild. So maybe you're right.
I do think an awful lot about him. I ask him for his help. I say,

"Hey, Dad, you know, when you were here you told me this was going to happen."

THERAPIST: What did he tell you?

VIC: He said, "Sonny boy, you better watch your attitude. You're going to end up like your mother." That's what he told me.

THERAPIST: Did you end up like your mother?

VIC: Damned close, if not right there. Sure.

THERAPIST: What kind of answers does he give you now when you talk to him?

VIC: I don't fantasize about answers. I just figure that his answer will be manifested in something. If I do the right thing, then he's probably there with me.

THERAPIST: Kind of indirect. If he were alive, what do you think he'd tell you about the present situation?

VIC: "I told you. You didn't want to listen."

THERAPIST: Have you been able to talk to anyone about missing your father? to Anna? any friends? your mother?

VIC: Definitely not my mother. Not really anyone else, either.

The therapist learned that Vic had had a strong reaction to his father's death, for the most part unexpressed. In fact, Vic did not talk about his feelings with anyone, a fact that sheds light on the level of desperation he was feeling about divorce. He had goals, but they seemed to come from his wish to win Anna back, as they addressed the criticisms she had of him.

The assessment of Anna's functioning indicated that she was sitting on the island of invulnerability, very reluctant to move toward Vic for fear that she would be hurt once again. The therapist learned that during her pregnancy her despair had led her to consider suicide, an idea she rejected because she did not want to hurt her family. Although she had a number of friends, she did not really have a language in which to talk with them personally. Her emotional state at the time she gave birth intensified the connection she developed with the baby.

DETERMINING THE STAGE OF THE CONFLICT

The evaluation of the Seligs took four weeks, but that does not mean that treatment began only in the fifth week. Efforts to lower the anxiety and to create a safe climate started when they first walked into the office. Some specific suggestions were also given during the evaluation period. For example, Vic was encouraged to give Anna as much room as possible and to move toward his son.

Because of the separation, the Seligs' marital conflict did not look intense. Anna felt that for the first time she had some control over the situation, and Vic was doing what he could to win her back. Nevertheless it was determined that their conflict was at stage III. The premorbid state of the family showed considerable conflict and several cutoffs, with dysfunction in several members of the system. On every single measure of the couple—communication, relationship time and activity together, position in the interactional sequence—Vic and Anna were clearly in stage III. The intensity and polarization of the many triangles surrounding their marriage were also indicative of intense stage III conflict. Finally, the projection, bitterness, and compromised level of functioning in both Vic and Anna as individuals confirmed a stage III diagnosis.

Planning the Treatment

Once the stage of conflict has been determined and the specifics of the couple's problems understood, the therapist is ready to formulate a treatment plan. The early steps of the plan for Vic and Anna focused heavily on triangles and on each of them as an individual. This plan reflected our belief that in stage III moving too quickly to strengthen the couple only intensifies the conflict. The therapist decided to focus the initial work on husband-wife-child triangle, thinking that Vic needed to stop pursuing Anna and to direct his energies toward developing a close relationship with his son, no matter what happened to the marriage. This move would take the pressure off Anna and demonstrate Vic's willingness to be available both to his family and to the therapy. Helping Anna to give Vic more access to her son would be a difficult but important part of the work on this triangle, given the overly close relationship between mother and son and Anna's bitterness toward Vic.

The therapist also planned to address the extended family triangles. Vic would need to reconnect with his own family as he pulled back from pursuing Anna. Both had work to do on their triangles with their parents. For Vic, this meant working to lower his reactivity to his mother and developing a more balanced view of his parents' marriage. Taking responsibility for his relationship with his mother would also detoxify the in-law triangle in this marriage. Anna would work on narrowing the distance with her father and on moving toward her mother in a different way. This approach would activate her triangle with her parents, bring her distress out into the open, and give her a more realistic view of her extended family.

On the individual level, Vic was full of self-recrimination about his part in the marriage, but he had very little real understanding about his behavior. That would need to be addressed in therapy. He also would need to develop relationships with others within and outside of his family, work on achieving the personal goals he had set for himself, and bridge the cutoffs in his extended family. Anna too would need to understand her part in the marriage, which would require her to sort out the various sources of her bitterness and then work on giving it up, in order to increase her self-focus. She would also need a clearer perspective on her family of origin and personal goals not exclusively related to her role as a mother.

Our treatment plan would address these issues. There is no guarantee about the outcome for a marriage, but we believe that this kind of work will give both spouses greater opportunities in their own lives and increase the chances for the relationship to thrive.

The next four chapters suggest specific treatment for each of the four stages of marital conflict.

7

The Treatment of Stage I

COUPLES in stage I are for the most part still in the beginnings of the relationship. The partners trust each other and, when tension appears or arguments arise, they are able to discuss what has happened. They feel safe and comfortable with one another and are often still cradled in a loving cocoon—the two of them against the world. Time, circumstances, illness, confusion, disappointment, betrayal, and the like are often still seen as things that happen to other people but will never erode their relationship if they can just stay on top of things and solve problems as soon as they happen. Marriage at this stage is more like an affair than a working relationship. It is a process of fresh discovery. There is no accumulation of hurt from earlier conflicts to impede progress.

Our experience with stage I couples has been through marriage enrichment courses sponsored by local churches, civic groups, libraries, and schools and through our own Family Systems Training courses offered at CFL. These experiences have led us to the conclusion that for these couples a psychoeducational program, with or without four to six sessions of

The authors wish to acknowledge gratefully the assistance of Eileen G. Pendagast in the writing of this chapter.

therapy, works best. The motivation and low level of anxiety of these couples make them able to use psychoeducational material in a functional way.

This chapter describes the educational process that we recommend for couples in stage I marital conflict and how these couples are able to make use of this information to strengthen their marriages against the inevitable ravages of time.

The Psychoeducational Program

Family Systems Training (FST) was originally developed by Eileen Pendagast and Charles O. Sherman in 1976. They developed a series of six-week training courses intended to teach families how family relationships work, the route that normal problems and personal relationships are likely to take, and the options for dealing effectively with these difficulties over time.

Both Pendagast and Sherman are former teachers, and the FST is set up as a class, with a curriculum, reprints of pertinent articles, recommended audiovisual material, worksheets, homework assignments, and final evaluations of the course. Continual anonymous feedback and input allow for changes in the curriculum and any other part of the program that is deemed ineffective. This feedback has also served another necessary function in informing the teacher about the level of problems in the relationships of the participants in any given course. This is important, because couples experiencing severe conflict in their relationships will take the information provided by an FST and use it to organize their conflict. For example, a wife may accuse her husband of being a "distant bastard, and distancers never change and never admit they were wrong."

The course outline originally designed in 1976 and still used most often is as follows:

1. The family as a developmental system
2. The genogram and the family as an emotional system
3. The marital relationship
4. Parenting young children and adolescents
5 and 6.   The extended family; the major issues of sex, alcohol, money, and death; and review.

Course Description

FIRST SESSION: THE FAMILY AS A DEVELOPMENTAL SYSTEM

The first session introduces the course participants to the concept of continuous, normative change as it takes place throughout the lifetime of each person, each relationship, and the family system as a whole. It combines the idea of individual physical, emotional, and spiritual growth with the ongoing task of interacting with family members, who are also developing and changing. Middle age, adolescence, old age, and retirement are given particular emphasis because they so often occur simultaneously within a family system, making developmental demands on members of the family and on their relationships with one another.

In each of the sessions a play, film, or short story is used as displacement material to provide a focus of discussion external to the couples' personal lives. In our experience this approach provides a measure of safety that greatly facilitates the learning process.

Robert Anderson's play *Double Solitaire* (1972) is a particularly useful piece of displacement material for the initial session. It depicts a three-generation family gathered to celebrate the grandparents' fiftieth anniversary. The middle generation, the marriage in serious difficulty, struggles with the question of whether or not to "renew their vows" as a symbolic gesture of marital solidarity. Meanwhile, the young adults and adolescents participate as observers of their elders and as actors in their own subplots. Course participants can volunteer to play parts in a reading, or a community theater group may be engaged to present specific scenes from the play.

Observing the relationship process in this play, course participants experience the buildup of tension within the family on all generational levels. It then is easy to teach the importance of viewing marriage as a part of a larger system in which tension places stress on the individual spouses and on their marriage. The course emphasizes the importance of knowing one's own emotional history as a way of measuring the obstacles that confront one's attempts to function. Most of us tend to measure our functioning against some abstract standard, rather than against the reality of our own emotional history and the state of our family relationships. As a homework assignment, couples are asked to try to identify with the younger adults in the play and to formulate a plan for preventing their marriages from ending up like the two generations of marriages before them.

SECOND SESSION: THE GENOGRAM AND THE FAMILY
AS AN EMOTIONAL SYSTEM

The second session reinforces the material of the first session by reviewing the homework assigned and then introduces the genogram. One of the best ways to do the latter is to use displacement material that presents several major parts of the family life cycle in rich detail. Guerin and Pendagast (1976) have found one of the most successful works to be the film version of Robert Anderson's *I Never Sang for My Father* (1968). This film is packed with normal human relationship dilemmas and clearly outlines times of acute cluster stress, chronic dysfunction, relationship cutoffs, and transgenerational issues. Course participants draw a genogram of the film family, list the basic facts and locate the major issues in the family, and then sit back and chart the emotional process in the family over time. As homework, each participant then prepares a genogram of his or her own family.

Anderson's *I Never Sang for My Father* is about the Garrisons, an upper-middle-class family. The major theme of the film is the relationship between fathers and sons across two generations. The father, Tom, and mother, Margaret, are in their eighties. They live in Westchester County, New York, in a house that has been theirs since their children were small. The father is a successful businessman, who was also once mayor of the small town. He has been retired for fifteen years. The mother is in poor health with a deteriorating cardiac condition. Anderson tells us nothing about her extended family, and she is clearly idealized by the author; however, there is a pattern of almost continual criticism from her aimed at her husband.

The father's extended family is presented through the father's eyes. He was the eldest of three children whose mother died when he was ten years old. She had been deserted by her husband, an alcoholic. Tom obviously saw his father as evil and idealized his mother. The process of idealization began while she was alive and was intensified after her premature death. Tom is presented as a self-made man, pompous and opinionated, invulnerable to feeling, who sees himself as devoted to his wife, whom he also idealizes.

The marriage of Tom and Margaret Garrison has produced two children. Their daughter, Alice, is married and living with her husband and children in Chicago. She has been cut off from her parents and her brother after having been "banished" by her father for marrying a Jew. Gene, the younger, is an author who lives in New York City but travels on tours to other parts of the country. His wife has died of cancer about a year before;

the couple had had no children. On a recent tour to California, Gene has met and fallen in love with a woman who has been married before and has children. The fate of her first marriage is not made known. This description should make it clear how useful this film is in introducing couples to the idea of the family as an emotional system.

The film opens with Gene picking his parents up on their return to New York from Florida and driving them to their home. To teach about the family as a system and how each of us gets caught up in the emotional process of our families, two segments are usually used. In the garage scene, the triangle that operates between an adult and his or her parents is beautifully illustrated. Gene, a compliant son who tries to please his aging parents, goes out to the garage to help his father start the "old Buick" that has been unused while the parents were on vacation. The father, having sensed from Gene's letters that he is contemplating remarriage and a move to California, carefully sets his triangular trap. First he talks of the mother's frailty: "The strain has been awful . . . You never know when she'll get one of those seizures." Next he makes explicit the special link between Gene and his mother: "You know, you're her whole life." Finally he deposits the responsibility and subsequent guilt: "If you went to California . . . it would kill your mother."

The second segment is a restaurant scene, in which we get to see the distance and the chronic conflict in the parents' marriage and hear in detail the father's often repeated diatribe on the horrors of his boyhood. "I was only ten, we hadn't seen my father in over a year . . . the four of us, living in a miserable two-room tenement and suddenly he shows up [at Tom's mother's funeral] weeping and begging, and drunk as usual . . . And I shoved him off the funeral cart . . . I never saw him again till some years later when he was dying in Bellevue." Tom's hatred and anger after all these years fascinate and frighten Gene.

After these two scenes have been shown, the class is given a break to process and dissipate the emotion that the film stimulates. Some people go off by themselves; others huddle together, comparing responses. The class is reconvened after ten or fifteen minutes, and a short debriefing is held to allow people to describe their emotional responses. The participants then begin the work of preparing a genogram on the family and elaborating what the film teaches about a multigenerational emotional system.

The course presenter draws a basic genogram and asks the group to help fill in the facts about the Garrisons from their own worksheets. The couples look for transition times, specific dysfunction such as alcoholism, relationship conflict, and cutoffs. They are introduced to the two different kinds of cutoffs—complete and ritualized (see chapter 1). Tom's part of the

extended family is marked by his mother's early death, his father's alcoholism and abandonment of the family, and the relationship conflict and
cutoff with his father following his mother's death. The course participants
are asked to speculate on what impact these events and characteristics of
Tom's family may have had on him, on his marriage, and on Margaret and
the children.

The husband in one stage I couple, in his early thirties and married
for three years, focused on Tom's pompous pride; he saw that as a cover-up
for Tom's shame about his father's drinking and abandonment. Such a
response, introducing the idea of shame or embarrassment about one's
extended family, gives the instructor an opportunity to encourage the
couples to learn as much as they can about their own families. If they
understand better what stresses led to events that are seen as shameful,
they should be able to be less judgmental and embarrassed and more
accepting of their family histories.

From the segments presented, most people end up sympathetic to
Gene and intensely reactive to Tom. It is important to discuss this relationship from the point of view of both the father and the son in order to get
the participants to begin to consider father/child relationships from more
than just the child's viewpoint. It is equally important to spend some time
on the role that Margaret plays, both as a wife to her critical, overbearing,
wounded mate, and as a mother to both her children. Did she have any
other options in either of these roles that might have helped things to work
more effectively in her family?

As the class discusses the garage scene, one of the first questions to
be entertained is the impact on Gene's first marriage of his intense triangle
with his parents. This leads nicely into a discussion of in-law triangles (see
chapter 4). The question that logically follows is what impact it will have
on his potential second marriage, and what difference it will make if he and
his new wife take up residence in California. This provides an opportunity
to discuss the types of relationship cutoffs and their impact on the marital
relationship. Tom cut off his father, and his mother died when he was ten,
yet their ghosts somehow haunted his marriage. The move to California
affords an opportunity to discuss the impact of physical distance on a
marriage and the cocoon effect discussed in chapter 1.

THIRD SESSION: THE MARITAL RELATIONSHIP

Like the first two sessions, the third combines lecture, discussion, and
displacement material. The first concepts taken up are the emotional climate and the interactional dance between the emotional pursuer and the

emotional distancer. A videotape of a brief playlet produced by ABC's *The Christopher Closeup* for an appearance by Thomas Fogarty is the first piece of displacement material used. The videotape opens with the homecoming of a fifty-year-old executive from his day in the city to his unemployed wife, who is in charge of managing their "empty nest." During the predinner cocktail-and-open-the-mail ritual, the wife asks a series of questions about her husband's day and gets angrier by the minute at his distracted half-replies. Initially she calms her anger by taking another drink.

After this segment is played, the instructor introduces the concepts of the emotional pursuer and the emotional distancer. A profile of each is presented and the segment is replayed. The participants are asked to identify which characteristics in the profiles fit the husband and which fit the wife. From this beginning the interactional sequence can be spelled out with the help of the class.

The instructor asks, "As John tunes out Mary's questions and becomes more distracted, what is she going to do?" Instinctively the class knows that she will intensify her pursuit with more intrusive questions, laced with increasing emotional intensity. The instructor then asks what John will do in response to that, and again the almost instinctive answer: "He will either change the subject or leave the room."

At this point the emotional pursuers in the class start to mobilize, the distancers fold their arms across their chests and become defensive, and a spontaneous discussion of married people's emotional reactivity to certain behaviors of their partners develops. The pursuers express their frustration with unsuccessful attempts to establish an emotional connection with distancers. The distancers usually have one or two spokespersons who defend their behaviors and describe the intense internal pressure they feel from the emotional demands of the pursuers.

For the most part this type of interchange remains playful, and the universality of the experience is validating. If the tension in the room begins to rise, it may be an indication that there are some stage III couples present who have not mastered the volatility of some of their bitterness. The instructor must then relax the tension and redirect the class to a more cognitive level.

From the playful blaming and complaining produced by the discussion of emotional pursuers and distancers, the ideas of self-focus and projection are introduced. The instructor asks people to describe the differences in themselves when they are under stress and when things are going well. The idea is presented that everyone has a "toxic" and a "nontoxic" self. People are asked whether married people have the right to expect their spouses to change or whether they should invest their energies in developing better ways of dealing with the "obnoxious" parts of their partners. This question leads nicely into a discussion of expectations and where they come from and to the concept of the expectation-to-alienation progression (see chapter 5).

Next a second segment of the displacement videotape is shown. The wife has obtained a job, and we see the impact of this change on her husband, first at the neighborhood bar and then when they meet at home, when the husband is more than a little drunk. This episode opens the discussion of changes in women's roles and of men's ability or inability to handle them, leading into a consideration of the shift that takes place in a marital relationship when the reciprocity between overfunctioning and underfunctioning spouses is shaken. Reciprocity is discussed in its most obvious forms, as when the alcohol-abusing spouse stops drinking and the nonabusing spouse becomes depressed, and also in the more subtle forms that occur daily in all relationships. Any further discussion of alcohol abuse as an issue for married couples is deferred for a later session.

As the session ends, the class is assigned to do some thinking about how much creativity they invest in making their marriages work, as opposed to the energy they invest in other aspects of their lives. They are also asked to reflect on how children affect the marital relationship, in preparation for the theme of the next session.

FOURTH SESSION: PARENTING TRIANGLES WITH YOUNG CHILDREN AND ADOLESCENTS

Because most of the couples in stage I are young adults with young marriages, the focus of the presentation on parenting is placed on the two extremes of the relationships of adult children with their parents and the impact of pregnancy and childbirth on the marital relationship. A final segment of the tape from the previous session is useful here. It depicts the impact on the relationship of John and Mary when their adult daughter asks them to watch the baby for the weekend so she and her husband can go skiing. This segment allows for the introduction of relationship triangles and the key types that surround the marital relationship, concepts that will be useful as the participants examine their positions as adult children and as parents and as they begin to consider, perhaps for the first time, that children are active participants in the family emotional process. They also begin to see that their style of parenting tends at least in part to react to or imitate the way in which they themselves were parented.

Since every FST attracts some middle-aged couples, the topic of adolescence is always covered. The parenting of adolescents by middle-aged parents experiencing some degree of crisis in almost every area of their own lives is a feat that deserves presentation in a forum that has been made safe with humor and understanding by a skilled teacher/therapist. In such an atmosphere, people can begin to examine their own adolescence from a different perspective, gaining insights that can be enormously helpful not only in doing the job of parenting in as nontoxic a way as possible but in dealing with their own parents.

Two other films may also be used as displacement material. *Breaking Away* (1979) focuses on adolescence and the family in a beautifully soft and humorous way, and *Shoot the Moon* (1982) is especially graphic in its depiction of child and adolescent triangles and parenting issues during severe stage III conflict, on through divorce and remarriage.

FIFTH AND SIXTH SESSIONS: THE EXTENDED FAMILY AND THE MAJOR ISSUES OF SEX, ALCOHOL, MONEY, AND DEATH

The fifth and sixth FST presentations demonstrate the relevance of extended family patterns and relationships to the marital relationship and deal with some of the toxic issues around which marital conflict is often organized.

The Extended Family

In teaching the extended family material, the instructor reviews the extended family process in *I Never Sang for My Father.* The triangles, the transgenerational issues, the cutoffs are all discussed. Then a question is posed: "Is it possible to have a personal relationship with a man like Tom Garrison or any difficult-to-reach parent?" To facilitate this discussion, we use the closing confrontation scene of the film. The participants are asked to look for any possible opening Gene might have to shift the process in his relationship with his father.

The scene begins with a superficial friendliness between Gene and his father. In spite of this superficiality, the mutual longing for closeness comes through. Again they try. Earlier, while talking with his sister about the days following their mother's death, Gene had complained that he wanted to talk with his father about his dead mother, but that his father wouldn't allow it. He is about to get his chance.

GENE: *(very tentatively)* You know, Dad, I've never seen a picture of your father. *(Tom looks at him a long time. Then finally, with his hatred showing in his face, he unwraps another tissue, and hands over a small picture.)*

GENE: *(Surprised)* He's just a boy!

TOM: That was taken about the time he was married . . . Oh, he was a fine-looking man before he started to drink. Big, square, high color. But he became my mortal enemy . . . Did I ever show you that? *(He takes out a small piece of paper, hands it to Gene)* Careful . . . When I set up a home for my brother and sister, one day we were all out, and he came around and ripped up all my sister's clothes and shoes. Drunk, of course. A few days later, he came around to apologize and ask for some money and I threw him out . . . The next day he left that note.

(Rumpled piece of paper. Scrawled on it: You are welcome to your burden.)

[Tom agains builds a case for how evil his father was and openly proclaims him as his mortal enemy. In response, Gene searches for something positive that might mitigate Tom's intensely negative stance.]

TOM: You are welcome to your burden.

GENE: And you kept it?

TOM: Yes, I never saw him again until many years later he was dying, in Bellevue, and someone got word to me, and I went down and asked him if he wanted anything. He said he'd like some fruit. So I sent him in a few oranges. He died the next day.

GENE: There must have been something there to love, to understand.

[Tom blocks Gene's attempt and shifts to the positive things about his relationship with Gene. It is as if each of them has made a pledge not to let their relationship with one another be a repeat of the previous generation.]

TOM: In my father? *(He shakes his head "no," and then shows Gene another card)* Do you remember this? "To the best dad in the world on Father's Day." That was in . . . *(Turns it over and reads the notation)* 1946 . . . Yes. *(Emotional)* I appreciate that, Gene. That's a lovely tribute. I think I have all your Father's Day cards here . . . You know, I didn't want children, coming from the background I did . . . and we didn't have Alice for a long time. But your mother finally persuaded me. She said they would be a comfort in our old age. And you are, Gene.

GENE: *(Touched, but embarrassed and uncomfortable)* Well . . .

TOM: *(Fishes in the drawer and brings out a program)* A program of yours from college . . . some glee club concert . . . I've got everything but the kitchen stove in here . . . Do you still sing?

GENE: *(Smiling)* Not in years.

TOM: That's too bad. You had a good voice. But we can't do everything . . . I remember your mother would sit at the piano, hour after hour, and I'd be up here at my desk, and I'd hear you singing.

[The theme of singing for your father is clearest here. We see the central triangle: Tom, alone in his room upstairs working; Gene downstairs singing to his mother's accompaniment. Here father and son almost touch in a real way, when the truth of how it really was surfaces, and the father is again thrown back into the past.]

GENE: You always asked me to sing "When I Grow Too Old To Dream."

TOM: Did I? . . . I don't remember your ever singing that . . . You always seemed to be just finishing as I came into the room. *(Looks at Gene)* Did you used to sing that for me?

GENE: *(Not a joke anymore)* No . . . But you always asked me to sing it for you.

TOM: Oh. *(Puts program away)* Well, I enjoyed sitting up here and listening. *(He pokes around in the drawer and takes something out . . . in tissue paper. He unwraps a picture carefully)* And that's my mother.

GENE: *(Gently)* Yes, I've seen that, Dad. It's lovely.

TOM: She was twenty-five when that was taken. She died the next year . . . I carried it in my wallet for years . . . and then I felt I was wearing it out. So I put it away . . . Just a little bit of a thing. *(He starts to cry, and the deep sobs finally come and his emaciated body is wracked by them. It is a terrible, almost soundless sobbing. Gene comes to his father and puts his arms around him and holds him. Then, after some moments)* I didn't think it would be this way . . . I always thought I'd go first. *(He sobs again, gasping for air. Gene continues to hold him, inevitably moved and touched by this genuine suffering. Finally, Tom gets a stern grip on himself.)* I'm sorry. *(Tries to shake it off)* It just comes over me. . . . It'll pass . . . I'll get a hold of myself.

GENE: Don't try, Dad . . . Believe me, it's best.

TOM: *(Angry with himself)* No . . . it's just that . . . I'll be all right. *(He turns and blows his nose)*

GENE: It's rough, Dad . . . It's bound to be rough.

TOM: *(Shakes his head to snap out of it)* It'll pass . . . It'll pass. *(Starts to wrap up the picture of his mother)*

GENE: Can I help you put these things away, Dad?

Gene misses his opportunity. His father, vulnerable in the face of pictures of his father and mother, might be open to Gene's talking about himself and how he experienced the loss of his wife and then his mother. Instead Gene responds on the object level, offering to help put the things away. This breaks the climate, and with magnificent timing Gene tells his father that he is going to marry Peggy and move to California. The opening is slammed shut, and the automatic reactive pattern is reestablished. Gene and his father now proceed, against both their wishes, to repeat a piece of painful process from the generation before. An angry confrontation ensues that ends with a cutoff between Gene and his father—a cutoff that is at once different from and the same as the one a generation ago.

Toxic Issues

Sex, alcohol, money, and death are the four major issues around which marital communication gets shut down. As "toxic" issues they are present in many marriages but often do not get talked about. Money and death are discussed together here because they are often related in family situations. Death often brings to the surface a family's attitudes toward money as difficulties and tensions arise in the handling of the estate. Death also brings out a family's problems in dealing with each other's intense emotional reactions. Money, whether or not it is connected with death, is a central issue that affects the balance of power in a marriage.

The presentation of the toxic issues has four goals:

1. To teach participants to observe and describe the emotional process in their own families around sex, alcohol, money, and death, and to trace these patterns back through the generations of their extended families
2. To provide participants with information about the physiological and emotional aspects of sex and alcohol
3. To provide a systems view of sex- and alcohol-related dysfunctions
4. To help participants understand the "emotional shock-wave" that follows a death in the family and to provide functional ways of dealing with it.

Discussion is a major part of the learning process for both the instructor and the course participants. Here is a transcript of a discussion that developed around a presentation by Philip Guerin on the issue of alcoholism. Dr. Guerin had just made the point that in systems terms any problem, including alcoholism, should be seen as being in both the system and the individual, rather than just in the individual, and that the individual must be viewed as being part of the relationship system.

QUESTION: Is it better to deal with the parents, or to move away and not deal with them? And if you are going to deal with them, how do you go about it?

DR. GUERIN: I think it is always better to deal with them. I don't think that physical distance is ever the answer, although physical distance can have some temporary value. A few days away from home can give you quite a new perspective on the trouble you may be having with your kids, or mother, or whomever. Begin by trying to identify your emotional triggers. Get in charge of your anxiety, and then invest some relationship time in which all you try to do is just not to become uptight in your parents' presence.

QUESTION: What I would like to know is, for an alcoholic father, for instance, wouldn't you suggest forgive and forget?

DR. GUERIN: No, but I might after I knew the facts. I would suggest a research project aimed at finding out what his alcoholism was all about, because you have only one side of the story.

QUESTION: Yes, but I've got the side that says that Mom worked two jobs to raise me while he was drunk, the bum!

DR. GUERIN: That may be true, but that's only understanding him in the view of the person who was responsible, as opposed to the bum who was irresponsible.

QUESTION: Yeah, but the bum had my address.

DR. GUERIN: I understand that. But the bum also had parents, and siblings perhaps, and was part of a family. If you get to know how that family worked and what the process was in it, your father's alcoholism and his desertion of you will be more understandable. In order to do that you are going to have to run against the feelings of a person who has been very responsible, who nurtured you and took care of you. That's very difficult. I can't suggest that everyone just run off and do that. But I would suggest that you entertain the thought.

In that connection, I have seen people do exactly that: connect with a father they haven't seen in thirty years, since the time of the divorce caused by the father's alcoholism. I have seen them learn fantastic things about the process that led into the alcoholism—how it was tied into the whole process of the mother's relationship with her parents, and the father's relationship with his mother, and the play between him and his in-laws, and how that exacerbated the drinking and even helped to trigger it. That is not whitewashing the father, or excusing his behavior or his alcoholism. But it is widening the frame to give more than just an emotional reaction to the past.

You can do this kind of thing for yourself, because if you can get a broader picture you may have more emotional freedom to relate to your father and to relate to future things that may develop in your life. You've got part of his biology in you, and your kids will have part of his biology. There is no way to wipe that out, even though he deserted you. That's a very emotional thing and I don't want to be glib about it. I realize that you had to live it. I just say, think about it.

QUESTION: I relate to one of the things you've been saying, because I've gone through it too—not necessarily with an alcoholic father, but the part where the mother uses the child to help her carry her burden. As a child you take on the burden, and you are never free of it until you finally see that you've been used.

DR. GUERIN: I agree except to suggest that you be careful not to swing into the position of becoming judgmental about your mother. Understand the pickle she was in and where she was coming from when she got locked into you as her emotional refuge in dealing with her husband.

QUESTION: Oh, right! That's what's the cause of it—trying to deal with an alcoholic husband. She didn't know what to do with him. If I could go back to the beginning: you said that difficulty in the marriage perhaps led the husband to alcoholism.

DR. GUERIN: That's one basic premise.

QUESTION: I see. In other words he had no difficulty with alcohol before he had trouble in the marriage?

DR. GUERIN: I don't know. I'm just saying that is one way of looking at it. You see, you can put your viewfinder on any part of the process, at any point. You can say there was alcoholism up there in the extended family—that there was a biological or psychological predisposition in the family's emotional vulnerability to alcohol—whatever. What you don't want to get into is blaming the wife for this. There is a part of the process that each of these two people played a part in, and the kids played a part in, and the families of origin also.

QUESTION: So, even if the relationship was idyllic, his predisposition might lead him to become one?

DR. GUERIN: People have different vulnerabilities. They can be vulnerable emotionally, psychologically, or biologically. When in difficulty or under stress, one person may develop a disease, another some other kind of symptom. I myself am a somatizer. When my anxiety level shoots up, I'm likely to have some sort of disease—and having gone to medical school, I have a whole encyclopedia-full to choose from!

QUESTION: May I review what you say? In Al-Anon terms we accept the
fact that we don't know what caused an alcoholic to become
an alcoholic, and it isn't terribly relevant. But in any situation
in which stress will be produced—in the marital situation, or
on the job, or in any family situation—actually, any kind of
situation can produce stress—then the person who uses alcohol as an escape from stress will run to alcohol. So in the
marital situation, from what you say, they are running away
from marriage into alcoholism. They may have run away
from high school, where they had poor grades, into alcoholism. They may have had army problems, or job problems,
whatever. In each case they escaped from stress by running
toward alcohol.

DR. GUERIN: Well, it's all part of a process, and more than just the alcoholic
is involved in that process.

A Stage I Couple: The Robinsons

The majority of stage I couples do not request clinical consultation, either
during or after the FST. Their only continued contact with the Center and
the Marital Project is through follow-up evaluation done through the mail
six months later. Those couples that respond to the request for feedback
after six months usually provide positive documentation of the impact the
course had on their relationships.

Some couples do ask to be seen, however, either during the course,
immediately after it, or within the first six months. Sandra and Mark
Robinson, both twenty-seven, had been married for a year and a half.
They had attended an FST around the time of their first anniversary.
Sandra called for an appointment, stating that she and Mark were beginning to fight about how to deal with their respective mothers and with
finances. They were concerned that the fighting might escalate and that
they wouldn't be able to slow it down.

Both appeared for the interview in their business suits. Sandra, in dark
blue with a striped shirt and a foulard tie, looked almost stern. Her short
hair and glasses added to the look. She was in business, and she meant
business. Mark on the contrary looked younger than his twenty-seven
years—too young to be married, and uncomfortable in his shirt and tie. He
had come because Sandra insisted.

They had met in college, broken up after graduation for about two years, and become reacquainted and reconnected when they ended up working for the same corporation. After three or four months of dating on and off, they moved in together and subsequently married. Some of the problems that had been involved in the original breakup after college had resurfaced. Both were eldest children and close to their parents while growing up. They had both distanced from their parents while at college, but they would distance only so far, and then they would miss the closeness and warmth at home and drift back. Sandra's family was Catholic and Mark's was Jewish. While Sandra and Mark were dating at college, the families had no objection to each other as long as they were not required to become in-laws. Both mothers had attempted to sabotage the reconciliation, and each had declared herself miffed at the wedding preparations.

Sandra could tolerate Mark's mother only in small doses. Mark did not want to visit his mother with Sandra, because his mother tended to make references to what she perceived as Sandra's personality problems. The longer they stayed, the more she warmed to the task of criticizing Sandra, her family, and her "insane" religious beliefs.

Nor was Mark fond of Sandra's mother. She seemed frivolous, addicted to spending money on lavish clothes and to playing tennis. Sandra didn't mind going to see her mother alone, because she understood Mark's feelings and in many ways agreed with them. Her mother often seemed vague, empty-headed, and uninteresting to talk to. The problem was that Sandra's mother liked to get visits, and she complained that Mark was ignoring her if he didn't come. When Mark was around her, however, she couldn't resist "trying to help him" by choosing his clothing, working on his hairstyle, encouraging him to go to the gym, and asking him embarrassing questions about what it was like to be Jewish. She made it sound like a disease.

Their other problem was money. Sandra stated that she didn't want to spend her life working; she wanted to enjoy the fruits of her labor. She wanted to travel extensively, even to purchase land and homes in other countries and rent them out to vacationing Americans, selling them after a while and buying new and grander ones. Eventually she would choose one to retire to somewhere around the age of forty-five. Mark reported that she read the *Wall Street Journal* with such intensity that he felt she lost touch with the real world. She would think and scheme and come up with money-saving and money-making schemes that sounded dishonest and maybe even illegal to Mark. He confessed to having great difficulty imagining himself retired at forty-five and living in Europe. He had trouble thinking of being forty-five when he wasn't yet thirty. He would listen to

Sandra and feel real panic at the scope of her desires and her relentless need for more and more money.

Mark was not particularly attracted to poverty, but he felt he had time on his side. He was not about to hurry through his life taking the risk of losing most of it or at least failing to appreciate it, while he amassed a fortune in real estate that he was too far away from to take care of and too busy working to visit. Besides, a nuclear device could blow it all up, anyway.

From the FST Sandra and Mark had been intrigued by the session on the extended family. The premise that each spouse was to take responsibility for his or her own side of the family was not surprising to them and not a problem for them. Neither one of them had had a chance to hand over their mothers to their spouses, and their mothers would not have stood for it. In six sessions spread out over three months, the therapist focused on working the interlocking in-law triangles and the primary parental triangles.

Initially Mark telephoned his mother and visited her more frequently by himself. She responded positively but did not moderate her negative comments about Sandra. The therapist next coached Mark to try two things: to talk to his father about the problem of feeling caught between Sandra and his mother and to respond to every negative comment from his mother about Sandra with a positive, flattering comment about his mother, with no defense of Sandra. (It was important that he do this in Sandra's absence lest she experience it as disloyalty.)

When Mark talked to his father he learned that his father had had a similar experience in which his mother had been incessantly critical of his wife. The father commiserated with Mark about how tough it was but had no suggestions on how to handle it. This information was all Mark needed. The next time he was with his mother he asked her about her relationship with his father's mother. She glossed over it and described it somewhat positively. Mark expressed his sadness that she and Sandra would never have a positive relationship like the one she had had with her mother-in-law. As he was leaving, he shouted to his father, "Hey, Dad, Mother disagrees with you about the relationship she had with Nana, and she says she won't have any trouble with her Jewish grandchildren, either."

Some observers would say that that was a dirty trick to play on one's middle-aged father. Perhaps, but one could also reason that if the father had done more of his homework on the problem with his own mother and his wife, less would have been left for Mark. The result, at any rate, was that Mark's mother stopped her critical comments and became much more civil to Sandra. Mark did not expect them to love each other, at least not right away. It was accomplishment enough that his mother was behaving more appropriately with Sandra.

On her extended family journey, Sandra discovered the precedent for her ambition and her obsession with financial gain. She was able to discuss it with her mother and was surprised at how down-to-earth her mother was and how intelligently she responded. It reminded Sandra that her mother had graduated from a prestigious college and had just never used her brain in occupational pursuits. She and her mother discussed the different opportunities for women these days and some of her mother's "might-have-beens."

Over the course of the three months, Sandra's intensity lessened. She and Mark discussed their differences more openly and decided to make a project of studying the differences between their cultures. The therapist gave them a check-up appointment for six months later.

8

The Treatment of Stage II

THE WORKMANS, a couple in their late twenties, came to CFL's clinic requesting marital therapy. Sheila Workman had called and described the presenting problem in the following way: "We are really getting on each other's nerves, and our marriage is in trouble for the first time. We're both really scared and hope you can help." They had been married for five years. All four parents were alive and well, and the couple lived about fifty miles from both families of origin. Each spouse had two siblings, all of whom were doing well with their lives except for Sheila's youngest sister, a senior in college, who was depressed over not getting into medical school and the breakup of a five-year relationship with her high school boyfriend. Jack's older sister had just delivered her first child, a daughter, and this event had reawakened in Sheila her long-held desire to be a mother. Jack was still unsure about when they should have their first child.

JACK: After five years of breaking my ass to please you and satisfy your every whim, not to mention your mother's, you can come in here and complain about our marriage. You're beyond being satisfied; nothing, nothing would be enough.

SHEILA: I know you've done a lot for me and that you love me, I just

feel disconnected from you at times—unneeded, even sometimes unwanted.

THERAPIST: She wants more of your soul, Jack.

JACK: Whatever the hell that means.

THERAPIST: A larger portion of the personal part of you—how you think,
how you feel about yourself.

JACK: [Pause] That's not my strong suit. I mostly keep things like
that to myself.

THERAPIST: How do you show Sheila you love her?

JACK: By trying to do everything she wants, even sometimes before
she thinks of it.

THERAPIST: So you love by doing, rather than talking about personal
thoughts and feelings.

JACK: I guess that's right.

THERAPIST: Are you ever more open about personal things than at other
times?

JACK: I don't think so.

SHEILA: Remember when we were dating and your father had a heart
attack? You talked to me for hours in the parking lot of the
hospital. You told me things about yourself and your father
and mother I've never heard before or since.

JACK: I don't remember that time awfully well.

THERAPIST: Does Sheila relate to you in ways that open you up or close
you down?

JACK: Both, in a way. I trust her more than anyone, but when she
gets critical and pushes me to talk, or worse yet to have a
feeling, I shut down for days, even weeks.

SHEILA: I can't stand being shut out.

THERAPIST: What does it do to you?

SHEILA: First I get hurt, then I try again to get in. If he shuts me out
long enough, I either blow up or begin to cut him apart a piece
at a time.

In this transcript from the initial session with the Workmans, the
patterns of emotional pursuit and distance are clear. These would form the
basis for an experiment for this couple directed at getting them back on
track. Before moving to set it up, however, the therapist would check out
the more positive aspects of the relationship and gauge the readiness of the
couple to begin playing with the patterns in their relationship.

In stage II conflict anxiety and emotional arousal are high enough to
override the ability of the relationship to contain them. In intensity the
conflict falls somewhere between the subclinical levels observed in stage

I and the severe conflict of stage III. There is usually only a moderate level of stress in the family system surrounding the marriage. For example, a couple attempting to decide when to have their first child may find themselves in significant conflict, but without a long history of past conflict and without a high number of other stresses in the larger family system. As a result, the general stress level is fairly low and relatively easy to contend with.

Stage II conflict usually lasts less than six months. Communication is still relatively open—benign exchanges of information flow easily, and misunderstandings are minor—but expressions of personal thoughts and feelings are either reactive or restricted, and intimacy is on the decline. Both spouses may complain about this decline in closeness, either because sex is on the wane or because there is little or no "sharing" anymore, or both.

All these factors, both positive and negative, account for a less intense and less fixed polarization in the triangles that surround the marriage. For this reason the therapist has direct access to, and may operate directly on, the marital relationship. In stages III and IV, by contrast, the triangles must be dealt with first.

The Treatment Protocol

The treatment of stage II marital conflict moves directly toward the marriage itself to provide the couple with ways to change their interaction, adopt more functional patterns, and solve future problems by themselves. After engaging the couple and lowering their anxiety about their marriage and about therapy, our stage II protocol has two major thrusts. The first is the restructuring of the marital dyad through pursuer-distancer experiments, and the second is the reinforcement of each spouse's self-focus through work in the extended family, work that will provide an awareness of actual and potential stress from the extended family and an increase in support from the multigenerational family system.

PURSUER–DISTANCER EXPERIMENTS

As we have seen, an emotional pursuer is oriented to relationships, freely expressing affect as well as personal thoughts and feelings and placing a high value on explicit human connectedness. The following clinical example from an evaluation session gives a vivid picture of the emotional pursuer in her own words.

JOAN: When I approach him and I want to talk to him, he doesn't want to talk. I get upset, because I've been holding these things inside me for a long time. It's in me and I want to get it out and I get very excitable and I raise my voice because I want to get it all out, but he doesn't want to listen. He's tired, he wants to go to sleep, he wants me to shut up.

DAN: You can't communicate with someone that's screaming.

JOAN: But I'm not screaming at the top of my lungs. That's not the way I start out, but he won't listen to me, and look at me, and talk to me. He's constantly going away, going away, and I want to tell him all these feelings inside me and I approach him and he pulls away and usually he goes out, or if I try to stop him by standing in front of him and saying, "Dan, please don't go." "Get out of my way," he tells me, and he says, "Get out of my way or I'll push you out of my way," and he usually does push me and I'll push him back and then it will just get more violent, back and forth. I don't want him to leave so I block the door and say, "Please stay, let's talk it out, let's talk about it." He says, "I'm not talking with you, you don't know how to talk."

DAN: But you don't talk, you're yelling and screaming at the top of your lungs.

JOAN: Dan works five nights a week, and during the day he does carpentry work with this other fellow. They do paneling when they get a job, roofing or something like that, so sometimes he's gone all day. Well, first of all, let's start at night. He's got to leave the house at 5:45, so I try to have supper on the table at 5:00. He leaves at 5:45, and he's gone all night and he gets home—well, last night was an exception, it was 3:00. When he's busy he gets home maybe 6:00–6:30, it ranges, it depends. I'm already up with the baby and it's light out and I still don't have my husband next to me, so I sleep alone and I wake up alone. It's a horrible feeling.

This brief interchange expresses clearly the experience of an emotional pursuer. We believe that such people are constitutionally primed to respond in this fashion in the majority of their relationships. Joan in fact was an intense pursuer of her husband and her children. She was distant from her parents, whose long-term conflict and preoccupation with her alcoholic brother had long since dampened her pursuit. Having given up any hope that her parents or brother would ever change, Joan had moved to protect herself with a ritualized cutoff from them. She displaced the emotional intensity from her family of origin into a connection with Dan that she hoped would meet her needs and provide a state of internal comfort. The more that didn't happen, the more she became obsessed with Dan and with changing him, especially changing his emotional distance from her.

In working with emotional pursuers individually or in conjoint sessions, it is important first to hear them out and elicit and validate their pain, and then to move to assist them in developing self-focus. When the timing was right with Joan and Dan, the therapist formulated an experimental plan to modify her behavior.

THERAPIST: What do you think would happen, Joan, if you just ignored Dan for a while? You know . . . assume he needs to be left alone.

DAN: She couldn't do it.

THERAPIST: There's a challenge for you.

JOAN: I'm afraid he'd just get worse, never be home.

THERAPIST: If you were going to try it, how would you set it up?

Joan was being asked to convert the struggle into a playful experiment. The experiment had at least two phases. In phase one, Joan was asked to stop some of her behavior patterns, such as her emotional demands, time demands, questions, criticisms, and comments. At the same time she was asked to monitor her own inner calm and Dan's responses, if any. As Joan successfully carried out this phase, she began to experience the level of her upset rising, and she found herself doing perhaps a different version of the behaviors she was trying to avoid. Joan reported this experience in therapy, where the therapist first validated her pain and her effort (demonstrated by the escalation of discomfort) and then helped her see how much her pursuing behaviors were serving the function of keeping her insides calm.

THERAPIST: When you were being most successful with the experiment, what did it feel like?

JOAN: I felt good, like I had some control over my emotions and behavior.

THERAPIST: And when you were failing?

JOAN: Mostly then it varied from feeling angry at Dan for making me have to go through this too, and at other times I felt like I was going to burst.

THERAPIST: These behaviors we're playing with, do you think they are what makes you a loving and caring person?

JOAN: Yes.

THERAPIST: Have you ever been able to determine the point when those same behaviors that make you a lover become just desperate attempts to keep your insides calm?

JOAN: No.

Joan was now ready to put this experiment into perspective and move on to phase two, which involved improving her skill at planned distance. She was encouraged to increase her emotional investment in object productivity and in other personal relationships. She was coached to accept as functional any movement toward her on Dan's part, even if it was done in anger, but she was cautioned not to respond to his movement toward her by overreacting and quickly closing off the distance between them, which would just reestablish the old equilibrium. As Joan carried out phase two, she would come to the realization that Dan's distance also served the function of keeping his inner calm, and this knowledge would help her not to take his behavior so personally.

Joan's husband Dan was a classic distancer, oriented to objects and productivity, who kept personal thoughts and feelings to himself and placed a high value on personal privacy and time alone. A detective on the White Plains police force, he spent a great deal of time at work, which included two extra jobs, one as a bartender and the other in a small construction business with a boyhood friend. As Joan successfully distanced herself in the relationship with Dan, he first experienced relief and was delighted with therapy. As her planned distance continued, however, he found himself angry at her and upset in ways he didn't understand. His functioning at work and at home began to suffer, and he eventually sought Joan out to talk, but only after she began to talk about a trial separation.

Emotional distancers possess a very efficient system of containment. When they have an emotional reaction to something, automatically the reaction is shunted into an inner compartment and closed off from awareness. This phenomenon contributes to the myth that emotional distancers don't have feelings, that they are cold and emotionless.

The following session occurred after Dan's wife had successfully distanced from him, and after his tightly sealed emotional compartments had begun to pop open in response to the change in his wife's behavior.

THERAPIST: Did you miss her, when she backed off?

DAN: Sure I did, I started to not do well on the job. Not being able to function at home. I couldn't do simple things; I couldn't do simple chores anymore. I couldn't look at anything and want to do it. It was also resentment; I resented her very much.

THERAPIST: So you also found out that you were addicted to her and you were in withdrawal.

DAN: That's a good one. I'm still in withdrawal, or maybe I kicked the habit. I guess it's like I saw Joan for the first time the other night, her face, everything. She looked so different. It was like she was someone that I've really wanted to be with.

THERAPIST: What are the most positive things of the old you that are left standing?

DAN: It's not all out. Like I said, it's been in there, but it's been buried.

THERAPIST: If you lined up Joan and all those folks that are important to you, like your mother and your father and your sister and your brother, and you paraded the old Dan by, how many of them would applaud?

DAN: I know my family would.

THERAPIST: So they would applaud. It's Act Two and we bring out the new Dan. Who is going to applaud and who isn't?

DAN: I guess they'll all be in shock and probably nobody will applaud.

THERAPIST: Joan will give you a standing ovation. You're caught between two very important poles for you. One says be one way, the other says be another, and how the hell do you find Dan in the middle of that?

DAN: I'm not going to be the way they want.

THERAPIST: You're not going to be defined by those people.

DAN: No, because Joan might like what she sees now, but I don't know if she's gotten to know me yet.

THERAPIST: You mean if she really gets to know you, she might not like you?

DAN: It's possible, but I don't know that.

THERAPIST: Are you going to give it to her slowly or all at once?

DAN: I would just like to do it as it comes.

THERAPIST: Have you had, in any of these past few very emotional days, the sense of being caught between Joan and your ties to her and your folks and your ties to them?

DAN: Oh, yeah, sure.

THERAPIST: Have you been able to get any perspective on that?

DAN: My mother said to me last night, you used to talk to me all the time, sometimes you would even wake me up at night to talk to me, but you don't talk to me anymore. And I thought about it, and I said yeah, because when I talked to her she directed me and gave me all this good advice, and I finally got to the point where I was distancing from her, because I guess that I just didn't want any more advice.

In this segment Dan teaches us that distancers have feelings too, but that they keep these feeling locked away in tightly sealed compartments. As these compartments open up in therapy, the pursuer may react with fright and upset even though she's been asking the distancer to tell her his feelings. What she really was asking for were his positive thoughts and feelings about her and perhaps his troubles with important others in his life. From an experience such as Dan's, an emotional distancer can learn how efficient his system of containment is and how much his emotional distance and productivity orientation serve to insulate him not only from his wife's emotional intensity but also from his own.

EXTENDED FAMILY WORK

The second part of the stage II protocol involves individual work by both spouses in their families of origin. The purpose of this work is threefold:

1. To establish a linkage between what is happening in the extended family and the interaction within the marriage
2. To increase each spouse's sense of belonging and support in his or her family
3. To bring out the connections between the key triangles of the extended family and the marital relationship. This step is important in case a surge of stress in the extended family later drives the marital conflict to stage III.

The most effective way of moving into this phase of the work is to establish a link between what is being worked on in the marriage and past or present experiences in the extended family. The simplest link is a comparison between the marriage under scrutiny and the marriages of each spouse's parents. When either or both spouses have been married before, it is also important to include in the comparison the previous marriages.

THERAPIST: How often do you compare your marriage with your parents' marriage?

JEANNE: I've always wanted mine to be different; they never fought, but mother would vacillate back and forth between idealizing my father to us and at the same time you got the idea she was never quite satisfied with him. As they've gotten older, it's like they live parallel lives.

THERAPIST: Would your parents agree with your evaluation?

JEANNE: I don't know. I've never talked to them about things like that. My mother would probably paint a glowing picture, and my father would laugh and change the subject.

THERAPIST: How often do you seen them?

JEANNE: About once a month. They only live in New Jersey.

THERAPIST: Do you get any time alone with either of your parents?

JEANNE: No, not really. Mostly it's my husband and I going over for Sunday dinner once a month.

THERAPIST: Which parent are you most comfortable with, find it easier to talk to?

JEANNE: Probably my father; he's difficult to pin down, but he listens better and is very slow to judge or criticize.

THERAPIST: Would your father be suspicious if you asked to meet him for lunch in the city one day?

JEANNE: He'd probably think I was getting a divorce or needed a loan.

THERAPIST: Would it make sense to you to spend some time with him and eventually ask him how he became such an expert at dealing with your mother?

JEANNE: I guess so. I'd have to think about it.

This transcript demonstrates an initial attempt to establish linkage between the conflictual marriage and the wife's extended family. As Jeanne began to investigate this link, she found that her parents' marriage manifested a process similar to her own. Her work here also allowed her to improve her relationship with her parents, which took some of the pressure off her own marriage.

In work with the extended family, it is important to coach the wife not to spend the time with her parents complaining about her husband. That would interfere with making a personal connection with her parents. In stage II it is still possible to make this restriction; in stages III and IV the marriage is such an intense source of pain that it is nearly impossible to prevent it from being discussed with the older generation. Even then, however, the therapist attempts to minimize the degree of complaining that people can do with their parents at a time of conflict in their marriages.

Timing

The clinical timing of the move to incorporate the extended family into the treatment process is important. In work with stage II couples, involvement usually begins in the middle of the pursuer-distancer experiments, when the emotional pursuer is attempting to hold her (or his) planned distance. At this time the pursuer can hear the suggestion to move toward relationships in the extended family as a way to hold her distance in the marital relationship while activating another source of potential emotional connection.

Extended family work may be introduced to the emotional distancer earlier in the therapy, while the distancer is struggling to become less reactive to the emotional intensity and demands of the pursuer and is having difficulty accepting the reactive nature of his distance. A simple question such as "Is this a new experience for you, dealing with this level of emotional intensity?" or "Who else in your life has had a similar kind of emotional impact on you?" can serve to introduce the extended family, as in the following brief segment of a session transcript.

THERAPIST: Who else in your life has had this kind of emotional impact on you?

HUSBAND: No one I can think of.

WIFE: Try your mother, for instance.

THERAPIST: Your wife thinks your mother makes her look like an amateur.

HUSBAND: Well, my mother, she's another story.

THERAPIST: Give me just the introductory chapter.

HUSBAND: My mother and I had a great relationship until I was about twelve, then she just asked too many questions and looked hurt when I gave her vague answers.

This segment suggests the beginning of a link to the extended family for a husband-distancer. More elaborate involvement of the distancer with the extended family is usually best saved for later in the course of therapy.

If the therapeutic intervention on such a couple is successful, two things usually happen. The pursuer gives up pressuring the distancer to change and moves toward her extended family while simultaneously returning to the distancer the responsibility for dealing with his extended family. And the distancer finds himself having to deal with his own side of the family as he observes his wife's progress in changing to more functional patterns in dealing with her family. In the best of outcomes, he then wants some of this "good medicine" for himself.

The Extended Family Expedition

Work with the extended family in marital therapy can be accomplished in a variety of ways. The two major clinical approaches are to involve the parents or siblings of each spouse directly in therapy sessions in various membership combinations or to coach each spouse in ways of experimenting with his or her extended family relationships. We use the direct involvement of family members more often in stages III and IV, or when attempts at the coaching process are unproductive. In stage II we prefer to coach the spouses. If coaching does not work, or if the couple is not interested in taking on the project and the marital conflict is significantly abated, we do not force the issue, because it is not necessary to what the couple considers a successful outcome.

The coaching process involves:

1. Picking a portion of the extended family that is most relevant to the marital conflict—usually the couples' triangles with their own parents, but occasionally a triangle involving an adult sibling
2. Spelling out the relationship process within that area and creating a plan to confirm that process, followed by an experiment that will open that portion of the extended family system to change
3. Lowering the spouse's anxiety about approaching the extended family prior to the contact, so that the family members who are approached will not become reactive to the anxiety being carried in and cause the experiment to fail.

A Stage II Couple: The Savalases

Greg and Maria Savalas, thirty-four and twenty-six, had been married for four years and had no children. They came to therapy because Greg was feeling restless in the relationship and Maria was fearful that he might leave. They periodically had intense arguments in which Greg would blow up and then not speak to Maria for several days. During the latest blowup, Greg told Maria that he was very attracted to a woman at work. In retaliation Maria told Greg that the previous year she too had had a crush on a man at work, but had simply talked herself out of it. Since then, a stony silence had prevailed, except for Maria's attempts to talk things out with

Greg. These had only resulted in Maria's becoming hysterical and Greg's being more silent and angry than ever.

Until several months before the couple sought treatment, the relationship had for the most part been satisfying. But each of them had some complaints. Maria thought Greg devoted too much time to working on the reconstruction of their house. Despite the fact that both of them had wanted to install a new kitchen, Maria had never expected Greg to come home from work and spend the entire evening working on it. When it was time to go to bed, Greg would drop off to sleep immediately. Maria was hurt and angry, as she felt that Greg had already given her short shrift because of his overinvolvement with work. When Maria let her disappointment show, Greg would first change the subject and then tune her out. If she pursued him he would eventually explode in anger—behavior he felt was not a usual part of his personality. He would tell Maria that he wasn't sure how he felt about her, that he wondered whether he loved her after all. Maria would then be consumed with fear that he would leave. She longed to have him listen to what bothered her, and for him to be reassuring rather than cold and rejecting.

Greg's complaints about Maria were less precise. He said he sometimes felt bored with marriage and wished he could feel more excitement. Greg used to be sure he wanted a family, but had recently been unable to look ahead to a future with Maria and children. He felt that if Maria were to leave him alone so that he could gather his thoughts, he might not feel so confused. The woman at work was a problem for him since he could not get her out of his head. On top of all his confusion, the pressure he was feeling from Maria was unbearable.

Maria and Greg agreed that when there was no conflict they had some very good times together. Greg liked Maria's bounciness and felt good around her. She tended to be an "up" person, providing a good balance to Greg's somewhat pessimistic outlook on life. Maria liked Greg's calm and quiet strength. She thought of him as a gentle man who was her best friend. They had a small network of close friends whom they saw often. Recently they had been spending less and less time together, which troubled both of them.

EXTENDED FAMILY INFORMATION

The genogram revealed that Maria had a brother five years older than herself, who lived at home with their widowed mother. Maria's father had died two years earlier from a stroke, at the age of fifty-five. He had been separated from Maria's mother off and on for the six years prior to his death. He was a musician, a profession that took him away from home throughout the marriage. Maria's mother asked him to leave when she found that a woman who was a close family friend had been her husband's lover for many years. After the separation he became ill with high blood pressure, and his wife took him back periodically for the rest of his life.

Maria remembered fights all through her childhood. Both of her parents came from Hungary and Maria thought their quarreling and chaos were "just being Hungarian." She had a distant relationship with her father, staying well out of his way in order to avoid his anger. In contrast, she remembered feeling like a mother to her mother, in that she often felt responsible for her.

Maria was very annoyed at her brother, seeing him as living off their mother. Mother often called Maria to complain about him and to ask Maria's advice on how to deal with him. Maria's relationship with her brother was distant. She spent only ritualized time with him, mostly on holidays. She had recently been calling him on the phone, trying to get him to be nicer to their mother. These calls usually ended in fights, with Maria hanging up on him.

The information that Maria's father had been having an affair with a close family friend, someone Maria had referred to as "aunt" all her life, had upset her a great deal. She felt angry at her father and this woman, and felt that her mother was a victim. Since her father's death, her mother had spoken to her several times about the affair. Lately her mother had confided in Maria that she had been dreaming about the other woman and her husband. The dreams were painful and Maria felt increasing anger and hurt that her father had been "that kind of man." She kept her feelings to herself, ashamed that her father had behaved in such an immoral way.

Greg had one brother, ten years older than he. His mother and father lived together. They came to the United States from Greece as small children and both worked in the family bakery business in Manhattan. Greg described his father as an alcoholic who was often out of control. His mother joined his father in drinking and the two of them would end up in verbal and physical conflict. Greg remembered his terror and loneliness as a child, as he listened to his parents carrying on. He tried to stay out of their way. A quiet boy by nature, he would retreat into his room to work on his model cars without being missed.

Greg left home at eighteen to join the air force. He clearly saw leaving as his way of surviving. He was sent to Germany, where he stayed for four years. He is not certain what would have happened to him if he had not left home. His older brother was a chip off his father's block: out of control. Greg could not relate to him. He had been married twice and now had four children whom Greg described as also out of control. Greg saw his family only on holidays. Often he and Maria invited both families to their house for holidays in the hope of "getting it over with all at once."

TREATMENT

Greg and Maria were easy for the therapist to engage. Both of these young people had a good sense of humor (a real asset in this kind of therapy) and an openness about them. They were intelligent and fairly well versed in psychology. Maria was an attractive, petite woman who loved to talk and was quite emphatic as she told her story. Greg, who was more reticent, made jokes about himself to hide his anxiety. He was a handsome man whose bookish style belied his athletic ability.

Pursuer-Distancer Experiments

As Maria and Greg began treatment, the therapist was able to see that each of them was locked in a predictable two-step in the relationship. Maria was clearly the emotional pursuer, moving toward Greg whenever her anxiety was up in an attempt to take hold of him and relieve her inner tension. Greg fit the description of the emotional distancer perfectly. He was a cautious, logical man, reluctant to allow anyone into his internal space. He tended to be reasonable with Maria's emotionality, but when pushed he would either "head for the hills" or blow up. If left alone he tended to think things between Maria and himself were just fine.

In order to show each of them their parts in the fixed movement in their relationship, the therapist early on began to label Maria's and Greg's behavior, introducing the concepts of pursuer and distancer. For example:

GREG: Maria was really carrying on and I had just walked in the door.

THERAPIST: What happens to your insides when Maria is upset like that?

GREG: I get all tight, like in a knot.

THERAPIST: What do you do?

GREG: I try not to get involved. I figure it will blow over. When it doesn't, sometimes I leave.

THERAPIST: You mean you need some distance to get rid of the knot you mentioned?

GREG: Yeah, I can't think when she's yelling. If I can get some space, or distance as you call it, I feel less trapped.

Greg easily latched onto the term *distancer;* it accurately described how he saw himself moving in relation to Maria's upset. Similarly, Maria could easily see herself as a pursuer of Greg, as she described the predictable chase in the relationship.

Both Greg and Maria acknowledged the fruitlessness of their behavior pattern. Like so many couples, they believed the solution for this nonproductive behavior was for the other to stop doing what he or she was doing. According to Greg, Maria should stop nagging, and according to Maria, Greg should stop withdrawing. Since both were tired from the dance of pursuit and distance, it was fairly easy for the therapist to interest both of them in experimenting with reversing their movement in the relationship.

The purpose of coaching the couple to behave differently with one another is to calm the emotional reactivity in the marriage and to teach each spouse that his or her behavior is automatic. As they focus on their own predictable reactions to each other's behavior, they become observers of self rather than experts on what is wrong with the other person. The reversal also takes away the sting of the other's behavior as personally directed against him or her. It is important for the therapist as well as the couple to understand that the pursuer-distancer experiments are not techniques to fix what is wrong in the relationship but rather learning experiences that will give husband and wife a self-focus in treatment and an understanding of what triggers the automatic emotional responses in the conflict.

The following is an excerpt from an early therapy session in which the therapist worked with Maria and Greg around beginning some pursuer-distancer experiments.

THERAPIST: Maria, you tell me that when Greg is working long hours, or out with his buddies, by the time he gets home you are upset. What do you do when he comes in the door?

MARIA: I usually promise myself that I'm not going to talk to him and I try, but when I see him I can't help myself. Then it usually ends up in a fight, because I try to get him to see how I'm feeling and he never does. The more I explain, the less he understands.

GREG: [turning to the therapist] Tell me, could you listen to someone who's shrieking at you?

THERAPIST: Maria, what's the longest you've gone keeping quiet when Greg comes home late? Two minutes, five minutes?

MARIA: [Laughs] Are you kidding? Maybe one minute. I can't help it; I've tried.

THERAPIST: Why don't you try imagining an experiment? Just pretend for a minute what it would be like if you pulled back from Greg instead of pursuing him. Imagine focusing on yourself when he comes in late instead of on him and what he is or isn't doing. What you're doing isn't working anyway. [Maria nods in agreement.] Perhaps you could use the time spent waiting and getting worked up about Greg to do something for yourself. You told me that you haven't seen some of your friends in a while. Why don't you give one of them a ring?

MARIA: I guess I could, but Greg will probably stay out all night if I do that. But I'm not supposed to be focused on him, right?

THERAPIST: Right.

By the time a couple like Maria and Greg comes to therapy, the problems have been going on long enough that the one who has been the emotional pursuer in the marriage is often burned out from trying to fix what is wrong. Moreover, the pursuer has often been noisily campaigning for change and therefore has the reputation of being the problem. It is usually the emotional pursuer who calls the therapist to set up the treatment, and she usually has had to sell her husband, the distancer, on coming for treatment. He comes, but hoping that somehow she will "get off his back." The pursuer is most frequently the uncomfortable one in the marital situation and sees herself as having done all the work.

Our treatment protocol recommends pulling Maria back from the unproductive pursuit of Greg. But this step asks the pursuer again to do the work in the relationship. It can be construed by the couple as a condemnation of the pursuer and an affirmation that the distancer is not doing anything wrong. Therefore it is very important for the therapist to be aware of the reaction of the couple as the experiments are explained. The tasks need to be framed in such a way that the pursuer does not end up feeling blamed or being defined as the problem.

As the therapist began to coach Maria to move away from her husband and become less focused on him and his behavior, she first validated the pain that Maria was experiencing because of Greg's distance. Then she asked questions such as, "Maria, does what you do work? Does it change Greg's behavior, or does it provide you with any comfort?" Of course the answer was no. The ground had then been broken for the therapist to suggest that Maria had options for movement in the relationship aside from running after Greg and coming up empty. Maria's curiosity was piqued and her involvement in doing something different was enlisted because it was keyed to helping her function better.

Although pulling back made sense to Maria intellectually and she thought it sounded like an easy homework assignment, emotionally she knew it would be difficult. The therapist confirmed her feeling and cautioned her that she might run into some difficulty, because she would be operating in direct opposition to her feelings. She was urged to focus on her "insides" as she pulled back from pursuing Greg the next time he was late coming home and to observe any differences in his response.

When the therapist has coached the emotional pursuer to pull back from her distancing husband, it is sometimes difficult to evaluate how much the pursuer actually pulls back. If the pursuer reports that she has pulled back from her husband but experiences no distress from having done so, the chances are she has not pulled back at all. The demands of the pursuer can be communicated in many ways other than verbally: a facial expression, a sigh, a shrug of the shoulder, feigned lack of interest in sex or other joint activity. Pulling back sounds easy, but it is most often very difficult.

Clinical or personal experience will help the therapist coach a spouse more successfully in pulling back and giving her partner some space. Predicting the difficulty the pursuer will have as she goes about this experiment and framing it as an opportunity to learn about herself will take some of the sting out of failures as she struggles to carry out the therapist's recommendations.

Maria found it hard to resist the temptation to move toward Greg. She became aware of the turmoil and reactivity within her. At the next session she reported to the therapist how she had "blown it." She had managed not to nag Greg when he went to a hockey game with an old college friend. She had been calm and noncritical when he came home late Monday night from a business meeting. But the night before the session he arrived home late again and failed to call. He had been particularly "insensitive" in response to her upset. That was when she "really lost it." As a result he slept in the guest room and she paced the floor all night. Maria playfully teased the therapist that she was making things worse rather than better; after all, what she really wanted was for the therapist to fix Greg, not to make her more uncomfortable!

As Maria struggled with her task, at times she needed to call the therapist between sessions for venting, validation, and encouragement. She began to talk more and more about the anxiety she was feeling as she focused less on what Greg was doing. She wondered, "Does he love me?" When asked by the therapist to describe more of the picture of what was underneath her anxiety, Maria spoke of her fear of being left alone. As she focused on describing more of what was going on inside her, she began to think about calling her brother (a task suggested earlier by the therapist). While she was thinking about her brother, thoughts of her childhood surfaced, especially about her father. She began to feel an immense sadness, like the sadness she felt after her father died. She described a fantasy of standing on a barren hillside, the wind blowing, not a soul in sight, her father lying alone in the grave, flesh deteriorating, a picture of his skeleton. As she spoke of this in a joint therapy session, Greg's eyes filled with tears and he grabbed her hand.

Thus as Maria moved into self-focus, the process led her directly back to her family of origin, where the second phase of stage II therapy awaited her attention.

As this was going on, what was happening with Greg? When working with the distancer in the marriage, the therapist should keep in mind the distancer's attitude toward the therapy. The emotional distancer is often unaware of relationship problems or, if he is aware of them, is much less interested in taking them to an outsider. The distancer prefers to leave the problems, and any work on their solution, implicit. Consequently, the therapist should avoid pursuing the distant spouse. If the distancer moves toward the therapist, the therapist may take that as an invitation. Otherwise, the therapist can work to engage the distancer and to communicate with him by behaving in a way that makes therapy a "safe" place. Many an eager therapist, with the best of motives, has chased away an emotional distancer by replicating in the therapy session what has been happening in the marriage.

Greg regularly attended the therapy sessions with Maria. The therapist was aware from the description of the problem and from Greg's attitude—polite and pleasant, but not eager—that he was in treatment as a way to calm Maria down. He did not see himself as part of the problem or as part of the solution. The therapist was patient and found a way to chat with Greg about their mutual interest in long distance running. While Maria struggled with her own reactivity in the relationship, the therapist, in a noncritical tone and with continued friendliness, would ask Greg to assess how much of the problem in the marriage he saw as his. When Greg guessed about 20 percent, the therapist asked what that 20 percent consisted of. Greg spoke of his absentmindedness and his angry silences. The therapist did not jump at the chance to pin a part of the problem on Greg, but gave him plenty of time and room.

Greg began gradually to move toward the therapist, asking her to guide him in handling Maria's upset so that he wouldn't get so mad. That gave the therapist an opportunity to coach Greg on how to handle Maria differently. With the therapist's suggestions in mind, Greg was able to stop defending himself when Maria accused him of various things when he came home late. Greg remembered that the therapist had said, "One need defend oneself only in court," and it helped him to be quiet.

When that advice worked well for him, he began to let the therapist know the inner upset he was experiencing in the absence of Maria's pursuit of him. The therapist reminded him of the old Irish saying, "Be careful what you wish for; you may get it." Greg laughed but acknowledged the truth of the saying. He never would have guessed it.

The therapist asked Greg in that session whether he had told Maria lately how dependent he was on her. He had not. He had never known it until now. The therapist turned to Maria and asked her whether she realized how much impact she had on Greg. Maria replied, "Just the opposite. I thought I had absolutely no impact on him, since I saw his distance as verification that he didn't value me."

This was the turning point for Greg, as he began to get a clearer sense of how his emotional side was misread by both Maria and himself. The following is a segment from the fourth session with Maria and Greg, in which Greg described his experience of self-discovery. As he noticed Maria's "blip" going off his internal radar screen, he became aware of an emotional process within himself that had gone unobserved so long as he was busy warding off Maria's attacks and defending himself.

GREG: Last night I had to stay at work to finish up this project. I tried to call Maria, my new program of being a more considerate husband, and there was no answer. I called twice, at four and at five.

THERAPIST: What were you worried about?

GREG: I guess about her driving home.

MARIA: He didn't tell me he was worried. He yelled at me because I never got around to taking the car in to have it serviced.

THERAPIST: Greg, I'm confused. Maria tells me you were angry at her, and you tell me you were worried about her. Which is it?

GREG: Uh, I guess worried. [He turns to Maria.] Was I yelling?

MARIA: Yelling? You gave me your "You've got to learn to take care of the car" routine, which always turns me off.

THERAPIST: When was the last time you said, "Maria, you're really important to me, I really depend on you?"

GREG: I think I expect her to know that. It's not me to say stuff like that. Anyway, I gave her a romantic Valentine card last year.

THERAPIST: Maybe there's hope for you yet, Greg. [Smiling] Where is the "lover" in you? How would you find him? Was he ever there?

GREG: I guess when Maria and I were dating and right after we were married.

THERAPIST: How about trying to rediscover the romantic Greg?

GREG: I might feel foolish. What if she didn't like it? [He literally squirms in the chair.]

THERAPIST: What if you just thought about it as a way to enlarge your repertoire, rather than expecting her to like it or not to like it? How would you do it?

GREG: I don't know.

THERAPIST: Are you uncomfortable with tenderness? Can you be tender with her?

GREG: I'd like to, but, uh, I don't know what to do or say.

MARIA: He used to be much more tender or romantic when we were dating. Typical, once he got married that all disappeared, especially lately, and when I try to tell him about it he either says it's not happening, which makes me crazy, or that it's because of the way I act, which makes me crazy.

THERAPIST: Greg, what are you thinking?

GREG: I feel bad for her. I guess some of it is me. Of course it is and I know it. I don't always pay her the attention I should, and when she gets upset I don't know what to do or say.

THERAPIST: What mistakes could you make?

GREG: [Laughs.] It looks like I already make them all. I thought it would be safer to say nothing.

THERAPIST: Would you be willing to try risking saying something about yourself to Maria during times like that? Like, "I don't know what to say or do when you're upset with me."

GREG: [Again laughing] Oh, that would be innovative!

In this segment the therapist began to coach Greg to move toward Maria by telling her he needed her and becoming more romantic in the relationship. These were attempts to help Greg develop ways of operating other than his critical-expert stance or just leaving the scene in anger. As the session progressed it became apparent that Maria's question about her lovableness and Greg's paralysis in responding to her upset played a big part in their conflict.

As therapy continued over the next two-and-a-half months, the couple gained more understanding of their own operating styles and how the movement in the relationship exacerbated the pursuer in Maria and the distancer in Greg. They learned to desensitize themselves to the part of the other that set them off in a chain of emotional reactivity. Maria stood still and waited when Greg moved away, and Greg got better at handling Maria's emotionality without leaving or getting angry.

Extended Family Work

We saw that as Maria pulled back from Greg, emotions connected to her extended family surfaced. Greg, too, saw that his having grown up in an alcoholic system had a lot to do with his avoiding conflict in his marriage. He acknowledged that he needed to learn more about his family, but his acknowledgment came reluctantly, and the thought of dealing with the situation raised his anxiety considerably.

Although the work in the extended family may seem to the therapist to be clearly relevant, it may seem beside the point to the couple. Many stage II couples want no more than symptom relief in their relationship. When they feel better about themselves and their marriages, they are satisfied with the treatment and ready to leave. They should be allowed to do so.

For some couples, however, what they have learned motivates them to move on and do more. For still others, new problems—perhaps with their children or their extended families—are raised in the therapy. In some cases, one or both spouses may complain of depression or some other problem that has emerged after the calming of the marital conflict. Extended family work may make sense to the couple when, through the experience of focusing on their own operating styles and the reactivity that they observe in themselves, they learn that the family from which they came still has an impact on them and on their behavior with their spouses. These couples are then available for the next step in the treatment of stage II marital conflict: working on their extended families. They can be moved first to a more complete understanding of the extended family system and then to begin work to make changes in triangles with their parents, cutoffs, and enmeshments.

As Maria and Greg progressed in therapy and became more self-focused, several family issues that were pressuring the marital relationship came to light. The most intense was the triangle involving Maria and her parents.

The fact that Maria had such a negative history with her father became more of an issue for her as she worked on her inner self. She realized that she believed that men would sooner or later do her in. Her memories of her father were primarily through her mother's bitter eyes. In a session alone with the therapist Maria talked about the nights she used to hear her parents arguing, her father's loud angry voice rising above her mother's muffled sobs. She recalled that when she was quite small her father used to play his clarinet for her, and that once he took her to one of his performances and she sat up on the bandstand. She remembered how excited she was and how he introduced her to everyone as his little girl. The therapist pointed out that despite many of her bad memories, there were also some good ones. Maria agreed, tears welling up in her eyes.

At the therapist's suggestion Maria agreed that perhaps she could enlarge her picture of her father by talking to some of the people in her family who were less negative about him. The therapist coached Maria to speak to her father's older sister whom she had not seen since her father's funeral. Maria came into the next session proud of herself that she had talked to her aunt. Her aunt had told her that when Maria was born her father was so happy to have a daughter that he bought cigars for everyone in the neighborhood. He thought she was the cutest baby he had ever seen and referred to her as his "little tootsie." Maria was surprised to learn about her father's enthusiasm for her. Her aunt also told Maria that her mother was seen by her father's family as a demanding wife, someone who was never satisfied.

As Maria began to get a different picture of her father, the therapist decided to raise the issue of her father's affair.

THERAPIST: Maria, have you ever wondered what was going on in your parents' marriage that might have contributed to your dad's moving toward this relationship with Sarah?

MARIA: Yes, as a matter of fact, I've thought about it a couple of times; once when Greg told me about his flirtation at work and the other time when I had this crush on a fellow at my job last year. I thought it was bad blood, you know, like father like daughter. It scared me, but now I'm wondering if it wasn't a symptom of trouble between Greg and me.

THERAPIST: That is often a big piece of it. If your dad were sitting here what do you think he'd say about how he ended up with Sarah?

MARIA: Oh, he'd probably say that my mother was cold, not affection- ate, maybe demanding. As a matter of fact I don't ever remem- ber my mother kissing my father. I remember his dancing around her and joking with her and her pushing him away and getting mad at him. Mostly, though, he would fight with her.

THERAPIST: How well do you know Sarah?

MARIA: I used to know her well. My parents used to take me to visit her and her family every month while I was growing up. I like her. She was kind to me and gave a lot of attention. She was very pretty and warm. She never married. My mother said the affair went on for many, many years.

THERAPIST: Sounds to me like that was a long-term relationship, not a roll in the hay.

MARIA: I guess, now that you mention it, maybe my father was really in love with her. I wonder why he couldn't just leave my mother.

THERAPIST: That's a good question. Could you imagine paying a visit to Sarah? Where is she?

MARIA: Oh, God. You mean talk about the affair? She moved away after my father died. But it's not far away.

THERAPIST: Well, what I had in mind is something initially less explicit. For example, paying her a visit because you were driving through and because you knew how much your dad valued her. A way of getting some information from someone who we can guess was positive about him. [Maria looks interested but nervous.] Would you tell your mother about such a visit?

MARIA: No way, she'd see me as being disloyal.

THERAPIST: [nodding in agreement] But you could try a trial balloon. You could tell your mother that you had a dream about Sarah too, and you dreamt you went to see her and your mother got mad at you.

MARIA: I could maybe do that. I could maybe begin to imagine seeing Sarah and talking to her. I hope I wouldn't cry.

As Maria became intrigued about her father and his relationship with Sarah, she began to question more how she fit into the process that had been going on in her parents' marriage and how that had an impact on her fear that Greg would abandon her.

During this time Greg, although less interested in doing work in his family of origin, did begin to talk about his allergy to anger and confrontation. He linked this allergy directly to his experience of growing up in his family. He was aware of how toxic he found his family and how little he wanted to do with them. He came to see his expectations that there should never be any problems between Maria and himself, and his belief that, if there were, all would be lost as the result of having lived in a battleground. The therapist suggested that Greg attend some meetings of ACOA (Adult Children of Alcoholics) in order to have a safe place to begin to talk about his childhood experiences. At first he was reluctant, using the pressures of business and the fact that he was not a "group person" as excuses. With Maria working so intently on her family, however, he decided that he did not want to be left behind. He began attending ACOA meetings and after a few uncomfortable sessions began to feel that he had found a group of people who understood exactly what it was like for him. They had had the same experience. He became enthusiastic, talking to Maria about what he was learning about alcoholism and families. A by-product of attending these meetings was that Greg began to bring into therapy sessions an interest in learning how he could become more comfortable when he was around his family.

The first part of the Savalases' therapy lasted six months. In that time the pursuer-distancer experiments gave them a structure through which to view their relationship and a method for self-focusing in the face of an exacerbation of conflict between them. Over the six months there were twenty-one sessions, during which the groundwork was laid for the extended family work. Greg and Maria continued this work for eighteen months, in a total of twenty-four sessions. They have continued to do well over the four years since then, during which they have returned to therapy separately or together a total of eight times.

9

The Treatment of
Stage III

Τ HE HALLMARKS of stage III marital conflict are high emotional
arousal, a polarized position of fixed distance, and a rampant projection
process in which each spouse blames the other for the state of the relationship and has little or no self-focus. Attempting to negotiate the conflictual
process or address it directly with structural tasks or experiments, without
first preparing the way, will inevitably fail. The first two goals in treating
stage III conflict are therefore to create a safe climate by lowering the
emotional arousal and to increase self-focus in each spouse, which will
help to neutralize the intensity of the reactive emotional process. These
goals must be achieved before the third major goal, strengthening the
marital relationship itself, can be addressed.

The work toward the first two goals begins during the engagement
process and continues throughout the entire course of therapy. To reach
these goals, the therapist and the couple work in three key areas:

1. *Reactivity in the marital dyad.* The intensity of reactivity in the marital
    relationship must be lowered. It is especially important in stage III
    that the therapist keep his or her own anxiety down and help the
    couple to discipline their automatic reactivity.

2. *Key triangles.* During the evaluation period the major active triangles are identified and the process within each is determined. The therapist needs to be aware of the intensity and importance of each triangle before deciding on the sequence in which to address them.

3. *The individual.* The focus of the individual work is on reducing bitterness and helping people to take greater responsibility for their own lives. The degree to which disappointment and anger have turned into bitterness is assessed in each spouse, and each is put to work neutralizing those feelings of bitterness. Once the bitterness is less intense, both spouses are encouraged to develop personal goals in the areas of productivity, personal relationships, and personal well-being.

If progress is made in these three areas, the climate will gradually improve. Spouses will be better able to see their own parts in the conflictual process and to accept responsibility for change. Direct access to the marital relationship is then possible. In the final phase of therapy, the therapist attempts to prepare the couple for the inevitable recycling of the conflict and to reinforce the positive forces in their relationship by working on partnership, companionship, and intimacy in the marriage.

Stage III couples enter treatment in two major ways: in overt conflict or in covert conflict that is camouflaged by another symptom in one of the spouses or in a child. The largest percentage enter therapy in overt conflict and explicitly label the marital relationship as the problem they want to address in treatment. The possibility of divorce may be an open issue, or one spouse may have privately decided on divorce and may be seeking to have the therapist validate his or her hopeless view of the marriage.

When the marital conflict is covered by dysfunction such as depression or alcohol abuse or by a problem in a child, the couple will want that symptom addressed in therapy. If the therapist attempts to bypass the symptom in order to bring to light the underlying marital conflict, the couple may well terminate therapy. On the other hand, if the therapist perceives the marital conflict but does not begin to link it up with the symptom, the marriage may be driven into irreversible conflict once the symptom is alleviated.

The stage III treatment plan varies from couple to couple. Some work in each of the three areas—reactivity, triangles, self-focus—is done with every couple in treatment, but the time and effort devoted to any one area differs from case to case, depending on the process in the marriage that is most central to the symptoms and most accessible to intervention, the issues that are presented, and the availability and motivation of each spouse to work in therapy. In each of the four cases used in this chapter a different area of the treatment protocol was emphasized or was very clearly illustrated.

The Treatment Protocol

Engagement with couples in stage III is made difficult by the intense emotionality that is always present. The efforts of even the most experienced therapists can be sabotaged by stage III couples who hold fast to their blaming stance and thwart the therapist's suggestions. In a successful engagement the therapist will calm both spouses' emotional upset, validate their pain without taking sides or necessarily agreeing with them, and instill hope for their individual emotional survival. This process of connection and validation or engagement must be maintained throughout the course of treatment.

REACTIVITY IN THE MARITAL COUPLE

The marriage, once a refuge from the pressure of the outside world, is now viewed as the source of pressure and pain. The therapy must provide a safe context for both spouses to explore themselves and their vulnerabilities. Therefore, lowering the intensity of reactivity from the very first session is essential to engage these couples successfully in treatment.

Decreasing Reactivity in the Sessions

The emotional climate in a stage III marriage is unsafe and stormy, with dramatic shifts in temperature and turbulence. Icy distance and heated conflict alternate in automatic cycles over which neither spouse seems to have any control. The couple's acute sensitivity to each other leads to volatile reactivity. Over time these cycles erode caring, open up emotional wounds, and create significant emotional damage.

The following case presented problems that required the therapist to create a safe climate in the session. Ellen and John D'Aiello, a couple in their mid-forties, married for sixteen years with four children, came for therapy in overt conflict. The battle began in the initial interview, as soon as the therapist asked each of them to describe the problem. Ellen was in a rage at John and attacked him for the affair he was having and for years of financial irresponsibility. John defended himself by picking on the details of her accusations and rationalizing his own actions as responses to her behavior. Had this process continued, duplicating their interaction at home, their anxiety would have increased and the therapist's effectiveness would have been compromised. The therapist therefore invoked a moratorium on the attacks and defense. He insisted that Ellen and John speak one at a time and direct their comments to the therapist rather than to each other. When one of them interrupted the other, the therapist gently but firmly reminded them that they would not get anywhere if that continued. If they had been unable to adhere in some fashion to this structure, the therapist would have divided the session and seen each of them alone.

When the therapist directed the discussion to the presenting problem, Ellen began to answer questions and describe events with an excess of detail. She wanted the therapist to know the time, date, and place of each atrocity that John had committed. When John got the floor, he questioned the accuracy of each of these details. To keep the session from filling up with this kind of content, which would have escalated the already high level of anxiety, the therapist elicited just enough detail to get each person's picture of the issue and then moved the discussion to more productive ground by asking process questions developed from the content. This procedure begins to get people thinking rather than just responding reactively. The following transcript demonstrates the technique as well as other methods for changing the emotional climate.

THERAPIST: Now I'd like each of you to give me your view of the problem.

JOHN: I find she's very closed. She thinks I lie.

THERAPIST: You've got a credibility problem with your wife.

[The therapist labels the problem instead of going for details about the lies.]

ELLEN: I don't trust him. He's lied so much in the past.

JOHN: I haven't lied.

THERAPIST: There's a difference of opinion. How do you resolve differences of opinion?

[Again, the therapist is avoiding details and going after a broader process. This is an attempt to get them to start thinking in process terms rather than remaining caught in runaway emotional reactivity.]

ELLEN: I don't know. He just says, "I don't want to discuss it. We'll discuss it when we get to the counselor." And I didn't discuss it until I called the girl. My husband's been seeing another woman who works in his office for a year.

JOHN: No, I haven't been seeing her for a year.

ELLEN: She invited me to have lunch to tell me it wasn't true. My husband has been protecting her. I called her December 21st to tell her to stop seeing my husband. She said it wasn't true. Then she wrote a letter to my husband saying, "How did she find out?" Which he told me.

THERAPIST: You believed him on that. So there are some things you believe and some you don't. How do you know whether to believe the first and third rather than the second and fourth?

[The therapist is again asking questions that bring out process rather than getting bogged down in content. He is also attempting to get Ellen to begin focusing on herself.]

ELLEN: I'm perceptive.

THERAPIST: So it's your insides you rely on?

ELLEN: Yes.

JOHN: I would say she *thinks* she's super-perceptive.

THERAPIST: You think she overvalues her perceptiveness, relies on it too much, and that sometimes it's inaccurate?

[The therapist restates attacks so that they are easier to hear.]

JOHN: You have to be very careful about what you say.

THERAPIST: Let me kind of roll the wheels back. This thing around the other woman has kind of spun things out. There's a lot of anxiety around it.

[The therapist tracks the presenting problem.]

ELLEN: It's not the first time, either.

THERAPIST: When did this one surface?

ELLEN: He started going to Gamblers Anonymous meetings in April. I noticed he started talking about this girl all the time. I thought he was mentioning her too much. I asked him to have her desk moved away from his office. He lied and said the manager refused. Then I called December 21st. He said he wasn't seeing her, which was another lie.

THERAPIST: So back in April you started to talk about it, but you were just noticing that he was talking about her. You were experiencing your husband as missing in action, and you tied this girl to it. You saw him as moving away from you and the kids toward her.

[The therapist has begun to bring out the process around the affair. He puts it in movement terms.]

ELLEN: He had been up in the air because of GA meetings. I was upset by the GA meetings.

THERAPIST: Before going to GA I'd like to try to get a sense of . . . to compartmentalize this piece. Because you've just described something that's maybe a picture of how this relationship works. John, you've got a different picture?

JOHN: We did work together . . . in May . . . job organizing.

[John was giving countless details; Ellen had trouble staying quiet.]

THERAPIST: Ellen, you're in the listening position. [She laughs.] John, I'd like to stop you, because you're giving a lot of details. I'd like to get a sense of where you are. I'm asking you not to defend yourself, even though you feel like you're being attacked. Did you feel like you were available to your family?

[The therapist takes control by stopping the old pattern of interrupting. He attempts to get each of them to do something differently, Ellen to listen and John to stop defending himself.]

JOHN: Not as much as I could. I was in business for myself and tried to keep it going longer than I should. I've been with this new company for a year, and I tried to continue my other business.

[He described great pressure and blamed Ellen for not supporting him enough.]

THERAPIST: You're telling me you've been stressed by work. You don't think Ellen appreciates you. The other thing I hear you saying is that when you're stretched out it's difficult to stay tuned in to her.

[The therapist restates the process in a way that allows John to self-focus. He proposes another reason for the distance and validates both John and Ellen.]

JOHN: That's true. I haven't made plans to do things with her and the kids, the way others might have.

THERAPIST: Is it your style to be an involved father and husband if you weren't so stressed?

JOHN: I haven't been that involved over the years.

[This exchange helps to validate the pain Ellen has experienced without blaming John.]

THERAPIST: So you tend to be a distant guy, and when you get a little more stressed, you get more distant, and Ellen doesn't know what to do about it.

[The therapist sums up the process and avoids being judgmental.]

The therapist in this example was operating from principles that are critical for a successful beginning. First, he kept his own anxiety down and established control of the session in order to create a safe context for treatment. Second, he defined and dissected the process to offer a different perspective to the couple, rather than getting bogged down trying to referee the content. Third, he maintained a systems perspective and avoided taking sides with either spouse.

Another procedure that helps to decrease the intensity of reactivity in the session is to teach the couple about transition times. Stage III couples are usually going through a period of transition when they initiate treatment. Most often the conflict has been going on for a long time, but the added stress that comes from the transitions the family is going through intensifies it and leads them to seek professional help. The transition times might include the loss of a job, a serious financial reversal, or a physical illness. It might also be a life-cycle crisis like the death of a parent, the birth of a child, the first or last child leaving home, or retirement.

The couple does not usually present these issues as particularly relevant to the current conflict. Their perspective is severely limited; they fall into rigid cause-and-effect thinking and tend to blame life's problems on their marriage and specifically on each other. By documenting the transition times the family has gone through, the therapist begins to introduce the idea that there are other reasons why the marriage is in trouble. The short-range goal is to broaden the couple's perspective and reduce anxiety by teaching them that a significant amount of stress has been building over the years as a result of these transitions and that it has had an impact on their marriage. The long-range goal is to help them to develop skills that will allow them to recognize when their relationship is being stressed by transition times so that they can avoid handling them with the familiar pattern of conflict.

When a transition time is mentioned by either husband or wife as the genogram information is gathered, the therapist takes time to explore the process around it in order to bring out the impact that the event had on the marriage. For example, if the wife mentions the birth of their youngest child, the therapist asks a series of process questions: Who had wanted the child? How had each of them responded to the pregnancy and delivery? What had changed at home after the baby's birth? Had either of them ever thought about the stress involved in adding a new member to the family?

As a number of transition times are mentioned, the therapist comments on the stress they must have produced. "You folks have been through a lot. I'm beginning to understand more about how your relationship got into this trouble." This says to the couple that their conflict is at least in part a result of stress and begins to teach them that marriage is a struggle that requires a great deal from husbands and wives. It also begins to address their secret fears that they are in this position because they are bad people.

Decreasing Reactivity at Home

If the couple is to experience the therapy as helpful, the therapist must begin early to give them suggestions for interacting differently at home. The therapist provides operating guidelines for each spouse that if followed will begin to calm the explosive system. During the evaluation of one stage III couple, Carol and Ed Rutkowski, who were in their early forties and had been married fifteen years, the therapist made two suggestions. First, they had to stop the physical violence in their relationship. Second, they had to take the pressure off the marriage.

Carol and Ed would go for days without talking to each other. Carol would break the silence to argue over one of the many toxic issues in the relationship, such as money, in-laws, or Ed's work. Their arguments frequently got out of control to the point of yelling and door slamming, and periodically they resulted in physical violence. Although Carol usually struck the first blow, she had sustained a number of injuries during their fights; the most severe had been a broken rib.

The first step in changing the climate at home was to address the physical violence. The therapist took a strong position, telling Ed and Carol that violence had to stop because nothing could change in a climate where people were frightened or worried about their physical safety. The therapist explored the process around the violence and learned that Ed usually knew when Carol was about to cross that line. Ed was advised to distance physically from her when that happened.

For example, in the week prior to their first session Carol had been trying to get Ed to respond to some questions while Ed was reading the paper. The more she asked, the more involved he became in his paper. She pulled the paper out of his hands and started ripping it up. Ed sat staring at her until she attacked him physically; he then slapped her across the face and pushed her into a wall. The therapist used this example to teach them more functional behavior. Ed was coached to move to another room as soon as he realized the intensity of Carol's pursuit. If she followed, then he was to leave the house. Carol was coached to move toward another person or activity when she felt that kind of rage escalating in her. The therapist helped her look for the most positive resources she had to move toward. During the following weeks this behavior was carefully monitored in therapy.

When one spouse is the aggressor in the fighting and the other habitually stays around for the beating, the latter needs to be aware of a number of alternatives. He or she might have to call the police or a hot line for domestic violence or perhaps take legal action. Therapists need to know the law regarding domestic violence in the area where they practice as well as the resources available in the community. Sometimes couples are unable to put a stop to these explosive outbursts, and the therapist may have to advise a temporary separation.

In stage III conflict husband and wife spend a great deal of time and energy focusing on their relationship, generating intense pressure that must be alleviated if the emotional climate is to change. Carol and Ed's marriage was always on the table for dissection; it had become the third leg of a triangle. Whenever they argued, she would threaten to end the marriage, and he would attack her for even thinking about divorce. By the end of the first session the therapist knew that their relationship would have to cool off before they could approach it directly. In other words it would not work to prescribe a weekend alone for this couple or to suggest that they find more time to talk about their marital problems. To decrease the pressure on the marriage, the therapist asked them to refrain from discussing the relationship or any of the toxic issues between them outside of the therapy sessions. They were also asked to stop all talk about therapy. They were told that the marriage was too hot to handle and needed to be put on the back burner temporarily. The therapist specifically stated that in treatment a number of things, like changing the emotional climate, would have to be accomplished before they would be able to address the marriage directly.

This approach raised two questions. First, how would the therapist make therapy relevant to Ed and Carol when they had come in wanting help for the marriage? Second, how were they supposed to deal with each other when almost all of their interaction was devoted to conflict over the toxic issues in the relationship? Ed and Carol agreed that discussing their marriage had been unproductive and exhausting but blamed each other for that fact. The therapist let them know that in our experience with intense marital conflict, attempts to tackle the marriage in a more direct way had repeatedly failed and that the approach we were recommending to them had proved more successful.

This does not mean we promise couples that the marriage will necessarily be saved; if the couple is talking about divorce, the therapist points out that this will always be an option but that it is not a solution and should be approached in a slow, thoughtful way. The therapist is saying that their best chance of turning the marriage into a satisfying or positive relationship, or at least of minimizing the emotional damage to themselves and their children, is to begin by working on themselves rather than on the marriage.

If Ed and Carol were to avoid toxic issues and discussion about the marriage, they needed guidelines for interacting with each other in a different way. The therapist coached them to treat each other decently, the way one might treat a business acquaintance. They did not have to like each other, but they did have to find a way to be civil. The therapist asked them to describe their ideas of being decent and learned that they each had different and unrealistically high expectations about each other's "decency," and these were addressed in the session. A few minutes at the beginning of each of the early sessions were devoted to monitoring their progress on these tasks.

KEY TRIANGLES

Triangles are always numerous and intense in stage III conflict. The following case illustrates our approach to triangles, as well as to lowering the reactivity in the couple and the bitterness in each spouse. The treatment focused on three goals with each triangle: (1) identifying the triangle and revealing the process; (2) shifting each person's part in the triangle so that each could have a close personal relationship with the other two people; and (3) working to lower reactivity in the interlocking triangles.

Bill O'Rourke, an attractive forty-year-old man who operated his own plastics company, had been married to Barbara, who was thirty-five, very pretty and petite, for seventeen years. Both were Irish Catholic. They had four children: Joe, aged sixteen, Tim, fourteen, and twin girls, Kathy and Mary, who were ten. Barbara had called to make the appointment because of the acute conflict in their marriage, which currently revolved around two issues, Barbara's quest for autonomy and problems with their elder son, Joe. During the evaluation sessions the therapist determined that each of these issues involved a very active and intense triangle. In the struggle around Barbara's quest for autonomy, there was a triangle with her social network, and they had been in conflict around their eldest child since the time of his conception.

Work on these two triangles became the major focus of the therapy and took place in forty sessions over sixteen months. Membership varied according to the focus of treatment but usually included husband and wife alone and in sessions together. The therapist considered the child triangle too intense to handle until the spouses were less reactive and so she developed a treatment plan that initially focused on the social network triangle, hoping that if they made some progress there they would be better able to address the child triangle. In order to remain relevant to the family, the therapist addressed the child triangle whenever an issue with the eldest son came up, and there was substantial discussion early in the treatment about the long-term changes each family member would need to make. For the sake of clarity each triangle will be discussed separately, although the work on them was interwoven through the course of therapy.

The Social Network Triangle

Five years before coming to therapy, Barbara had started going to Al-Anon during a period when Bill had been drinking heavily. She and six other women from Al-Anon had formed a support group that had continued to meet up to the time she entered treatment. Encouraged by her group, Barbara had begun to explore ways to change her life. By the time therapy began she had been taking courses at a local community college for several years, had started a part-time job, and had begun pressuring Bill to allow her more control of the family finances.

Bill, who had started with practically nothing when they were first married and now owned and directed a very successful company, flew into a rage whenever she broached the subject of money. There was no way he would give her more financial responsibility, he felt, because she could not handle what she already had. Suspicious and negative, he believed that her every move was orchestrated by her "group." He would counter her requests for more financial control with "Whose idea was that one?" and would suggest that the group pay for the taxes incurred by "your ridiculous job that costs me money." Barbara would defend herself and her group, and the pattern would be repeated over and over again. This almost daily sequence was usually triggered by Barbara's absence from home at dinnertime, by a call from one of her group members, or by one of her demands for more financial autonomy.

Early in the therapy the therapist supported Barbara's goal of achieving greater autonomy and maturity. At the same time, she encouraged Barbara to review the three major efforts she was making and evaluate how well they were working. Barbara decided that her return to school was constructive and that she needed to focus her energy on academic goals. She decided to continue her part-time job but to postpone an increase in her hours in order to give the family a chance to adjust. A review of her request for more financial control revealed it to be premature. On the one hand, she was attempting to persuade Bill to put more of their financial holdings in her name and to give her more access to their bank accounts. On the other hand, she frequently wrote checks against insufficient funds and then would appeal to Bill to help her straighten out the mess when the monthly statement arrived. Barbara was demanding more financial autonomy from Bill rather than taking greater responsibility for the money matters already in her control. In therapy Barbara explored the sources of sensitization to this issue in the extended family, worked to objectify her perception of the conflict with Bill, and experimented with her behavior patterns in order to increase her functioning in the financial area.

If a couple is to have a decent chance of surviving a shift like Barbara's move toward autonomy, the spouse who is making the changes needs to be sensitive to the impact those changes have on the family. At first Barbara was defensive when the therapist explored this area. She said she thought her four children were supportive and proud of her and expressed little concern about the change. She labeled her husband a male chauvinist and attributed his angry response to his desire for absolute power and his lack of sensitivity to her needs. Not only did his critical reaction disappoint her expectations for approval, but it also triggered that part of her that was ambivalent about the steps she was taking. Her own fears about the changes surfaced and were explored, and the therapist then worked with her to understand the impact her new direction had already made, to observe the current reactivity of other family members objectively, and to predict what was likely to occur with each new step she took. The goal was to help Barbara stop her defensive behavior and lower her own reactivity while she continued her steps toward personal growth.

The therapist encouraged Barbara to address the way the group from Al-Anon was influencing her thinking and behavior. Clearly she valued their support, but she decided that some of their suggestions had increased her bitterness, which had led to an increase in provocative behavior toward Bill. When she used the group as a sounding board for her rage at Bill, they responded with direct advice that when followed inevitably escalated the conflict. Barbara worried about how the group would see her if she did not "stand up for her rights" with Bill. Coached to explore and experiment, she learned that moving toward individuals in the group for emotional connection and companionship, organized around her own struggle and without the negative discussions about Bill, worked in a much more functional way.

Bill's experience of the triangle was that he had lost influence over his wife. She was listening to someone else, the group. He was encouraged to reach for neutrality and to stop attacking Barbara's group. Bill discovered that part of his emotional discomfort was linked to Barbara's absence when she was not doing what she was "supposed" to be doing. He spoke of his fantasies of finding another woman, one who would appreciate him. As his dependence on Barbara continued to surface, he became more aware of his feelings of loss and their connection to his critical and angry behavior. When Barbara heard him talk about his sense of loss and his fear that if she had more financial independence she would leave him, she was surprised that he could admit his emotional vulnerability. She began to listen in a different way and to modify some of her polarized perceptions of their relationship.

Early in the work on this triangle, the therapist asked that the couple be seen by another therapist in consultation. The following transcript is from that session.

BARBARA: I have experienced things that now have led me into becoming more independent, more self-reliant. I feel more like a partner, and I don't think Bill likes it.

THERAPIST: Do you think he liked you as a victim?

BARBARA: Yes.

THERAPIST: What's your evidence for that?

BARBARA: I think Bill enjoyed that pattern of fighting and making up, and I accepted that for a very long time, and he expressed it monetarily on many occasions. Whether it had to do with his drinking or not is another question.

THERAPIST: You mean he'd make it up to you by giving you more money?

BARBARA: Yeah. You know, like mink coats and stuff like that. And it worked.

THERAPIST: So you've become more independent, and instead of giving you mink coats, Bill's complaining about $250 phone bills. Your independence has cost you a lot.

BARBARA: I know.

THERAPIST: Did your independence cost you anything in the relationship apart from money?

BARBARA: I think that I've been able to become independent very slowly, and that Bill has accepted it very slowly. I feel now he's become very resentful of my new job.

BILL: It interferes with my dinner.

BARBARA: It's interfering now with his life, and I recall him saying last night that he felt that the reason our son was having problems was that I was never home.

THERAPIST: Do you think it's really the absence of dinner, or is it something else?

BARBARA: I don't think I'll ever be able to please him at this time in the way he'd like me to.

THERAPIST: Have you stopped trying?

BARBARA: Yes.

THERAPIST: How long ago did you stop trying?

BARBARA: Not too long ago. I'd say ever since I started school this semester.

THERAPIST: So you're on the track of getting independent, and are you on strike as far as Bill goes?

BARBARA: I'm not on strike. I have to honestly say that the things Bill has asked me to do have been very low priority for me . . . and on the other hand, I try to do everything and be the supermother so I can have time to do things that are important for me.

THERAPIST: But have you lost in that whole process the ability to let Bill know how important he is to you?

BARBARA: I think, maybe it isn't important to me anymore.

THERAPIST: Do you feel bad about that?

BARBARA: I guess I do feel bad about that. I feel our relationship has been clouded by many things: family issues with our children, his health, my going to school, and I do feel—Bill is important to me, and I do love him, but I'm tired of trying to express certain things to him, and I feel very frustrated. It's like I don't want to bother any more.

THERAPIST: How come he doesn't hear you? What's the frustration?

BARBARA: I don't think he does hear me. I think Bill is devastated by my small steps toward independence.

THERAPIST: You mean like if you really loved him you'd stay in place and march to the same tune?

BARBARA: Right.

THERAPIST: And you mean what you'd like is to get a piece for yourself and somehow have him understand that doesn't mean you don't love him?

BARBARA: Exactly.

[In this exchange the therapist spells out the direction of Barbara's movement away from Bill in pursuit of other things. At the same time he attempts to validate her experience of the bind she finds herself in. He then proceeds to explore Barbara's expectations about what response her move for autonomy would evoke.]

THERAPIST: Did you expect your moving out to have fallout with Bill and the kids?

BARBARA: Yes, and I think that's why it's been so delayed.

THERAPIST: That's why you've hesitated for so long?

BARBARA: Yes. I think I've tried and pulled back and tried and pulled back, but I feel like nothing's going to stop me now. I feel better about myself.

THERAPIST: How come that isn't carrying over to everybody feeling better about themselves?

BARBARA: I don't know.

THERAPIST: If Bill ever said to you, "Dammit, Barbara, I never realized how dependent I am on you until you moved out and got all involved." Has he ever said that?

BARBARA: No.

THERAPIST: What would be your response?

BARBARA: I feel like it might put us back on the same ground again.

THERAPIST: Is it hard for Bill to make statements like that, even if he realized it?

BARBARA: I think so, yes.

[In addition to exploring Barbara's expectations, the therapist begins to bring out Bill's dependency and loss, at the same time modeling alternative ways Bill might communicate with Barbara. The focus then turns to Bill to see if he has picked up the message.]

THERAPIST: Bill, how many beers would it take to put that into words?

BILL: I guess I'm a cold person in that respect, and I suppose that's why I give gifts. I supported her college education. I was annoyed when she took the job from 6 P.M. to 9 P.M.; dinner's at 7:30.

THERAPIST: Let me go back. Are you cold inside or outside?

BILL: Probably outside.

THERAPIST: Inside you're not so cold. You have trouble getting it out there? You think that's because you never learned it?

BILL: Probably never learned it.

THERAPIST: Have you made an effort? You think an effort would be worthwhile?

BILL: Could be.

THERAPIST: Do you think Barbara would pick it up, or would it fall on rock?

BILL: I don't think it would make a difference. Now there are new conflicts coming into play. The kids' vacations don't coincide with Barbara's vacation, so Barbara says she'll have to take her own vacation. I don't know how to react to that.

THERAPIST: When you agreed to Barbara's going to school and being out there, did you know it would be as hard as it has been?

BILL: I thought it would be a daytime thing. I never gave a thought to vacations being cancelled.

THERAPIST: So it wasn't going to be on Bill-time; it was going to be on free time, and now it's gone over into Bill-time. Did it have more of an impact on you than you thought it would? Did you feel it?

BILL: I think she's going out faster than she should. My daughters don't like it either, coming home to an empty house.

[At this point the therapist decided he had done what he could to validate Bill, to give him a potential new pathway of perception, and to engage him in the process of therapy. He now turned and attempted to slow down Barbara's movement and modify her reactivity. Finally, he closed by reminding Bill of his dependency.]

THERAPIST: Now what do you think, Barbara, without defending yourself? Have you overcorrected? Have you gone too fast?

BARBARA: No.

THERAPIST: But as you pull out, there's bound to be fallout from it. That's totally predictable. The pace at which you pull out and the way you handle your move out will have more or less fallout depending on how you do it. That's not your responsibility to control all of that. The other folks have to handle their piece of it, but how do you know when you're moving out too fast or too slow, or losing your momentum or whatever? Or haven't you bothered to evaluate that?

[Barbara again becomes very defensive, intermittently crying.]

THERAPIST: It's such a toxic issue for you that it's hard for you to entertain questions about what you're doing without getting defensive and without getting scared of falling back, and that doesn't allow you to see the whole picture and deal with some of the pieces of it. I'd encourage you to do that. Bill, I want to get back to something. When I asked you before whether you could say to Barbara that you never realized how dependent you were on her, if you experienced that, could you tell her?

BILL: I think I have told her. As far as holding down the home fort, and keeping the kids in line.

THERAPIST: How about just your internal feeling of well-being?

BILL: Well, I haven't thought about that.

THERAPIST: If Barbara is going to look at the impact of what she is doing on the family, I think you need to look at your anger and at the internal, deeper feelings that it is covering up.

The couple's reaction to this session was mixed. Bill found it helpful and felt supported by the therapist. Barbara initially felt angry and defensive. She heard the therapist telling her that the steps she was taking toward independence, which she had considered painfully slow, were too ambitious. In the ongoing therapy, the regular therapist supported Barbara's frustration but continued to encourage her to evaluate the impact her change was making on the family. By the time they watched the videotape of the consultation several months later, Barbara's reactivity was significantly lower, and she was able to hear what was being said with much more objectivity.

Bill and Barbara made progress in their work on this triangle, although the process was slow because of the intensity of their conflict. In time Barbara learned to use her group in a more productive way. During one session, when she and the therapist were discussing why she sometimes felt weak for staying in the marriage (a pattern we have noted with many women today), she was able to connect her feeling with the group's influence. She realized that she was the only one of the seven women who had not left a husband or a lover and felt that there was an underlying theme in the group that a strong woman strikes out on her own. Barbara began to entertain the possibility that it takes a great deal of strength to stay in a marriage and to work on making it better without giving up the goal of autonomy. When Bill fell back into criticism, she was often able to say with sincerity that she was sorry he was having trouble with her movement instead of defending herself. She learned to pace her moves in a way that minimized the impact on the family, and she made progress in taking more responsibility for financial matters. Bill learned to control some of his criticism and began to take risks in exposing to Barbara his vulnerability about his dependence. He also took steps in giving up some of the financial control.

To summarize, the clinical management of the social network triangle involves the following steps:

1. The triangle must be identified and the process brought out. Most commonly the wife is moving toward a woman, a group of women, or a body of feminist literature for support in her struggle for autonomy and away from her husband, whom she labels the enemy. The husband, in reaction to his wife's absence, pursues her with personal criticism and blames the outside influence for her betrayal.

2. Husband and wife need to shift their parts in the triangle. The husband must stop criticizing his wife, give her room to grow, and stop blaming the third party. He needs to identify his dependence

on his wife and to explore the feelings of loss he is experiencing. The wife has to look at the way she has been influenced and the way she uses the other women and determine what is productive for her and what is not. She needs to set her own agenda for change, one that is based on a careful assessment of her needs but reflects sensitivity toward the family. When the steps that she takes conflict with her husband's desires, she must avoid being defensive.

3.   To reinforce these shifts, both spouses need to focus on the interlocking triangles, which take them back to their families of origin to study the source of their scripting in the social network triangle.

The Child Triangle

Early in therapy the therapist brought to the surface the process in the triangle with Joe. Barbara was concerned about Joe's behavior in school and out. He was failing a number of courses and seemed completely unmotivated. She worried about his use of alcohol and about the group he associated with, and she feared that he might be using drugs. Bill agreed that Joe had problems but attributed them to the fact that his mother had overprotected him. That comment elicited a hostile diatribe from Barbara about the poor example Bill had set for his son. The intensity of conflict around Joe was immediately apparent to the therapist.

In this triangle, Barbara was moving toward Joe to protect him from his father and from the various schools he attended. She had initially felt that Bill was inconsistent and insensitive with Joe, but over the years her perception of his fathering had grown even more negative. By the time they started therapy she felt that Bill had always hated Joe and had wanted to get rid of him. She also considered her husband an alcoholic and blamed him for Joe's use of alcohol. Bill was extremely critical of Barbara's overprotective treatment of Joe, and the two of them were involved in a continuous attack-counterattack pattern.

Joe had felt protective of his mother since he was a very young boy. He remembered standing on his bed with his ear cupped to the wall, listening to his parents' raging fights and wanting to kill his father. When Bill and Barbara began therapy, Joe said his father was always picking on him, and he vowed he would never come in for a session alone with him.

A graphic example of the process in the triangle occurred whenever Joe and Bill got into a fight. These fights always happened when Barbara was within hearing range. Bill would tell Joe to do something and then be enraged by Joe's passive or negative response. The interaction would quickly escalate until Bill was challenging Joe to fight "if you're so damned tough." The two of them would go into Joe's room, Bill would lock the door, and they would taunt each other until Bill finally hit Joe. Barbara, who had been listening from the sidelines and demanding that they stop, would run to Joe's room, screaming that she would call the police, and pound on the door until Bill opened it. Days of coldness between them would follow.

Once the triangle is identified and the process understood, work with parents who have lost control over their acting-out adolescent usually proceeds in one of two ways. Depending on the nature of the process, we might coach them to join forces in establishing critical but minimal rules and then to use the leverage they still have with their child in order to enforce them, or we might put one parent in charge of the child and move the other in another direction. In this case the conflict over the son was too intense to begin with either of these approaches. Getting the mother to join forces with the father when she was convinced he would rather see the son dead would only have fueled the conflict. Putting either one in charge and asking the other to move back when they were so hostile and critical about each other's parenting would have had the same effect.

The therapist began by taking a position on the existing level of violence. She said that any physical violence had to stop, because no one would be able to change in that kind of climate and there was a potential for something very serious to happen. Both spouses were encouraged to move away from the situation when they felt themselves losing control over their anger, and the way anger was being expressed was monitored from week to week.

This much was done early in therapy, and the primary focus then shifted to the social network triangle. Once Barbara and Bill made progress there, their capacity to change their thinking and behavior around the child triangle improved. When the therapist began to concentrate on the child triangle, she decided on a plan in which the mother would initially work only to stay out of the interaction between father and son but not back away from her relationship with her son. Meantime, the father would be working on improving his relationship with his son. The son would be encouraged to take more responsibility for himself in school and with the family.

Letting Bill and Joe handle their own disagreements was an extremely difficult task for Barbara. She seemed to know whenever there was a possibility that Bill and Joe would cross paths, and she made sure she was there. When the three of them were together, she always felt very tense and watched carefully for the moment when she would have to rescue Joe.

The first thing the therapist asked her to do was to monitor her own thoughts at those times when Bill and Joe were arguing. She reported a continuous inner dialogue filled with vituperative, blaming thoughts about her husband, which included the rehashing of specific incidents from the past when she felt Bill had been unfair or abusive to Joe. In order to stop monitoring father and son she needed to do something about the bitterness that had built up over the seventeen years of their marriage. The therapist followed the steps we use in working with bitterness, which are explained in detail in the next section of this chapter.

As work on the bitterness progressed, Barbara was coached to change her behavior when Bill and Joe were together. She began by leaving the room when things were calm, which was difficult enough for her because of her fear of the consequences. She viewed her role as Joe's protector in life-and-death terms. Gradually she was able to leave them alone together when stress was reasonably low.

The therapist's initial goals with Bill were to engage him in improving his relationship with his son, to bring out any softness and concern he felt for him, to explore his expectations of Joe, and to get him moving toward Joe in a more positive way. In his sessions alone, Bill expressed a desire for a better relationship with Joe, but in Barbara's presence he was cynical and negative about him. The therapist explored his model for fathering. He had always had a distant and conflictual relationship with his own father but a warm, satisfying relationship with his maternal grandfather. When Bill looked at the way in which his grandfather related to him, he realized that it was fairly close to the way he related to his second son, Tim. He treated Joe more as his father had treated him.

Five months after therapy began, an incident occurred that accelerated the very slow progress they were making on this triangle. Bill had had back surgery and was recuperating at home. Joe came home from a party obviously drunk and demanded the keys to the car. Barbara was out, and Bill told Joe that under no circumstances would he allow Joe to go back out because of the shape he was in. Joe became very aggressive, insisting he was fine, and began to push his way past Bill. Bill grabbed an antique gun from the closest and used it to block Joe's way, knocking him in the nose, which bled profusely. Bill, concerned that Joe's nose was broken, took him to the hospital emergency room for X rays. By the time Barbara came home, father and son were sitting calmly watching television, Joe's nose bruised but not broken. The younger children told her about the fight, including the fact that Bill had used a gun. She flew into a rage, screaming that she had always known Bill wanted Joe dead. She threatened to call the police but called the therapist first.

Once it was clear that both father and son were calm, the therapist encouraged her not to call the police but to bring the family in for a session the next day.

When they came in, Barbara was still raging about Bill's use of the gun. The therapist said she knew Barbara was very upset and could understand how the gun had really scared her. She asked Barbara just to sit and listen while she talked to Bill and Joe about the previous night. Bill summarized the events and defended his use of the gun by saying that he knew the gun, a collector's item, had missing parts and had not worked in years. He said he reached for it because he thought that it might stop Joe, and he knew he could not stop him without help because of his bad back.

The following is a segment from that session.

THERAPIST: What were you thinking about when Joe first came home?

BILL: I thought, "This kid is wasted—he'll kill himself or someone else if he gets behind the wheel of a car."

THERAPIST: So you were worried about him?

BILL: There was no way I was going to let him leave. Yes, I was worried.

THERAPIST: When you saw that he wasn't going to listen to you, did you consider other ways of stopping him?

BILL: I don't think I did such a bad job. I'm sorry about his nose, but it's probably the first time Joe and I have settled a fight. We were fine by the time Barbara got home, and she went completely crazy anyway. She should have stayed out of it. She thinks I should have called the police instead of stopping him myself. I never would have done that.

THERAPIST: What has prevented you from settling fights in the past? Why was this one different?

BILL: Probably because Barbara wasn't home. Usually we end up fighting whenever I'm pissed off at Joe.

THERAPIST: So then it's you against the two of them?

BILL: Yes.

THERAPIST: Joe, what do you think? You think you and your father worked it out?

JOE: Yeah. I think Mom made a big deal of it.

[Note that the process has shifted.]

THERAPIST: Did you know that your father was worried about you?

JOE: I heard him say it.

THERAPIST: Bill, you said Barbara wanted you to call the police and that you would never do that. Sometimes bringing someone in who's completely outside the family can help calm things down. Why do you feel so strongly about it?

BILL: My father once did that to me, and I wound up in jail for three days.

THERAPIST: Joe, has your father ever told you that story?

JOE: No. My mother told me something about jail, but I didn't know the details.

THERAPIST: How much do you know about him when he was your age?

JOE: I know he was wild, but not really too much else.

THERAPIST: Maybe that's something the two of you can do, Bill. Maybe you can fill Joe in about you at his age and about your relationship with your father. I think all three of you could do something different. Barbara, for you I think it goes back to what we've been talking about—taking the risk of letting the two of them work it out. Bill, for you it's working on controlling your anger when you're dealing with Joe, and whether Barbara intervenes or not, because that's going to be very hard for her. And it's working on not fighting with her. And Joe, how are you going to stop providing the ammunition for your parents' fights?

JOE: I guess by not getting into trouble.

THERAPIST: What do you think they would do without you to fight over?

JOE: Fight over something else, probably.

THERAPIST: [To Bill and Barbara] Is he right?

BARBARA: We'd come up with something.

THERAPIST: Why don't you try that, Joe? Because it seems to me you keep yourself in a lousy position in the family by giving them so much ammunition.

The rest of the session focused on the couple's need for an issue to fight over and their uncertainty about what the marriage would be like without one.

The next important piece of work with this triangle was done around the choice of a new school for Joe. The advisors at his school, a large public high school, had recommended that he not return because he had not passed the year, and they felt the school could not provide the kind of individual attention he needed. Both parents agreed that it was not the right place for him, but they were in conflict over an alternative. Most of the choices were boarding schools, which Barbara saw as Bill's way of getting rid of Joe. Bill had gone to boarding school as an adolescent and thought it might be a positive experience for Joe. He also admitted that it would be a relief not to have to deal with him on a daily basis. Joe ultimately chose one of the boarding schools. The therapist took the position that living away from home might be beneficial as long as nobody saw it as a solution to their relationship problems. They would all need to continue working. She also recommended that Joe work with a counselor or therapist at school.

Joe's initial adjustment to school was very positive. Bill went through periods of missing him and would occasionally go to sit in Joe's room—something he had difficulty admitting to Barbara. He also wrote letters to him, and there were phone calls and visits. After Christmas vacation Joe's grades began to deteriorate, and with eight more weeks left in the school year he was suspended for a week after he got into a drunken fight. He came home and wanted to stay there. Bill took the position that he had to finish the year, that coming home was not an option, and for the first time Barbara backed him up. Joe came in for a session with Bill during that week and said he never remembered his mother agreeing with his father on an issue that related to him. All three experienced the process as very different. Joe calmed down and spent the rest of the week painting the basement. He returned to school and did fairly well for the rest of the year, getting reasonably good progress reports from his teachers.

Barbara was able to join with Bill in saying that Joe had to return to school, but she described it as one of the hardest things she had ever done. Her struggle was by no means over. She continued to get caught defending Joe, although not as often, when she failed to make a conscious effort not to. She recognized that her interference only escalated the problems between Bill and Joe, and she developed some confidence that if she left the two of them alone they would eventually work it out.

Bill, too, had more work to do on this triangle. He still sometimes moved toward Barbara with his complaints about Joe, and he easily fell into a harsh critical posture with him. However, there was a softening in his overall approach to his son, and he was able to handle difficult issues in a much more functional way. For example, when Joe came home for the summer, Bill initiated a family meeting to establish house rules, allowing Joe to contribute his ideas and thereby minimizing the potential for heated conflict. Bill's expectations of Joe became much more realistic and flexible. He also became more sensitive to Barbara's difficulty in separating from Joe, and he was often able to keep his reactivity down when she got upset.

Joe began functioning at a higher level, having passed the school year and holding down a full-time summer job. He continued to have difficulty controlling his anger with his father and still moved toward his mother with complaints about him.

To reinforce the progress that each of them had made in shifting their parts in this triangle, the therapist focused on two of the interlocking triangles, one of which involved Bill, Joe, and Tim, the second son, and a second involving Bill, Barbara, and Tim. In the first, Bill and Tim were in a close positive relationship, and Joe was on the outside in conflict with both of them. Joe would criticize Tim for trying to be just like his father, precipitating a fight between them. When Bill intervened, it would be on Tim's side. The process of triangulation with Bill, Barbara, and Tim was triggered whenever Barbara felt Bill was being unfair or abusive to Joe. She automatically turned on Tim with criticism or some kind of harsh behavior. As Bill went to work on his relationship with Joe, Tim began to act out, throwing tantrums at home and having problems in school. In a session with Bill, Barbara, and Tim, Tim was able to talk about the resentment he felt about all the attention Joe had been getting. Barbara, who had always focused so much on Joe, recognized her reactive behavior with Tim. She began to spend more time with Tim alone and to work on keeping her relationship with Tim separate from her relationship with Bill and Joe. Both parents were able to support Tim through a difficult period he was having in school, and he began to calm down.

The progress on the child triangle is exemplified by two brief anecdotes. On a family trip to Chicago each of the children had a different agenda for the day. Bill encouraged Barbara to go off with Joe, while he took the other three, a clear shift from his old position of raging about any time Barbara and Joe spent together. Second, Bill supported Barbara's desire to visit friends for a long weekend while he stayed with the four children. For the first time she trusted him alone with Joe, and Bill and the children had a very positive weekend, during which Joe assumed some of the responsibility for the younger children.

In summary, the clinical management of this child triangle involved the following steps:

1. The triangle was identified and the process brought to light. The wife was in an overly close position with the eldest son, and the father was in a distant, conflictual relationship with his wife and son.

2. The husband, wife, and son all needed to shift their parts in the triangle. The wife had to give up her role of protecting her son from his father and work on establishing a separate relationship with each of them. The husband had to stop taking his complaints about his son to his wife and work on a more positive relationship with both of them. The son had to stop complaining to his mother about his

father and work on taking more responsibility for his own life. The husband and wife had to join forces around the important parenting decisions, and all three of them had to take responsibility for the way in which they expressed anger.

3. To reinforce these shifts, the major interlocking triangles were addressed.

ADDRESSING BITTERNESS

In stage III conflict husband and wife have gone beyond being disappointed and angry that their expectations for marriage have not been met. Bitterness has built up in each of them, and one or both may have turned off the emotional switch that keeps them vulnerable to the pain in the relationship. If the bitterness is not addressed and reduced in therapy, neither will be able to begin taking responsibility for the self, which is essential for a resolution of conflict and successful treatment.

When a stage III couple presents for treatment, one spouse, usually the wife, articulates the bitterness first. Alan and Jan Goldman were a good example of the clinical picture we see most frequently. They had been married for seven years, and for the two years prior to therapy they had been in stage III conflict. They married after college, and Jan immediately gave responsibility for handling all important decisions to Alan. He took care of the finances and decided where they would live, when they would buy a house, take vacations, or buy a car. Jan was initially comfortable with the arrangement, but several years into the marriage she began to resent it. She pursued Alan to change, wanting him to be more supportive and understanding and to encourage her independence. When she attempted to do something on her own, efforts that were fueled by her voracious appetite for consciousness-raising literature, she found him critical, unsupportive, and undermining.

Alan did not respond to her pleas for therapy until she had gone into a deep freeze and talked repeatedly about leaving him. When he did come in, he was much more in touch with his fear about losing her than he was with his own bitterness, which did not surface until the threat of divorce diminished.

The effort to decrease Jan's bitterness included seven steps typical of our approach to bitterness in stage III couples:

1. Bringing out and working on the fantasy solution
2. Identifying and labelling the "bitter bank" and reframing it as self-destructive

3. Tracking bitterness back through the progression from expectation to alienation
4. Researching the bitterness as a generational pattern
5. Changing the perception of Alan as the enemy
6. Working with the emptiness that comes when the bitterness is gone
7. Developing personal goals and working to reach them.

Working on the Fantasy Solution

In stage III conflict at least one of the spouses has a fantasy solution, an idealized answer to the problems of life and marriage: the death of the other spouse by natural or unnatural means, divorce, life with another person, or living alone. The person reactively moves away from the spouse and marriage and toward the fantasy. He or she is usually not doing anything active to reach the solution but is spending a great deal of time thinking or dreaming about it. When people create fantasies that involve life without the spouse, they have given up the hope that life would be better if the spouse changed, because they no longer believe the spouse can change. As long as they are absorbed in this kind of fantasy thinking, their motivation to look at their part in the process and begin work on the accumulation of bitterness will be minimal.

In some cases the fantasy solution spills out in the first session, and in other cases the therapist needs to bring it out. During the first two sessions with Alan and Jan, the therapist asked them what would have to happen for things to improve, and Jan responded that she did not see any way out of the mess they were in. However, when the therapist saw each of them alone during the third week, Jan started her session by saying that, in fact, she did often think about a solution to their situation: for one of them to die. She had no thoughts about committing suicide or murder, but she often thought about Alan's dying. She did not focus on the way he would die but rather on the fact of his being dead. She could picture the funeral and people coming back to the house afterwards. She imagined feeling a mixture of sadness and relief. Her fantasy did not extend into the future except that she was aware of the sense that the slate would be wiped clean and that the future would at least hold possibilities. The therapist asked how much time was devoted to these thoughts and learned that they occupied her mind at least some portion of every day.

This exploration became a valuable stepping-off point for further treatment. For instance, the fact that Jan had settled on this particular solution rather than looking at other options like separation or divorce or changing the relationship revealed her inability to make active decisions and choices in all aspects of her life. The therapist tracked this powerlessness back into her family of origin, where her father had made all important decisions for her mother, her older sister, and herself. They identified this as a problem she would need to work on.

Once the fantasy had surfaced, the therapist began to test the reality of its central elements. What would life really be like without Alan? Had she thought much about the kinds of decisions she would make? Would there be anything she would miss about Alan? What would she regret about the marriage? The therapist's goal was to get Jan thinking about a more active and functional plan for the resolution of her problems. It is important that the therapist explore the fantasy solution rather than fight it, in order to avoid winding up in a triangle with the creator of the solution. Through these questions the therapist must convey the idea that it is dysfunctional to spend so much time and energy dreaming about life without the other spouse, because that is a way to avoid changing.

Sometimes the person does not give up the fantasy and moves toward playing it out, particularly when it involves leaving the marriage. The therapist must point out that there is a functional way to leave a marriage, which is to do it as nonreactively as possible, without blame, and knowing one's own part in the relationship.

When the fantasy solution is an open issue in the relationship, the other spouse often tries to fight it, and the therapist has to coach that person to pull back. In one case, for example, whenever the wife began talking about her desire to live alone, her husband attacked her. He said she would never be able to do it because she did not know the first thing about supporting herself, and he labeled her immoral for even thinking about leaving her children. The therapist asked him to refrain from this kind of behavior, pointing out that it only intensified his wife's desire to leave.

When the fantasy solution is not open in the relationship and is described in an individual session, the therapist must use clinical judgment about making it known to the other spouse. In a case like Alan and Jan's, where the solution involves the imagined death of one spouse, revealing it is sure to add more fuel to the fire, but themes inherent in the fantasy can be introduced into conjoint sessions. For example, the therapist might bring up with the other spouse present the feeling of powerlessness and futility that are inevitably a part of that kind of wish.

The "Bitter Bank"

Once the fantasy solution has been explored and the person has in some fashion agreed to do some work before making a decision to leave, the focus of treatment turns to what we call the "bitter bank": the accumulation of bitterness that builds up over time. People in stage III marriages come into therapy so focused on their spouses as the cause of all hostile feelings that they have little awareness of the degree to which bitterness has taken over their own emotional lives.

The "bitter bank" is a useful term for a variety of reasons. People generally respond to it in a positive way and usually take part in embellishing the image with additional banking vocabulary. It creates a tangible image that helps to draw the attention of the bitter person back from the spouse to himself or herself. The therapist labels the complaints one spouse relates about the other as coming from his or her bitter bank. For example, in one of the early sessions Jan began describing the sins Alan had committed through the course of the marriage.

THERAPIST: It sounds like you've been storing up a lot of bad memories for a very long time, and that maybe a kind of bitter bank has built up.

JAN: Yeah, I guess it has.

THERAPIST: Do you have a sense of how often those old tapes play in your head?

JAN: You mean any negative thoughts about Alan? [She laughs.] How many times do these thoughts cross my mind? I guess pretty much of the time. He'll say something, or do something, or something will happen that will just remind me of something that happened in the past.

THERAPIST: You mean something happens that triggers the old tapes, and you'd say that that's a pretty constant kind of thing?

JAN: It's so constant because he keeps doing the same old things. Like he'll say something critical of me in front of other people and then that will remind me of all the times he's totally humiliated me in the past, to the point that I try to avoid going out with other people or having friends home.

THERAPIST: That's really what I mean by a bitter bank. Each time something happens you make a new deposit, and over the years it all collects interest until by now you're really sitting on top of something big.

JAN: Yeah, God, if it were only money, I'd be a very rich lady.

THERAPIST: Have you ever thought about the kind of price you pay for living with so much bitterness? I mean you're telling me you think about it most of the time.

JAN: Sometimes I wake up in the middle of the night with those same tapes playing, or else I can't get to sleep.

THERAPIST: So the feelings affect your sleep. How much do they interfere with your job or with having a good time?

JAN: Who has a good time? I'm okay at work most of the time. Sometimes I can't really shake it at work.

THERAPIST: Where do you think you'd be five years from now if this were all to continue?

JAN: I worry about that because I can see that it's eating me up, but I can't see it getting better as long as I'm with Alan.

THERAPIST: I've seen people end a marriage filled with the same kind of bitterness you've got, and it doesn't automatically go away.

Jan, like other stage III spouses, needed to recognize that living with that bitterness had become a way of life that was more destructive to her than to anyone else. In order to get her to see that, the therapist helped her to identify the bitter bank as something that was hers and to see that the time and energy she devoted to it prevented her from developing more productive aspects of her life. The therapist did not at that point challenge her notion that Alan was a scoundrel—that would have inhibited the engagement process—but rather emphasized that she needed to get her emotional life back under her own control.

Tracking Bitterness Back

Once the person accepts the view that there is something to be gained from working on this bitterness, the therapist begins to guide him or her back through the steps of the expectation-to-alienation progression. Jan was encouraged to study the emotional roller coaster she had been on through the course of her marriage. When she started therapy, she was very clearly on an island of invulnerability. She was reluctant to get out of that position, because it would mean again being vulnerable to the old hurt.

The therapist guessed, and Jan agreed, that since she was probably getting more of a response from Alan than she had in the past, she might be worried that he would go back to his old ways if she ventured off that island. The therapist acknowledged that possibility but emphasized that the purpose of giving up the bitterness is not to get more from Alan but rather to save herself from a dysfunctional and unhappy life.

The research began with the numb phase that Jan was in. The therapist asked her to describe it and to try to pin down when it began. She thought her switch had gone off three or four months before they came to therapy. Alan had described this period as "her deep freeze" in the first session and it was what had gotten him into therapy. The therapist explored what led up to her reactive distance and then got her to look at the stages prior to it.

THERAPIST: If you had been keeping a journal of your thoughts and feelings through the marriage, what would the recent entries say?

JAN: It would sound pathetic probably, so defeated, trapped and defeated. I'm trapped because I've wasted all these years with a man who's incapable of loving. I would write things like "slow death" and "terminal torture" to describe what this marriage has been like. I'm scared about leaving because he's made me so dependent. I know I allowed myself to get that way, but that's the way he wanted it. I don't have the energy to start over; by the time I did it would be too late to have kids so I just feel stuck and defeated.

THERAPIST: Were you saying much to Alan about your thoughts in recent months?

JAN: We've gone through periods of not talking before, but this one has been different. I feel different, and I know exactly when it started. A few months ago an old friend of mine was in town. I hadn't seen her in years; we grew up together. She stayed for a weekend and it was a disaster. Alan was so rude, terrible to her and horrible to me, insulting me, and he kept turning the heat down. It was freezing; we could see our breath. That's something we've been fighting about for years. He thinks the heating bills are too high. He was at his worst, and I just gave up. I fell apart, and I've been shut down ever since. I just don't care anymore.

THERAPIST: So before that, when you cared, how was it different? What would your journal say about that period?

JAN: I was angry all the time, raging; most of the time I wanted to kill him. That's how I was for years, since the time when I started trying to change, to grow up, and he was trying to hold me back every step of the way with his criticism and negativity.

THERAPIST: Tell me what it felt like to be that angry. Try to describe it.

JAN: When it was really bad, it was like acid burning a hole through me. I wouldn't be able to focus on anything else. If I tried to read or do anything, my mind would jump back to whatever he did. Some people talk about seeing red when they're angry; I had a headache. Most of the time I had a headache.

THERAPIST: Do you remember a time when you weren't angry with Alan?
      JAN: That would be hard. No, it wouldn't. I wasn't angry before we
             got married, and for the first few years things were okay. They
             really weren't okay, but they were quiet. I'd get my feelings
             hurt a lot, but I wouldn't say anything. I remember being very
             sensitive and surprised when Alan wouldn't respond to me. He
             wasn't affectionate after we got married, and he had been
             before. If I made some tiny attempt to talk to him, he'd clam
             up or act like I was crazy.
THERAPIST: You had expected that the affection and all that good stuff
             from your dating days would continue?
      JAN: I guess I did. Stupid, huh?
THERAPIST: So if I read this journal, the story of the wife's emotional life,
             I'd learn about a woman who had certain expectations about
             the marriage and who spent a few years being disappointed
             and hurt when those expectations weren't met. Then she got
             angry about it all and spent a lot of years raging at her husband
             until she just gave up and got numb to the old hurts. Is that
             about it?
      JAN: Pretty close. I said it was a pathetic story.
THERAPIST: If it ended there, I'd have to agree. It wouldn't be a very
             cheerful story, but I don't know where you're going to end up:
             stuck on this island sitting on a mountain of bitterness or back
             in charge of your own life.

The purpose of tracking the course of each spouse's emotional life
through the marriage is to begin to get them focused on themselves rather
than each other. By labelling the steps they have gone through, it begins
to give shape to the painful and powerful feelings that have controlled
their lives. It attempts an answer to the question, "How did I get to this
point?" and begins the process of saying "These are your feelings. You
have gone through a process that has brought you to this point. You have
to take responsibility for changing this course." It also provides an opportunity for the therapist to be supportive by listening to the struggle the
individual has been through without fueling the fire by encouraging the
unstructured ventilation of feelings.

In the segment just quoted, the therapist took Jan from her island of
invulnerability back through the bitterness, rage, hurt, and disappointment to the expectations that were not met in the marriage. This step is
taken more than once during treatment, with the purpose of getting the
person to describe each of the stages. There is a tendency for stage III

people to say, "I was in a rage all the time because he (or she) did this and this to me." Our effort is to help people learn to articulate their own feelings: "I was in a rage, and this is what it felt like."

This is not the time to confront people when they make blaming statements. If a wife says, "I'm bitter because he made me dependent on him," the therapist guides her back to a discussion about her own experience with bitterness rather than asking her what her part in the process is. (That will be addressed when the bitterness is less intense.) The therapist who sees the expectation-to-alienation progression operating in person after person will be able to convey the fact that it is a predictable pattern in people with severe marital conflict. Knowing this helps people to build confidence in the capacity of the therapist to help them through what had felt like a hopeless situation. The exploration of the progression should end up presenting a challenge to the individual: "This is how you got to this point; now what is your next step? Do you stay on the island, or are you ready to begin to move in a new direction?"

The exploration of the progression also provides the therapist with the opportunity to move into the extended family, reinforcing the idea that one had an emotional life before marriage. After the person has described a particular stage, the therapist asks whether those feelings are familiar. This question often triggers memories of a particular period in the past and of a relationship that evoked the same feelings. Jan said she had felt the same kind of hurt she experienced in her marriage with only one other person, her mother. Her mother, who had been hospitalized twice for depression, had never been able to respond positively to anything Jan was pleased about, from school achievements to efforts she had made around the house.

Sometimes the person denies that there is anything to compare these feelings to, holding fast to the story that "I was a happy person until I met him." Rather than fighting this stance, the therapist might simply ask the person to think about it during the week.

We spend a fair amount of time with people focusing on the expectations that began the emotional progression. One of the phenomena about expectations that is particularly interesting and clinically relevant is the way in which people in conflictual marriages have pitched their expectations toward their spouses' greatest weaknesses rather than toward their strengths. For example, one woman complained bitterly about the fact that her husband never verbally expressed affection. He never said he loved her or complimented her on the way she looked. The expectation that this kind of behavior should be a part of any marriage had led to years of bitter disappointment. The reality was that this man had never been good at expressing affection. In his family of origin he had been nicknamed "The Stone" and was seen as a "chip off the old block," his father. Silent men with disappointed wives were scattered throughout the genogram. What this woman was expecting from her husband was probably one of his greatest areas of incompetence. In therapy we point out this incongruity and encourage people to work on identifying the strengths in their spouses and then pitching their expectations in that direction.

Bitterness as a Generational Pattern

The effort to decrease the blame directed at one's spouse and take responsibility for one's bitter feelings can be helped by exploring bitterness in the family of origin. We have found that when there is a great deal of bitterness in one person, there is usually a pattern of bitterness in other family members across the generations. By asking questions such as, "Whom would you describe as bitter in your family?" "Did anyone see himself or herself as a victim?" "How much blaming did you hear as a child?" the therapist enables the person in treatment to see that his or her feelings are not unique in the family.

Jan and her sister often heard their mother's litany against her husband. He had destroyed her life because he was miserly and sour and had prevented her from having friends or doing anything worthwhile. Jan could remember these laments going back to her early childhood. Her maternal grandmother had been abandoned by her husband and forever after lectured her offspring on the injustice men perpetrated against women. As she surveyed her genogram on her maternal side, she realized she had heard only negative stories about men. She believed that her father also lived with a great deal of bitterness, but he had been less verbal about it. His dissatisfaction was expressed around his job and politics.

Jan began to see that bitterness was common in her family and recognized that she would have to struggle to avoid a pattern that was part of her heritage and that was fast becoming a way of life for her. This process further developed the idea that there was more to the making of her emotional state than Alan's behavior. The therapist did not try to convince Jan that bitterness had been passed down through the genes in her family, but rather that there was a possible connection between her own feelings and those of significant members in her family of origin. Perhaps bitterness in previous generations has an effect on the expectations offspring take into their marriages, making them greater in order to compensate for the disappointment that others have experienced.

Changing the Perception of Enemies and Victims

In stage III conflict each spouse sees the other as the enemy and himself or herself as victim; each believes that the other is motivated by the desire to hurt. Changing this perception so that people begin to understand that they have more power in the relationship than they believe is a critical step in letting go the accumulation of bitterness. We address this problem through a process of behavioral change on the part of the "victim" and by expanding the view that the person has of the spouse. The change in behavior involves three steps: identifying the enemy/victim behavior pattern, changing the behavior, and evaluating the system's response to the change.

To identify the enemy/victim behavior pattern, the therapist working with Jan looked for specific situations in which Jan was clearly operating as a victim. For example, Jan had complained bitterly about Alan's excessive reaction when anything happened to the car. If she got a flat tire, a parking or speeding ticket, or a dent, Alan would fly into a rage.

THERAPIST: What happened when you first saw the dent? What were your first thoughts?

JAN: I was thinking, oh, Christ, he's going to be pissed. He goes nuts about the car.

THERAPIST: So your very first thoughts were about Alan's reaction?

JAN: Yeah. Yes, definitely.

THERAPIST: What did you do when you got home?

JAN: I was really nervous. I didn't say anything at first. I was afraid he'd notice it, but he didn't come in through the garage. Then he had to take the car after dinner, so I knew I had to say something. I guess I just blurted it out, and he started screaming, and I screamed back, so it turned into a major brawl, all over a stupid dent.

THERAPIST: You really had him pegged from the beginning, huh? I'm struck by the amount of fear you felt. You really saw him as the enemy in that situation.

JAN: I know how he reacts to those things, so, yes, I saw him as the enemy.

THERAPIST: It's funny how your own reaction to the dent wasn't even a part of the discussion with Alan. If you were living with a friend, and you came home after seeing that dent, what would you have done?

JAN: I probably would have told her that some jerk ran into my car in the parking lot and didn't even have the decency to identify himself. I'd probably say how frustrated I was.

THERAPIST: Have you ever tried that with Alan? You know, acting as if he were a friend in one of those situations where you expect him to blow up?

During the next session when Alan was present, Alan said that in situations like the dent episode he felt enraged because he never felt as though he had heard the full story. He saw Jan as a sneak, clearly the enemy, and believed she hid things from him in a malicious way. That was a pattern that went on in his parents' marriage. His mother often kept things from his father and confided in Alan; he viewed his father as a weakling for believing her ridiculous stories.

Once the therapist had brought out Jan's pattern of behavior in situations where she saw Alan as the enemy—becoming overly focused on Alan's reaction and in a high state of anxiety withholding information, blurting it out only when it was certain to be discovered—the second step was to change her victimlike behavior. By asking Jan how she would respond in a similar situation with a friend, someone she did not fear or see as all-powerful and larger than life, the therapist helped her identify a more functional behavior. The therapist then coached Jan to introduce that behavior into the relationship with Alan. This was extremely difficult for her to do, as it is for most people. She was being asked to change her part of the process with no guarantee that Alan would change his.

The therapist encouraged Jan to talk about the fear she felt when she even contemplated dealing with Alan in this straight, "friendly" way. They tracked that fear back to her family of origin, where the stakes seemed so high for any infraction that Jan learned to be a perfect little girl who carefully hid anything that might displease her parents. Her automatic response to Alan had its origins in a pattern that began long before she met him.

Jan's attempt to change this pattern occurred in stages. At first she was able to recognize the situations where she was triggered but was unable to change her behavior. Then she would catch herself in midstream and make awkward attempts to correct her part. Finally she was able to exercise enough control to change her behavior before she fell into the old pattern. The therapist predicted these steps and supported her through them.

After the person succeeds in some attempts at changing the victim behavior, the final step is to evaluate the system's response to that change. What does the spouse do in response to the new behavior? The therapist warns that the spouse might be unsettled by it and try to get it back on familiar ground, even escalating his or her behavior to do so.

In Jan and Alan's case Alan was at times able to step out of his pattern and respond in a calmer way. Jan saw that the old pattern shifted when she changed her behavior, and recognizing that her behavior clearly had an impact on their relationship helped to change her perception of herself as a powerless victim. Her perception of Alan had also been altered through the course of treatment as she learned that he had been as reactive to her as she had been to him. The sources of this reactivity were explored in their sessions together, and Jan began periodically to rekindle some of the sensitivity she had felt toward Alan early in their relationship.

Working with the Emptiness

People who struggle through this work and give up the bitterness that has been consuming a substantial part of their emotional lives are likely to feel depleted and drained. Much of the content and process of their lives have been organized around bitter feelings, and when these are gone, people often experience a profound emptiness. There is nothing to take the place of the internal dialogues replete with blame and anger. People are left without a language to speak or a framework for their thoughts. This is a vulnerable, raw time, which must be handled with sensitivity by the therapist.

Fogarty has written extensively on this aspect of treatment (1976b, 1976c, 1979a), and we rely heavily on his thinking. We teach people to describe the emotions they are experiencing and through that process to develop a new personal language to replace the old bitter dialogues.

Personal Goals

As long as people are consumed with the kind of anger and bitterness that is part of stage III conflict, they typically have little energy for working on personal goals. Once they have stopped blaming their spouses for the disappointments in their lives, there is at least the potential for developing goals and working to achieve them. The therapist can help this process by encouraging the person to evaluate his or her functioning in the areas of productivity, personal relationships, and personal well-being (see chapter 5). For example, in evaluating productivity one would ask about the person's level of satisfaction with and functioning in work and something about the kinds of career dreams he or she has had in the past and present. When the person develops a goal, the therapist helps to identify the strengths and limitations that might either aid in achieving the goal or make it more difficult to reach. The same process is followed in the areas of personal well-being (health, diet, exercise, grooming) and personal relationships (social network, nuclear and extended family)—always with an eye to current functioning.

Jan made progress on developing and achieving personal goals in all three areas. For example, she had been a special education teacher since her college graduation, and after the first few years she had grown to hate the job. She tended to become overly responsible for the students in her class and finished each day physically exhausted and emotionally drained. Once her life was less dominated by the bitterness toward her husband, she was able to focus on getting greater satisfaction from her work. She made an effort to increase her functioning at her teaching job by addressing the issue of overresponsibility, but at the same time she began to explore two fantasies she had had over the years: writing and owning a restaurant.

The process Jan went through to explore her writing ability clearly illustrates the ways in which the marriage can be used to inhibit personal growth. She began taking a creative writing course at night in the city, which quickly became a source of conflict with her husband. Alan would stress the danger in driving at that late hour to a "bad" part of the city. He pointed out that she would have trouble parking, and that weather conditions were likely to be bad during the winter. Jan's automatic reaction was to become defensive and to accuse him of not wanting her to do anything positive for herself. The process between them covered over her own very great fears about driving to the city and about taking the course, where she would be exposing her writing to the scrutiny and criticism of others.

The therapist worked to shift her attention from her husband's reaction back to herself, to explore her own personal fears. Jan was coached to give up her defensive behavior with her husband, to thank him for his concern, and even to agree with him periodically: "You know, you're probably right; I may be crazy to go out on a night like this."

To reinforce her new effort to get unhooked from Alan's reaction, the therapist helped her to track the issue back to her own extended family. How difficult was it to grow, to take on new challenges in her family of origin? Jan felt that every move out of her family had been frowned upon. She thought her father had a strong need to keep his women at home, and her mother seemed unable to go against his wishes but blamed him bitterly for prohibiting her growth. She never struggled to establish or achieve her own goals. When Jan studied the families each of her parents had come from, their roles began to make more sense.

This process is typical of the way we approach work on personal goals in any of the three areas of productivity, relationships, and personal well-being. First we assess the current level of satisfaction and functioning in a given area. Then we encourage people to define goals for themselves. These goals may come from dreams or ambitions they once had and had given up, or they may simply be the next step in improving their level of functioning in a given area. Next we help people develop a plan for achieving the goal and we focus on the ways in which marital or personal factors may be inhibiting progress. Finally we track those factors back to the family of origin.

Working with the Other Spouse

Husbands and wives rarely go through this individual work on bitterness and its accompanying problems at the same rate. The difference often throws a relationship off balance, with one growing faster than the other. In the ideal situation, both get to the point where they have stopped blaming one another and are taking responsibility for themselves. They are then ready to focus on strengthening their marriage.

Situations like Alan and Jan's are much more typical. One spouse comes in consumed by bitterness, while the other's bitter feelings are less available, concealed because of a long-established pattern of distancing— including distancing from his or her own feelings—or because the fear of losing the relationship takes precedence over bitterness for the time being.

This situation leaves the therapist with the task of working with two spouses who are at very different points. The beginning steps that the bitter spouse is taking through the bitterness protocol are likely to be very difficult for the other spouse to sit through. To detoxify that process for the other spouse, we do much of the initial work on bitterness in sessions alone. We also help the other spouse to understand the necessity of that work and find the personal strength to handle it, perhaps exploring the strengths that got him or her through particularly difficult times in the past. Then we attempt to engage the other spouse in work on one of the key triangles. When the bitter spouse has made progress in minimizing the bitterness and has set to work on personal goals, the other spouse may be just beginning to experience some of his or her own bitterness. This bitterness can be exacerbated by the belief that the other is moving away. At that point we try to decrease reactivity to the work the other is doing on goals and shift attention back to personal growth.

Severe as is the conflict in stage III, the goal of these couples is still to stay married. For some couples in severe conflict, however, that goal has been abandoned, and at least one of the spouses has begun the process of divorce. That act signals the onset of stage IV, which we turn to in the next chapter.

10

The Treatment of Stage IV

SOMEWHERE between stages III and IV, perhaps at 3.9, there is a "no-man's land." Lawyers have not yet been engaged, but hopelessness about the marriage has set in, and emotional fatigue and bitterness are forcing a decision on whether to hire a lawyer and sue for divorce. When couples present to us in this situation or end up there in the midst of marital therapy, we attempt to do three things: (1) help each spouse determine his or her bottom line, which represents the point of no return; (2) define what options remain open other than divorce; and (3) help each spouse understand how his or her own limitations have contributed to the failure of the marriage.

Some couples begin treatment in what we call pseudo–stage III, in which one spouse has divorce as a covert agenda before treatment begins. In some cases that person wants to be able to say, "I did everything I could. I even went to therapy so I would be able to leave the marriage without self-recrimination and guilt." In others the person wants to place a distressed, poorly functioning spouse in the hands of a therapist who will assume responsibility for his or her well-being. And in still others the person may be looking for support for the decision to divorce out of fear of an angry or violent response from his or her spouse. The conflict shifts overtly to stage IV when this agenda is revealed and a lawyer is engaged.

For still other couples, the decision to divorce has already been made when treatment begins and one or both spouses have already engaged lawyers, defining stage IV conflict. Frequently one spouse wants the divorce and the other does not, and only one of them is interested in therapy—usually the one who does not want the divorce, who sees in therapy one last hope for the marriage. Less frequently the one who wants the divorce looks to therapy for support in getting through the divorce process. A spouse may explain a lack of interest in therapy by saying that he or she is already immersed in individual therapy or that the lawyers involved have discouraged conjoint therapy. Underlying these explanations is often the fear that the therapy might attempt to put the marriage back together or that a hidden factor like an extramarital affair will be disclosed.

There are also couples who have decided to divorce and enter treatment together, usually expressing a desire to work on the mechanics of the divorce and to minimize the emotional repercussions for the children. In an ideal world most couples who divorce would make the decision and proceed with the process in a civilized fashion. In our experience only the minority of divorcing couples are able to do this; the rest relate in a style in keeping with the way they have related to each other over time. Marriages, like people, most often die as they have lived.

Involving an attorney automatically shifts the marriage into an adversarial context and makes reconciliation much less likely. In the ideal outcome of treatment for stage IV, both of the former spouses would be emotionally free to develop other primary relationships, able to communicate about children and money with minimal reactivity, and functionally connected to their families of origin and social networks. Both they and their children would be symptom-free.

Therapists who work with one or both members of a couple in this phase of marital dissolution are faced with several difficult tasks: first, trying to help each person reduce his or her level of reactivity enough to be able to function through the crisis; second, addressing the major triangles; and third, helping each person gain sufficient objectivity about the relationship to reduce bitterness and make it possible to achieve personal goals.

The Treatment Protocol

Our treatment protocol is basically the same for all couples in stage IV conflict. We first attempt to lower the reactivity between husband and wife so that they can disconnect from the marriage in a functional way. Then the work focuses on the central triangles and on the individuals. Ideally both spouses are committed to the therapy, with children and members of the extended family periodically involved. When this is the case, we begin with an emphasis on conjoint sessions if they are productive and then shift to a more individual focus as treatment progresses.

LOWERING THE REACTIVITY IN THE MARITAL COUPLE

The initial task in the treatment of stage IV is to help people through the crisis period that follows the decision to divorce. The high level of anxiety that these people experience calls for a therapist who can convey a sense of confidence about the case. People need to know that the therapist has been through this period with other divorcing couples and that, although the process was difficult, it was productive and everyone survived.

Lowering the reactivity is critical, because the emotional climate in stage IV families is usually turbulent, ranging in temperature from icy cold to explosively hot, and very unsafe. One wife compared her family to a solar system that had lost its sun: "We're all out there in a cold dark space, out of orbit, and crashing into each other." The picture of the future that parents and children once held is gone, and the uncertainty is frequently terrifying. The children in these families worry about everything from who will feed them to who will pay for college. Grandparents become convinced they will never see their grandchildren. Physical violence, vandalism, and bizarre behavior are frequently present in divorcing families. People do things they have never done before. One woman went to her husband's office, stood on his desk, and gave a detailed inventory of his transgressions to his coworkers. Another man spent hours on the phone every day calling his wife's family and friends to try to gain support. In order to lower this reactivity, we focus on four areas:

1. The level of functioning of each spouse
2. The couple's approach to the legal system

3. The couple's approach to parenting
4. The couple's approach to the extended family.

The Level of Functioning of Each Spouse

Most people's level of functioning is reduced during the crisis period that follows the decision to divorce. One of the factors that adds fuel to the reactivity and impairs functioning is that one spouse wants the divorce while the other does not. We find this imbalance present in most of the stage IV cases we treat.

The spouse who is holding on to the marriage comes in feeling devastated. These people are almost universally hurt and angry. They have a significant degree of anxiety about the future and often report disturbed eating and sleeping patterns, periodic dizziness, palpitations, and an inability to concentrate. The level of functioning of the person in this position is usually dramatically compromised. The therapist's first priority is to get the anxiety down and to mobilize the devastated person's personal and relationship resources. It is important to listen to and to validate the upset by conveying the message that the powerful emotional reaction being experienced is normal in this kind of crisis and that it takes time to regain one's stability. Then we take steps to help people to mobilize their own resources, to determine priorities in their daily responsibilities in order to make them more manageable, to verbalize their fears and do some reality testing around them, and to connect with a support system. If the person is still pursuing the spouse in an attempt to hold on to the marriage, we work on helping him or her pull back and let go.

The spouse who wants the divorce often comes in calmer, thinking that a solution to life's problems has been found or covering over the anxiety with a new relationship. To the degree that this person's functioning is impaired, we take the same steps mentioned for the other spouse. One of the main tasks for this spouse is to adjust the pace of the move away from the marriage, so that he or she can think clearly and function adequately. People in this position usually move too quickly and need to slow down. Often they are running faster in response to their spouses' desperate behavior, afraid that they might look back at their own ambivalence and change their minds. We try to teach people that they are not responsible for their spouses' lives but that they are responsible for their own behavior and its repercussions. The task here is to define a position of real responsibility. For example, if one spouse is concerned about the other's safety, it is that person's responsibility to inform members of the other spouse's family or close friends about the fears. We coach the person to enlist the support of the member of the spouse's family with whom he or she has the best relationship.

The Couple's Approach to the Legal System

Although the therapist should avoid giving any legal advice to a divorcing couple, we recommend providing the following functional guidelines for dealing with the legal system:

1. If a spouse has not already engaged a lawyer, he or she should move slowly, going for a consultation first to learn more about the various ways of proceeding. The lawyer should be asked to explain terms like mediation, legal custody, joint custody, shared custody, visitation, alimony, and child support. In therapy we help people formulate and organize questions to pose to the lawyer.
2. Before retaining lawyers, people should define what they need, what they would like, and what they are willing to settle for in terms of money and custody. Identifying their own wants and needs and the areas where they can compromise gives them a base to work from.
3. It is more important to hire a competent lawyer who is sensitive to the impact of divorce on the entire family than to engage one who believes in a big victory at any cost.
4. People need to be in charge of their lawyers. The decision to follow a lawyer's advice does not absolve the client from responsibility.
5. A legal separation allows more time for unfinished business than does a quick divorce. It also avoids some of the bitterness that surfaces when grounds are used.
6. Children do better when the custody agreement includes free access to both parents.
7. The emotional damage of a court-contested custody battle is extensive and should be avoided if at all possible.

The Couple's Approach to Parenting

There are countless ways that parenting can become dysfunctional in stage IV. Probably the most common is when one parent criticizes and blames the other to the children in an attempt to gain allies. Parents often pump children for information or use them as confidants, expecting them to take sides. Frequently children are the recipients of displaced anger. Many parents withhold important information from the children or tell them lies. One mother told her children that their father had moved out so that he could be closer to his work. The therapist must inform the parents of the potential damage of this kind of behavior, telling them that it makes an already complicated situation worse and may lead to serious problems for the children. Sympathizing with the parents' pain while labeling the behavior as less than functional is often helpful.

The work around parenting involves separating the marital problems from parental responsibilities and creating a cooperative climate in which each parent supports and encourages the children's relationship with the other parent. Practical issues involving the children, such as when and how to tell them about the divorce, are discussed. There are no hard and fast rules about the timing, but one guideline is that once the parents have made the decision to divorce and know when the physical separation will occur, it is time to tell the children. If the actual separation date is months away, however, then it may be advisable to wait before telling young children. We discourage premature threats of divorce, and we also warn against waiting so long that children may hear of it through the grapevine. We caution parents not to reassure a child falsely if the child asks whether they are considering divorce.

We encourage parents to stress three things in telling their children of the decision to divorce: that the children are not responsible for the divorce, that both parents will continue to love them, and that they will continue to be cared for. Parents should find a way to minimize blaming the other spouse when talking to children, but they do not necessarily have to present a united front. We have had children come in utterly baffled about the reasons for divorce, because their parents were so polite and cautious when they presented the situation to their children. A husband who is opposed to the divorce will have a difficult time going along with a script that requires him to say, "Your mother and I think it would be best to separate." There is nothing wrong with a child knowing that divorce is one parent's idea, as long as the child knows that both parents played a part in the failure of the marriage.

We help parents predict the ways in which their children will respond to the divorce by encouraging them to talk about each child's strengths, limitations, and behavior around past stressful events. We also give parents information from our own clinical experience about potential responses from children at various stages of development, informing them about markers to watch for, such as withdrawal, self-destructive behavior, acting-out behavior, sleeping and eating disorders, or a decrease in functioning in school, at home, or with friends.

The children in divorcing families are seen in sessions with their parents and alone. Without their parents present children may feel freer to express rage and frustration. The therapist can then coach them on ways to open communication with their parents and encourage them to share their upset with friends and other family members. Parents who want to keep the news in the family and forbid children to talk about the divorce are doing them a disservice.

We try to orchestrate family sessions so that each member talks about himself or herself with a minimum of defensiveness and blaming. During one session an eight-year-old boy screamed at his mother, in much the same style that his father had used, that no one would be able to stay with a bitch like her. The therapist took the position that it would be pretty hard for any mother to listen to that kind of talk from a son, and that that was a shame, because it sounded like he was hurting so much that he needed a mother who could listen to him. The therapist helped the boy find other ways to talk about his hurt, and her efforts served as a model for the mother.

We emphasize for children the fact that they are not responsible for the divorce or for getting their parents back together. We study the parent-child triangle and explore the children's fantasies, and when there is evidence that a child is feeling or acting overly responsible for the marriage or for the welfare of one or both parents, we try to "fire" the child from that job and encourage him or her to get back to age-appropriate responsibilities. One seventh-grade girl had been staying home from school to take care of her mother after a divorce. The therapist told her that she was working very hard, but at the wrong job. Her job was to learn how to make the transition to junior high school, to make and keep friends, and to be a responsible member of her family. This led to a discussion of what "responsible" meant, and they concluded that she could not take charge of her mother's happiness any more than her mother could do her school work.

The Couple's Approach to the Extended Family

One goal of the work in the extended family is to lower the anxiety that surfaces around the divorce. Husbands and wives in treatment are asked to keep their parents and siblings informed about the divorce process and to be direct and specific in their requests for support. When possible, spouses' parents are asked to an early session so that the therapist can hear their fears, get their views, and to focus on what can be expected in the near future.

A second goal is to facilitate connections between children and their grandparents, aunts, uncles, and cousins. In some cases this involves the continuation of already strong relationships, and in others it requires building new relationships.

A third goal is to restructure the relationship between spouses and their in-laws. Husbands and wives who have had close positive relationships with their in-laws often expect them to be supportive during the divorce and are surprised when they are not. People need to be reminded that blood is usually thicker than water, and they have to lower their expectations accordingly. Conflictual or cut-off relationships between spouses and their in-laws are addressed so that they do not interfere with the children's connection to that family.

KEY TRIANGLES

Triangles in stage IV conflict can be intensely reactive. We have identified seven that are particularly common around divorce.

1. Husband-wife-lawyer. One spouse has been taken over by his or her lawyer, blindly following inappropriate coaching on personal matters as opposed to legal matters, with the result that the conflict between the divorcing spouses has been intensified.
2. Husband–wife–social network. One spouse is being overly influenced by people in his or her social network and is acting out this influence in the relationship with the spouse.
3. Husband-wife-child. One or more of the children are drawn into an alliance with one parent and are angry at and distant from the other.
4. Husband–wife–in-laws. One spouse has sought refuge in his or her family of origin, and one of the parents is leading a crusade against the other spouse.
5. Grandparent-parent-child. A parent of one spouse links in an overly close position with a grandchild and fosters conflict with the other spouse.
6. Husband-wife-lover. One spouse is leaving the marriage and moving toward the lover.
7. Husband-wife-therapist. The therapist is in an overly close position with one spouse and is distant from or negative about the other.

The therapist must decide on the order in which to address the triangles. In stage IV, however, there is often very little choice because the intensity of certain triangles demands immediate attention. The work involves identifying the triangle and the process that is involved and then shifting both spouses' parts so that they are able to function at a higher level.

WORKING WITH THE INDIVIDUALS

After a divorce people need to let go of the marriage and get on with their lives. To let go they must accept the fact that a marriage that ends in divorce is a personal failure. It did not turn out the way the husband and wife had hoped it would, and each of them needs to understand why it failed. What were the limitations in each of them that did not allow the relationship to flourish? What events inside and outside of the family contributed to its demise?

People have to let go of the bitterness and the blame. If a wife really sees her part in the failure of the marriage, it will be difficult to hold on to her perception of her husband as the enemy. As in stage III treatment, the therapist walks people back from a position of alienation through their bitterness, anger, and hurt, to look at the expectations they once had. Letting go of the bitterness takes time. People often need to hold on to their anger to get through the adversarial process. They are afraid that if they soften, doubts about getting a divorce will surface. People who are able to give up the blame and reexamine their expectations learn that they may have looked for the impossible from the marriage.

Powerful feelings of loss are a predictable part of the mourning process that should follow a divorce, and the therapist encourages people to allow themselves to experience and express them. Sometimes anger is an appropriate response to the brutal mistreatment that can occur in a divorce. The therapist's task is to mobilize the individual's ability to deal with the mistreatment in a constructive way and avoid falling into the role of victim.

Getting on with life after a divorce requires taking risks that often seem overwhelming to newly divorced people. The therapist works to help them gradually increase the amounts of responsibility they take for themselves. Treatment focuses on relationships, strengthening old ones and beginning new ones; personal productivity both at work and at home; and increasing efforts at improving one's personal well-being.

A Stage IV Couple: The Martins

Lilly and Sam Martin, thirty-four and thirty-eight respectively, had been married for twelve years and had two children, a girl ten and a boy eight. When they began treatment, Lilly knew that she wanted to separate but had not consulted a lawyer or expressed her position emphatically enough for Sam to have lost all hope. Although their stated purpose in coming in was to address the conflict in the marriage, Lilly's motivation for treatment came from her fear that she would not be able to get through a divorce without support. Sam's secret hope was that in therapy she might change her mind and decide to stay married.

They had met while Sam was in graduate school and Lilly was finishing her bachelor's degree. He had been a teaching assistant in one of her classes, and she had been impressed with his intelligence and ability to express himself. He had liked her determination and curiosity. During their two-year courtship they established a teacher/pupil pattern that was to continue after they married. Lilly moved toward Sam for support and validation, valuing his opinions much more than her own, and he enjoyed being her guide. A daughter was born two years after they married and a son two years after that. Both of them found parenting very satisfying.

When her second child started nursery school, Lilly began working on her doctorate, a plan she had had since high school and one that Sam had known about and supported. Her enthusiasm about starting graduate school coincided with Sam's increasing dissatisfaction with his own work; he had dropped out of his graduate program and taken a job that he did not find challenging. Lilly still looked to Sam for his opinions on her papers and problems, but when she asked, she found him irritable and critical. As she put more energy into school and less into the house, Sam's criticism intensified. He felt he was doing more than his share, working full-time and splitting the responsibility for the cooking and children. He resented the fact that she had no financial responsibilities and yet could not manage to have the house straightened up or the refrigerator stocked. Lilly felt that in Sam's eyes she could not do anything right. Initially his criticism devastated her, and she tried to avoid it by working harder to please him. When that failed, she directed her efforts into her academic work, where the feedback from professors and fellow students was more positive.

Over the next four years the process intensified. Sam became more critical, and Lilly became more immersed in her studies. Somewhere along the way she learned to tune him out, letting his bitterly sarcastic remarks roll off her back. Comments from her new friends about her husband's hostility provided her with fuel for her frequent daydreams about divorce. Their relationship had become cold and distant, punctuated by raging fights or hopeless discussions about going into therapy. Neither of them took action until Sam intercepted a letter to Lilly from a man in her doctoral program and discovered she had started an affair. After a marathon of talking, screaming, and crying Lilly said she wanted to separate. Sam begged her to consider therapy to see if they could salvage the marriage. The arguing escalated as Sam grew more frustrated with Lilly's determination to separate, and he hit her, something that had never happened before. It was at this point, which Lilly later called "the point of no return," that she left the house. She spent the night with a friend and the next day called the therapist.

LOWERING THE LEVEL OF REACTIVITY

The first five sessions, in which Sam and Lilly were seen together three times and individually once each, were devoted to engagement, evaluation, and the clarification of their conflicting agendas for therapy. The therapist worked to create a safe climate in the sessions by following the approach discussed in chapter 6.

It became clear during this period that Lilly was intent on divorce and that she did not plan to end her affair, although she did not believe one had anything to do with the other. Her theory about the failure of the marriage was that she had had very little self-esteem when she and Sam had married and that as she had grown over the years, largely because of her work, the common ground between them had evaporated. The therapist did two things with her. First, she talked to her about the options available, emphasizing the idea that divorce was always an option, but that it was not a solution. Another option might be to put divorce on the back burner while they worked to understand how the relationship got to this point and to determine whether it had any future. Second, the therapist did some reality testing with Lilly. How far had she moved toward a divorce? Had she contacted a lawyer? Had she discussed it with anyone? Did she have a plan for the mechanics of separation? What was her picture of life without Sam?

As Sam saw more clearly that Lilly was not in therapy to work on the marriage, his anger escalated. He began to question whether he should still come to therapy. Why should he come to help her get out of the marriage more easily? The therapist listened to his feelings and did not fight them but held to her own position that whatever happened to the marriage, he and his children would be better off if he understood his own limitations, which played a part in the failure of the relationship. She clarified the way therapy could be used around a divorce to minimize the emotional repercussions. By the end of the five sessions, the agenda was set. Although they did not agree about separation, both Sam and Lilly were clear that the relationship was headed for divorce.

The Martins' Level of Functioning

Once Sam had accepted the reality of the situation, he said that he felt as though he were stumbling around in a nightmare. He did not go to work for four days and was barely able to get out of bed in the morning. The first task was to get Sam's anxiety down and to stabilize his functioning. After validating his upset, the therapist said that he could expect to continue to feel alternately anxious and depressed, but that he should begin to find ways of moving and organizing his life that would help him to manage his anxiety.

The therapist got Sam to enumerate his basic daily responsibilities and helped him divide the list into those that were absolutely necessary to resume and those that could wait. He decided that he had to get back to work right away, plan and fix meals for himself and his two children, who were with him, and keep the apartment livable. The therapist learned through brief checks in subsequent sessions that he was able to keep up with these tasks.

Sam was asked to try to verbalize his fears. He was afraid of losing his children, thinking that after Lilly got her own apartment she would want them and that there would be a custody battle which he would lose. He also thought he would be wiped out financially with lawyers' fees and two homes to support. He did not like the idea of being alone but was afraid he would never be able to risk trusting someone again. He was not even sure how desirable he might be to another woman.

Without offering false reassurances or stepping into legal territory, the therapist did some reality testing with him. For instance, Lilly had made it clear that she had no intention of taking the children away from him, and although her credibility was very low with him, they had always functioned well together as parents. Lilly was also headed for a career that would prohibit full-time parenting. The therapist pointed out that people who had really worked at it had been able to avoid some of the devastating outcomes he feared. She coached him to take one day at a time. When he caught himself dwelling on his fears, which would only pump up his anxiety, he would need to get back to his responsibilities for that day.

It is important for a person in this emotional state to be connected with people in the family and the social network. If the therapist is concerned about a possible suicide or violence, he or she asks to have important family members come to an early session. The therapist asked Sam how many people knew that Lilly had left and learned that he had told no one. He was told to move toward the people who would be easiest for him first, telling them the facts and something about his emotional state. He was urged not to dwell on his complaints about Lilly; families are likely to take sides anyway, and it is not helpful to add more fuel to the fire.

The spouse who wants the divorce also presents for treatment in a state of anxiety. Lilly said that before she left she had felt certain that divorce was the only solution, but once out of the house she felt on very shaky ground. She did not want to go back to Sam, but she was frightened about what lay ahead. She felt raw and exposed one minute and guilty the next, and she likened her experience to being on a runaway train.

The early work with her covered some of the same ground as with Sam. She had already told members of her family and her close friends, but she had to work on minimizing the complaining she did about Sam. Her fears were ones that divorcing women frequently report. She worried that she would be blamed by their mutual friends for leaving, that no one would understand. She was afraid the children would never forgive her and would always be closer to their father. She thought that Sam would get back at her by cutting off financial support. Everything about money frightened her, because Sam had managed it all, from tax returns to insurance payments. When responsibilities are rigidly divided in a marriage and spouses let their own skills for certain tasks atrophy, splitting up can be particularly frightening. Lilly was also worried that Sam would fall apart; she could picture him becoming either suicidal or violent. The therapist helped her develop a plan of action for either alternative. She also coached Lilly to keep a day-by-day perspective and to set up priorities based on her real responsibilities.

In order to improve functioning it is important to look at the direction each spouse is moving in around the divorce. Sam had been putting his energy into fruitless conversations with Lilly, getting to her mail before she did, reading anything that looked suspicious, and making copies of letters from her lover. The therapist asked him to describe the way he felt following these activities, and he reported feeling humiliated and ashamed. He agreed that they did not accomplish anything and that trying to hold on to someone who was moving away was unproductive. The therapist brought out his expectation that therapy could somehow change her mind, and he began to relinquish it. The therapist worked with him to monitor his pursuing behavior and to move toward his children and other more productive activities instead of going after Lilly.

Lilly was moving quickly toward a new relationship, and the therapist encouraged her to put it on hold until she had finished some of the business in her marriage. The therapist said that although it would be painful, she would have a better chance of having a successful relationship if she postponed a close involvement, and it would be better for the children. Getting people who are involved in an affair to slow down when that relationship feels like the only positive thing in their lives is not easy. Sometimes people will go along with at least a part of the plan. For example, they might refrain from moving in with the new person after the therapist stresses the importance of establishing their own household.

As Sam and Lilly's daily functioning stabilized, the focus of treatment shifted to their involvement with the legal system.

The Legal System

Sam and Lilly looked for and engaged lawyers who seemed sensitive to family issues and supported the fact that they were in treatment. The therapist asked both spouses to think about their own positions on custody and property but to avoid discussing them outside of the sessions. This injunction presented a problem for Sam, who pursued Lilly for her decisions on various issues. She withdrew, and when he pressed her, she would tell him to have his lawyer talk to her lawyer, at which point he would blow up, labeling her inflexible.

The therapist explored this reactive pattern with them. She asked each to imagine what was going on for the other during this kind of exchange and then had them correct each other's pictures. They learned that when Sam pressed Lilly for an opinion and she was not sure what she thought about the issue, she got very anxious and felt invaded and vulnerable, and her reactive response was to withdraw. When Sam did not get a response from her, he thought she was plotting something to hurt him, his anxiety went up, and he felt betrayed and vulnerable. His reactive response was to pursue in anger. This was the same process that had occurred throughout their marriage and could be tracked back to their families of origin. The therapist asked them to try to hold onto this information when they ran into difficulty during the negotiating period, and she kept referring to it herself. She also asked them to predict the issues that were likely to trigger these old familiar responses.

Sam and Lilly reached agreement on some of the basic points before they began working actively with their lawyers. Among other things, they knew they wanted joint custody with equal time for each parent. Much of the continued conflict was organized around money and the division of property. In therapy they worked to sort out the important issues from those that just served to keep the conflict going.

The therapist predicted that there would be an emotional response to each legal step; some steps might evoke tender feelings, and others might intensify the conflict. When Lilly's lawyer drew up the separation agreement, the therapist warned that seeing it in black and white and in legal jargon would be difficult for them. She suggested that Sam read it in as comfortable a situation as possible. If he were reactive to the contents, he should call the therapist and his lawyer before calling Lilly. Lilly was asked to minimize the surprises as much as possible by informing Sam about the contents before he got the document.

The greatest difficulty they had around the legal process had to do with timing. Lilly was eager to conclude the separation agreement and felt that Sam was procrastinating. Her pattern was to contain her frustration until she reached her limit and then to explode at Sam on the phone. Lilly described feeling utterly powerless, as she had felt frequently in her marriage and also during childhood. She had to learn a way of acting that was more likely to lead to a successful outcome, and she needed to know that she had other options if that failed. Ultimately, if Sam did not complete his part of the agreement so that they could sign it, she could follow another legal track. Lilly very much wanted to avoid suing Sam, but she felt calmer knowing she could do so as a last resort.

Sam had to sort out the difficulty he was having completing his work on the separation agreement. He basically saw his problem as part of a familiar pattern of procrastination and a result of a very stressful life with a demanding full-time job and the care of his two children half of each week. He also realized that some of his difficulty in compromising came from the feeling that this divorce was "Lilly's doing" in the first place.

The therapist's job consisted of monitoring how each of them functioned, coaching them through areas where they needed to change their behavior, dealing with the intense feelings that surfaced, and predicting potential pitfalls each step of the way.

Parenting

Sam and Lilly had questions about when to tell the children about the divorce, and the therapist advised them to do it as soon as they were sure they were being divorced. She had them role-play the conversation, giving each parent the experience of playing the roles of both parents and both children. The therapist also suggested various books to them, and one in particular, Ciji Ware's *Sharing Parenthood After Divorce,* was helpful. It raises countless issues about joint custody and suggests many creative ideas and solutions. There are scores of popular books that deal with every aspect of parenting around divorce; having a number of them to recommend is important, because reading can provide a structure that lowers anxiety for many people. The therapist should watch for a potentially negative effect from reading, however; some people use it to substitute for behavior change.

Sam and Lilly ran into problems with the mechanics of sharing parenthood. If a custody plan is to be successful over the course of a child's growing-up years, it needs flexibility. We have found it advisable, however, to start with as much structure as possible, to help families handle the predictable anxiety as they put the plan into effect. To get them through the periods when the emotional climate was particularly hot, Sam and Lilly had to learn to exchange facts rather than feelings about the children. Lilly, who had moved into a nearby apartment, became upset every time she brought the children back to their father. She would go into the apartment at the children's request, and each time she would find something that enraged her and led to a battle with Sam. Once she discovered that the inside works of a grandfather's clock that had been a wedding present from her family were missing. When Sam came to her apartment, she felt invaded. He would flip through the mail on her desk or ask long, involved questions. Both realized that they were too emotionally raw to continue going to each other's apartments and that the children did not need them to do it, so they stopped. The children were seen periodically throughout the treatment, in sessions alone and with each parent separately.

One of Sam's greatest irritations around the children had to do with the way they were dressed when they came back to him. He felt that Lilly was lax about clean clothes and about dressing them appropriately for the weather. He was also particularly sensitive about her borrowing items like party shoes or a certain dress from his house and then not returning them. His tendency was to let a few incidents build and then to blow up, setting off an angry response from Lilly and guaranteeing a lack of cooperation. In therapy alone, he worked on ways to keep his reactivity down and to sort out the important needs from those he could let pass, and then to express the important ones to Lilly without anger. Lilly looked at ways in which she could afford to meet Sam's requests without damaging herself.

Of course, issues like these, which look fairly simple on the surface, can always be traced back to deeper power struggles in the relationship. For example, Sam's anger about clothes was hard to separate from his anger and hurt about the divorce, but that is exactly what must be done in therapy. People need to know the sources of their anger when they are overreacting to an incident, in order to get their behavior under control.

The Extended Family

Early in the therapy Sam's parents, who lived nearby, came in for a session with Sam alone. The therapist wanted to get their view of their son's marriage and its dissolution and to get a sense of the anxiety they were experiencing. As is often the case, both of them were upset with their daughter-in-law for leaving and raised a number of issues that had troubled them throughout the marriage. Both felt that she had been more involved with school than with the home, leaving too much responsibility on their son's shoulders. They were concerned that the legal system would work against their son and worried that they would not have as much contact with their grandchildren. Sam talked about the kind of custody arrangement he wanted, and they discussed ways in which they could be helpful. The therapist discussed the predictable ups and downs that lay ahead and encouraged Sam to keep them informed.

In Lilly's family, which consisted of her parents, two brothers, and two sisters, the most common reaction to the news of the separation was that they had thought all along that the marriage was a mistake. The therapist worked with Lilly to understand the kind of impact their negativity had had on the marriage. The amount of support Lilly could get from them was limited by the cluster stress they were under—shortly after Lilly separated from Sam, her father left her mother after forty years of marriage and went off with another woman—and by the feelings of some of them that Lilly was moving too quickly into a new relationship. Much of the initial work with Lilly around her extended family dealt with her automatic defensive reaction.

KEY TRIANGLES

Numerous triangles were addressed through the course of therapy: the husband-wife-children triangle, the triangles with their parents, the husband-wife-lawyer triangle, and husband-wife-lover triangle.

In the latter triangle, Lilly was moving away from Sam and toward her lover, John. Sam was enraged at John but had never met him. Initially, Sam needed to stop trying to hold on to Lilly, and she needed to slow down her movement toward John. Lilly had planned to move very slowly in her relationship with John, and at first that seemed possible because he lived in a different city and was in the midst of a divorce himself. A few months later, however, he moved to New York, and the pacing became more difficult to control. Although we believe that one is better off completing a divorce process and spending some time alone before beginning a new relationship, the reality is that people often will not wait. Given the fact that the relationship with John was not going to disappear, the therapist worked with Sam and Lilly to shift their parts in the triangle so that each could move toward divorce and into a post-divorce relationship as functionally as possible.

To shift his part in the triangle, Sam needed to detoxify the subject of John. Initially John was just a name on a letter, but one that held enormous destructive power. Sam had several months to build up a monstrous fantasy about John before they met unexpectedly in Lilly's apartment. Sam was furious, but coming up against the reality of the "other man" standing there in flesh and blood actually started the process of detoxification. In sessions alone, the therapist encouraged Sam to express and explore the painful feelings that kept coming up, especially in relation to John's increasing involvement with Sam's children. The following dialogue is from a session with Sam one month after he had met John.

SAM: She's so damn irresponsible. I go to pick the kids up after school, which had been the plan, and find out that John had already taken them home. I could have killed her, and I'm pissed off at the school for letting them go. I went into my son's teacher like a madman.

THERAPIST: What had you most upset—that Lilly had changed the plan without telling you, or that it was John who picked them up?

SAM: Both. Lilly says she left a message for me. I never got it. Something about John getting them, though . . .

THERAPIST: What about that?

SAM: I don't know—that he was at the school—that he talked to one of their teachers.

THERAPIST: That's the first time I've heard you mention John doing something alone with the kids. Is that right?

SAM: I think so. I guess it is. The kids talk about him some. My daughter more than my son, but it's always about something

THERAPIST: they all did together. This was different—like it's moving in a new direction.

THERAPIST: What's got you scared about that new direction? Where do you think it will end up?

SAM: Rationally or in my gut?

THERAPIST: Pure gut.

SAM: He and Lilly will get married. The kids will like being with them better—more like a family—and I'll lose them. There won't be any room left for me.

In order for Sam to put John into a perspective that he could deal with, he had to bring out his fears and track them back to personal feelings of inadequacy. All Sam's doubts about himself funneled into the fantasy that he might lose the children. He had been so busy trying to make up for his own father's failures as a father that he had not acknowledged those personal doubts.

Over the next months, up to and beyond the time when John and Lilly began living together, Sam continued the process of detoxification by taking John in gradually increasing doses. He began by simply greeting John on the phone and eventually reached the point where he could sit down with John and talk about the children if they happened to cross paths. The therapist suggested that Sam actually ask John's help with something regarding the children. For example, Sam might ask John's opinion about how his son was doing, saying something like, "I'm a little worried about my son. You're with him a lot; how do you think he's doing?" Taking this approach is a way of staying out of the victim position, which in turn helps to build self-respect. Lilly was surprised when she walked into the apartment one Saturday to find Sam and John in the living room chatting amiably.

Probably the most significant ingredient that made it possible for Sam to become less reactive to John was the effort Sam had been making on his own life in the areas of productivity, personal well-being, and personal relationships. If someone in Sam's position has not begun to sort out the pieces of his own life, it is very difficult to accept a former spouse's moving on to a new relationship.

THE INDIVIDUALS

In order to move functionally through the divorce, both Sam and Lilly had to let go of their anger and blame and accept responsibility for the failure of the marriage. Sam's anger was mostly focused on the fact that

Lilly had left and that she had not been willing to try to work on staying together once they were in therapy. The therapist encouraged him to look at the separation as part of a much larger process—one that had started even before he met Lilly. Sam tracked back through the resentment and anger to the disappointment that had come from unmet expectations and then looked at the sources of those expectations in his family. As his anger lessened, a number of feelings surfaced, most notably a tremendous sadness and sense of loss. Sometimes it centered around his children, whom he missed a great deal when they went to Lilly, and sometimes he was very much aware of missing Lilly.

Sam was not particularly comfortable expressing feelings of vulnerability, which he saw as part of his contribution to the failure of the marriage. His automatic reaction was to cover up and assume an all-knowing kind of bravado. Much of his work in his family of origin was around this pattern. The sessions became a practice ground for letting some of his vulnerability show. He was coached to do the same thing with the important people in his life, particularly his father and his sister. In this phase of treatment both father and sister came back in for sessions.

The final focus of Sam's work in therapy was around the goal of productivity. He had to balance his desire for career advancement with his responsibilities for his children. He discovered that people at work were charmed and impressed when they learned that he had his children half the time, but they expected him to do the caretaking and housekeeping at no cost to his job and had little tolerance when he couldn't stay overtime at work or had to rush home to a very sick child.

Lilly's anger was largely covered over by her feelings of guilt about leaving and by her intellectualizing about the failure of the marriage. Her theory was that she had been very passive through most of the marriage and that as she had gained confidence through success in her graduate work and her friends, she had grown in a different direction from Sam. The theory is not necessarily inaccurate, but it is incomplete. She had been in treatment for over a year before she was able to verbalize the emotional progression she had been through in her marriage. Her feelings of not being valued or special to Sam surfaced and were very familiar to her, easily traceable to her family.

Lilly's remaining work in therapy went in two directions: addressing the issues that came up in her relationship with John, whom she planned to marry, and working in her family of origin. The latter was difficult because of the turmoil her parents were in. Lilly had been highly reactive to both parents and had a tendency to be overresponsible when they appeared helpless. She worked on staying in contact with them with very low expectations and without jumping in to rescue them or to play go-between. The fact that Lilly and her mother were both going through a separation provided a bond, and their relationship grew closer. Lilly made some headway on accepting her mother's limitations as a grandmother—her mother was not as involved as Lilly would have liked her to be.

Sam and Lilly made significant progress over the two years they were in treatment. In a follow-up session six months after therapy ended, they appeared to meet all four of our criteria for success.

Problems for the Therapist

We have identified five potential problems for therapists who deal with divorcing couples. They are:

1. A lack of awareness and/or control of the ways in which the therapist's value system and personal experience affect the treatment
2. Too much concern about the success or failure of the marriage
3. A victim/villain perception of the spouses
4. Anxiety about excessive emotional damage
5. Anxiety about dealing with lawyers.

THE THERAPIST'S VALUE SYSTEM

However strong and firmly entrenched our values, whether political, religious, or personal, we as therapists must separate them from the values of the people we treat. A therapist who believes on the one hand that marriage should be forever or on the other that marriage with intense conflict should be ended will find it difficult to be objective when working with a couple struggling with the issue of whether to divorce.

One therapist in training had difficulty working with a couple who seemed headed for divorce. Both the husband and wife had been married twice. The therapist, a practicing Catholic, found himself reactive when this couple sought divorce as a solution to their problems. His disapproval of their attitude made it difficult for him to see the emotional process that had led them to their present situation. When he recognized that his reactivity was rooted in his own religious beliefs, he was able to get past his emotional response and focus on helping the couple work on their problems.

Similarly, the therapist who has been divorced may try to breathe life into a dead marriage or encourage a divorce when there is still hope for the relationship. Neither position is functional. If the therapist has not accepted part of the responsibility in his or her own failed marriage, the chance of a skewed clinical view will be greater.

A woman who had made the decision to leave her husband came in for therapy. She had been married for three years and had a year-old baby. She reported that her husband pulled her hair and punched her when he was upset about the way she handled the finances. In the next session she brought her husband, who told the therapist that he wanted to continue the relationship and insisted that his wife needed to change. She deserved his anger, he said, because she was deceitful. The therapist recognized her own reactivity when she found herself thinking almost immediately that leaving this man was probably the best solution for the wife. She realized that it was based on her own failed marriage, in which she had been physically abused. She had viewed that abuse as an unforgiveable sin. She knew she had to find a functional way to deal with the physical violence in this case. It was hard for her to separate her own experience from the wife's, but once she recognized what was going on within herself she was more effective with this couple.

THE PERSONAL STAKE IN THE MARRIAGE

The therapist's personal pride may be wrapped up in success that is defined in terms of the therapist's own values. Many therapists have a personal stake in saving marriages: if they save a marriage, they are competent, and if they do not, they are failures. Feelings of omnipotence such as this are not useful and show lack of respect for the families being treated.

Therapists who focus on success or failure will concentrate on the results of therapy rather than on the process. They may become anxious over how to fix things, or, at the other extreme, they may wish that a family who reminds them of failure would terminate therapy. Developing a functional definition of a successful outcome in treatment will serve as an antidote to this kind of narcissism.

Another trigger for the therapist is hypersensitivity to a resurgence of tenderness in a divorcing couple. In a session with a young couple who were about to sign their separation papers, one therapist found himself moved as the couple spoke of their sadness over the end of their relationship. The tenderness between them awakened the therapist's hope that he could save the marriage. Although this marriage was at the point of no return, the therapist's sense of omnipotence took over, and he began to suggest that they postpone signing their papers. The moment of tenderness passed quickly, and the husband and wife began to argue. When affection and caring are observed in a divorcing couple, the therapist should use these positive feelings to foster a better adjustment for each spouse as they proceed through separation and divorce.

THE VILLAIN/VICTIM PERCEPTION

At any stage of marital conflict, it is important for the therapist to avoid seeing husband or wife as victim or villain. Otherwise he or she will become caught up in an intense polarization between the couple when the couple is divorcing. An angry or hurt spouse is often looking for an ally, and the therapist must make a special effort not to become part of a triangle supportive of one spouse and critical of the other.

Siding with one spouse may initially stabilize the clinical situation and the emotional state of the aggrieved spouse, but in the long run it fosters dependency on the therapist and renders the spouse helpless. Taking sides may also intensify an already volatile situation and may distort the therapist's thinking. For example, stories of a husband who will not give his wife money for the children's food or of a wife who dresses her children in rags when her husband picks them up for a visit to his law office should be viewed by the therapist as process rather than the truth about the other spouse. The stories may all be true, but accepting them as the whole view rather than as expressions of hurt and anger will make it difficult for the therapist to calm the situation and help the spouses deal with their crisis.

One therapist grew increasingly reactive to the wife in a divorcing couple because of her continuous demands for more money from her husband. The therapist believed that the husband had been making a sincere attempt to provide for his wife and children since the separation, while the wife had made no effort to supplement her income with even a part-time job and was openly critical of her husband to the children, telling them to "Go ask your father why you can't go on the class trip," for example. The therapist knew she was caught when she began to dread sessions with this woman and heard herself cutting off discussions about money.

The origins of this response were not hard to trace. The therapist, who came from a family that placed a high value on self-reliant women, was married to a man whose former wife was still asking for money after fifteen years. To free herself she met with the divorcing wife alone and tried to uncover the fears that kept this woman locked into a dependent relationship with her husband. She also asked a colleague to see the wife in consultation. The consultant took a firm position about the wife's dependency and presented a plan for taking more responsibility—a plan that significantly raised the wife's anxiety, in turn allowing the therapist to empathize with her regarding the difficulty of the task that lay ahead. If the therapist had not been able to control her reactivity so that she could work effectively with this woman, she might have had to refer the case to someone else.

In much of the stage IV work we do, only one spouse is interested in therapy. It is particularly difficult to maintain objectivity when this is the case. Our treatment goals remain the same whether we are working with one spouse or two. It is still important to guide the spouse through the work on the couple, the triangles, and the individual, but there are many potential traps when working with only one side of the equation. The therapist may have to wrestle with a bias against a spouse who is unwilling to come to therapy. Against the background of unwillingness to cooperate, it may be especially difficult to maintain a systems perspective if the spouse who is coming in is telling atrocity stories about the absent spouse. The therapist's tendency to encourage dependency may be greater when seeing one spouse. In a high percentage of these cases it is the spouse who has been left who comes in for therapy, feeling angry, helpless, and overwhelmed, and expecting a great deal from the therapist.

To minimize the difficulties in working with only one spouse, we encourage therapists to consider several steps:

1. To neutralize a bias about the absent spouse, it is important to try to understand the fears that have contributed to the decision not to come. Not everyone is geared for therapy, and there are many factors that might influence such a decision.

2. We make an attempt to see the other spouse at least once. We can usually bring this about by coaching the spouse in therapy in a more functional way to approach the other or by getting permission to contact the other spouse directly. We let the absent spouse know that his or her point of view is critical to the therapist in helping the family, even if it means just one session. If there are children, we emphasize the value of his or her role in minimizing the emotional damage to them.

3. We give special emphasis to helping the spouse in therapy build a strong support system in order to minimize dependence on the therapist.

4. We encourage the spouse in therapy to bring into sessions people from the extended family and social network who have a positive relationship with both spouses and a less biased view of the divorce, in order to fill in the blanks for the therapist.

5. We freely use consultations and peer supervision when we feel our
    perspective may be skewed.

ANXIETY ABOUT EXCESSIVE REPERCUSSIONS

It is not unusual in the treatment of intensely conflictual stage IV
families for the therapist to become anxious about excessive repercussions
during the crisis. Threats of or actual physical violence, drunkenness,
bizarre behavior, talk of suicide, the onset of serious health problems, or
the suffering of children all serve to increase the therapist's anxiety. It is
important for the therapist to remain levelheaded while exploring the
reality of the situation and providing direct advice to the family. The
therapist can use medical and psychiatric consultants, bring in extended
family members, and connect people to their social and religious networks
and to the legal system, if necessary, to provide supplementary assistance
to a family in crisis.

One woman, married to a twice-divorced police officer who had recently been fired from the force, came to therapy for help in getting out
of her marriage. The husband was seen twice and left treatment when it
became clear that his wife would not change her mind. In the following
weeks, the wife began to discuss her long-term fear of him and revealed
that he had forced himself on her sexually. She also mentioned that he had
a gun, which he kept in the night table drawer. His drinking had increased,
and most of their arguments occurred when he was drunk.

The therapist took this woman's fears seriously and at the same time
realized that his own level of anxiety was rising. He worked with the wife
to develop a plan of action that would reduce her fears. He encouraged the
wife to talk to her family about her desire to leave the marriage and also
told her to contact her husband's priest and friends, since he had no family,
and inform them of his upset. The wife was sent to her lawyer to tell him
about the gun and to find out how to obtain an order of protection. The
therapist coached her to monitor the signals that indicated that her husband was drinking and to leave her home when she felt she was in danger.
He urged the wife to move slowly and carefully through the legal process
to give her extremely upset husband time to adjust to the situation.

DEALING WITH LAWYERS

The involvement of lawyers in stage IV marital conflict presents special problems for the therapist. The intensity of these problems depends
on whether the couple is proceeding toward a no-fault divorce or a long-

drawn-out legal battle that may involve a property dispute or a custody fight. Although most of the stage IV couples we see divide marital property and determine the custody arrangement without litigation, the potential for triangles among spouses, therapist, and lawyers is always present.

It is important for the therapist to be aware of the pitfalls of getting caught in such triangles. Husbands and wives often ask the therapist for legal advice or check with the therapist about whether the lawyer is giving them correct information. It is sometimes difficult to avoid falling into the trap of becoming an armchair lawyer. The therapist should monitor the legal activity but without giving legal advice.

Despite the best efforts of a therapist, some cases do go to litigation, and then the therapist has to deal with many emotional issues. Just hearing the word *court* produces a reaction that we have observed in ourselves and in many other therapists who work with divorcing couples. We have labeled it *legal paranoia*. Ignorance of matrimonial laws and the legal process creates a good deal of anxiety. Therapists called to testify in court feel vulnerable: "If I had done things differently, would this couple be moving toward litigation? Will I be sued for malpractice, either because I have assets or because I am being blamed by one spouse for not saving the marriage? If I am subpoenaed, will I be able to hold up under intense questioning from clever attorneys who do not understand our family systems view?"

The therapist who is intimidated by the possibility of becoming a part of the legal battle between husband and wife is no longer free to operate. He or she may feel constrained about what is said in the session and written in the record. The spouses are often careful about what they say to their therapist, having been warned by their lawyers not to incriminate themselves. In some cases that go to court, the therapist may get the impression that at least one of the spouses is building a case on facts told in therapy.

In one case, a husband and wife were preparing for what might become a custody battle over their ten-year-old daughter. In their separate therapy sessions they said they wanted to settle things peacefully. Each admitted that their daughter would be the loser if they went to court. The therapist found, however, that the behavior of the spouses outside therapy gave no indication that peace was the goal. There were threats, physical violence, and lawsuits. When the therapist questioned them about their behavior, it became clear that each was leaving the de-escalation of hostilities to the other. Moreover, each spouse's attorney had cautioned his client not to show any weakness to the other spouse. The therapist, although frustrated by both lawyers' tactics, continued to urge both of them to devise a creative way to reopen the negotiations so that an armistice could take place. It takes patience for a therapist to maintain a firm yet nonreactive position with a couple like this. The couple must be reminded that continuing the battle over their daughter is irresponsible parenting and is potentially devastating to the child.

The authors have found that the consistent use of consultations with colleagues and peer supervision lends support to the therapist and encourages clear thinking. The involvement of colleagues also helps to lower anxiety when one is dealing with extremely complicated and intense treatment issues.

The therapist is wise to explore his or her potential legal vulnerability with an attorney. For example, in New York State licensed physicians, psychologists, and social workers have a nondisclosure privilege that can be waived by either spouse in a custody dispute. Knowing this fact may alter the way the therapist handles a particular clinical situation. Some therapists may be concerned about being sued for malpractice once attorneys are in the picture. Although the likelihood of this event is remote, therapists concerned about their liability in a clinical situation should consult an attorney.

In a case where the therapist may be subpoenaed, role-playing is a useful way to reduce anxiety. One of the authors benefitted from a mock courtroom situation in which she was realistically interrogated by a litigator. The litigator's manner of questioning was explained and the reasoning behind the questions was discussed. The therapist was able to experience how she would be dealt with if she ever went to court. Talking about her reactions with her attorney proved useful and lessened her concern about being subpoenaed.

The model presented in this book represents eight years of reflection, discussion, and clinical work. It provides a theoretical frame of reference and a clinical methodology for the treatment of marital conflict. It does not attempt to address the issue of quantifiable measures that would permit the theory and the methods of intervention to be tested in a controlled way. It is the authors' hope that their own work and the continuing work of interested colleagues will provide a refinement of the model over time.

BIBLIOGRAPHY

Ackerman, N. W. 1937. The family as a social and emotional unit. In *The strength of family therapy: Selected papers of Nathan W. Ackerman,* ed. D. Bloch and R. Simon. New York: Brunner/Mazel, 1982.
———. 1954. The diagnosis of neurotic marital interaction. In *The strength of family therapy: Selected papers of Nathan W. Ackerman,* ed. D. Bloch and R. Simon. New York: Brunner/Mazel, 1982.
———. 1955. Mental hygiene and social work, today and tomorrow. In *The strength of family therapy: Selected papers of Nathan W. Ackerman,* ed. D. Bloch and R. Simon. New York: Brunner/Mazel, 1982.
———. 1965. The family approach to marital disorders. In *The strength of family therapy: Selected papers of Nathan W. Ackerman,* ed. D. Bloch and R. Simon. New York: Brunner/Mazel, 1982.
———. 1967. The emergence of family diagnosis and treatment: A personal view. *Psychotherapy: Theory, Research and Practice* 4: 125–29.
Anderson, R. 1968. *I never sang for my father.* New York: Random House.
———. 1972. *Double solitaire.* New York: Random House.

Barbach, L. G. 1975. For yourself: The fulfillment of female sexuality. New York: Doubleday.
———. 1983. *For Each Other.* New York: Doubleday.
Bauman, M. H. 1982. Marital affairs and counter affairs. In *Questions and answers in the practice of family therapy,* vol. 2., ed. A. S. Gurman. New York: Brunner/Mazel.
Bloch, D., and Simon, R., eds. 1982. *The strength of family therapy: Selected papers of Nathan W. Ackerman.* New York: Brunner/Mazel.
Bodin, A. M. 1981. The interactional view: Family therapy approaches of the Mental Research Institute. In *Handbook of family therapy,* ed. A. S. Gurman and D. P. Kniskern. New York: Brunner/Mazel.
Bowen, M. 1957. Treatment of family groups with a schizophrenic member. Paper presented at the annual meeting of the American Orthopsychiatric Association, Chicago. In M. Bowen, *Family therapy in clinical practice.* New York: Jason Aronson, 1978.
———. 1966. The use of family theory in clinical practice. *Comprehensive Psychiatry* 7: 345–74. Reprinted in M. Bowen, *Family therapy in clinical practice.* New York: Jason Aronson, 1978.
———. 1976. Theory in the practice of psychotherapy. In *Family therapy: Theory and practice,* ed. P. J. Guerin. New York: Gardner.
———. 1978. *Family therapy in clinical practice.* New York: Jason Aronson.
Broderick, C. B., and Schrader, S. S. 1981. The history of professional marriage and family therapy. In *Handbook of family therapy,* ed. A. S. Gurman and D. P. Kniskern. New York: Brunner/Mazel.
Burden, S. and Gilbert, J. 1982. Stage III marital conflict. *The Family* 10: 27–39.

Carr, A. C. 1980. Psychological testing of personality. In H. I. Kaplan, A. M. Freedman, and B. J. Sadock, eds., *Comprehensive textbook of psychiatry,* 3d ed. Baltimore: Williams and Wilkins.

Carter, E. A., and McGoldrick, M. 1980. *The family life cycle: A framework for family therapy.* New York: Gardner.

Coles, R. 1967. *Children of crisis: A study of courage and fear.* Boston: Little, Brown.

Davatz, U. 1979. The concept of fusion in Bowen family systems theory and in biology. *The Family* 6: 83–86.

Duvall, E. M. 1977. *Marriage and family development,* 5th ed. Philadelphia: J. B. Lippincott.

Eshleman, J. R. 1981. *The family: An introduction.* Boston: Allyn and Bacon.

Fay, L. F. 1980. *The family in the diocese.* Unpublished manuscript.

Fogarty, T. F. 1974. Emotional climate in the family and therapy. *The Family* 2: 17–26.

———. 1975. Triangles. *The Family* 2: 11–20.

———. 1976a. Marital crisis. In *Family therapy: Theory and practice,* ed. P. J. Guerin. New York: Gardner.

———. 1976b. On emptiness and closeness, Part I. *The Family* 3: 3–12.

———. 1976c. On emptiness and closeness, Part II. *The Family* 3: 47–56.

———. 1977. Fusion. *The Family* 4: 49–58.

———. 1979a. The therapy of hopelessness. *The Family* 6: 57–62.

———. 1979b. The distancer and the pursuer. *The Family* 7: 11–16.

Freud, S. 1957. The origin and development of psychoanalysis. In *A general selection from the works of Sigmund Freud,* ed. R. Rickman. Garden City: Doubleday.

Gelfand, R. 1980. Glossary. In H. I. Kaplan, A. M. Freedman, and B. J. Sadock, eds., *Comprehensive textbook of psychiatry,* 3d ed. Baltimore: Williams and Wilkins.

Greeley, A. M. 1981. *The Irish-Americans: The rise to money and power.* New York: Harper and Row.

Guerin, P. J. 1976a. The use of the arts in family therapy: *I never sang for my father.* In *Family therapy: Theory and practice,* ed. P. J. Guerin. New York: Gardner.

———, ed. 1976b. *Family therapy: Theory and practice.* New York: Gardner.

———. 1977. A systems view of the alcoholic family. *The Family* 4: 29–36.

———. 1982. The stages of marital conflict. *The Family* 10: 15–26.

Guerin, P. J., and Fay, L. F. 1982. The envelope of marital conflict: Social context and family factors. *The Family* 10: 3–14.

Guerin, P. J., and Fogarty, T. F. 1972. The family therapist's own family. *International Journal of Psychiatry* 10: 6–22.

Guerin, P. J., and Gordon, E. M. 1986. Trees, triangles and temperament in the child-centered family. In *Evolving models for family change: A volume in honor of Salvador Minuchin,* ed. H. C. Fishman and B. L. Rosman. New York: Guilford Press.

Guerin, P. J., and Guerin, K. B. 1976. Theoretical aspects and clinical relevance of the multi-generational model of family therapy. In *Family therapy: Theory and practice,* ed. P. J. Guerin. New York: Gardner.

Guerin, P. J., and Pendagast, E. G. 1976. Evaluation of family system and genogram. In *Family therapy: Theory and practice,* ed. P. J. Guerin. New York: Gardner.

Gurman, A. S. 1978. Contemporary marital therapies: A critique and comparative analysis of psychoanalytic, behavioral and systems theory approaches. In *Marriage and marital therapy,* ed. T. J. Paolino and B. S. McCrady. New York: Brunner/Mazel.

———, and Kniskern, D. P., eds. 1981. *Handbook of family therapy.* New York: Brunner/Mazel.

Haley, J. 1967. Toward a theory of pathological systems. In *Family therapy and disturbed families,* ed. G. H. Zuk and I. Boszormenyi-Nagy. Palo Alto, Calif.: Science and Behavior Books.

———. 1973. *Uncommon therapy: The psychiatric techniques of Milton Erickson, M.D.* New York: Norton.

Haley, J., and Hoffman, L. 1967. *Techniques of family therapy.* New York: Basic Books.

Hall, C. M. 1981. *The Bowen family theory and its uses.* New York: Jason Aronson.

Harper, R.A. 1961. Extramarital sexual relations. In *The encyclopedia of sexual behavior,* ed. A. Ellis and A. Abarbanel. New York: Hawthorn.

Hoffman, L. 1981. *Foundations of family therapy: A conceptual framework for systems change.* New York: Basic Books.

Holmes, T. H., and Rahe, R. H. 1967. The social readjustment rating scale. *Journal of Psychosomatic Research* 11: 213–18.

Hunt, M. 1969. *The affair: A portrait of extra-marital love in contemporary America.* New York: World.

———. 1974. *Sexual behavior in the 1970s.* Chicago: Playboy Press.

Jackson, D. 1967. Aspects of conjoint family therapy. In *Family therapy and disturbed families,* ed. G. H. Zuk and I. Boszormenyi-Nagy. Palo Alto, Calif.: Science and Behavior Books.

Jacobson, N. S. 1981. Behavioral marital therapy. In *Handbook of family therapy,* ed. A. S. Gurman and D. P. Kniskern. New York: Brunner/Mazel.

Kaplan, H. I., Freedman, A. M., and Sadock, B. J., eds. 1980. *Comprehensive Textbook of Psychiatry,* 3d ed. Baltimore: Williams and Wilkins.

Keniston, K. 1965. *The uncommitted: Alienated youth in American society.* New York: Harcourt, Brace and World.

Kerr, M. E. 1981. Family systems theory and therapy. In *Handbook of family therapy,* ed. A. S. Gurman and D. P. Kniskern. New York: Brunner/Mazel.

Kinsey, A. C., et al. 1948. *Sexual behavior in the human male.* Philadelphia: W. B. Saunders.

———. 1953. *Sexual behavior in the human female.* Philadelphia: W. B. Saunders.

Komarovsky, M. 1967. *Blue-collar marriage.* New York: Vintage.

Lederer, W. J., and Jackson, D. 1968. *The mirages of marriage.* New York: Norton.

Leslie, G. R. 1982. *The family in social context.* New York: Oxford.

Lewin, K. 1951. *Field theory in social science: Selected theoretical papers.* New York: Harper Torchbooks.

Martin, P. A. 1976. *A marital therapy manual.* New York: Brunner/Mazel.

Meissner, W. W. 1978. The conceptualization of marriage and family dynamics from a psychoanalytic perspective. In *Marriage and marital therapy,* ed. T. J. Paolino and B. S. McCrady. New York: Brunner/Mazel.

Miller, J. G. 1980. General living systems theory. In H. I. Kaplan, A. M. Freedman, and B. J. Sadock, eds., *Comprehensive textbook of psychiatry,* 3d ed. Baltimore: Williams and Wilkins.

Mills, C. W. 1959. *The sociological imagination.* New York: Oxford.

Minuchin, S. 1974. *Families and family therapy.* Cambridge: Harvard University Press.

———, Baker, L., Rosman, B., et al. 1975. A conceptual model of psychosomatic illness in children. *Archives of General Psychiatry* 32: 1031–38.

Mittelman, B. 1948. Concurrent analysis of marital couples. *Psychoanalytic Quarterly* 17: 182–97.

Nadelson, C. C. 1978. Marital therapy from a psychoanalytic perspective. In *Marriage and marital therapy,* ed. T. J. Paolino and B. S. McCrady. New York: Brunner/Mazel.

Nichols, M. 1984. *Family therapy: Concepts and methods.* New York: Gardner.

Paolino, T. J., and McCrady, B. S., eds. 1978. *Marriage and marital therapy: Psychoanalytic, behavioral and systems theory perspectives.* New York: Brunner/Mazel.

Pendagast, E., and Sherman, C. O. 1977. A guide to the genogram family systems training. *The Family* 5: 3–14.

Sager, C. J. 1976. *Marriage contracts and couple therapy: Hidden forces in intimate relationships.* New York: Brunner/Mazel.

———, Brown, H. S., Crohn, H., Engel, T., Rodstein, E., and Walker, L. 1983. *Treating the remarried family.* New York: Brunner/Mazel.

Satir, V. 1967. *Conjoint family therapy.* Palo Alto, Calif.: Science and Behavior Books.

Steinglass, P. 1978. The conceptualization of marriage from a systems theory perspective. In *Marriage and marital therapy,* ed. T. J. Paolino and B. S. McCrady. New York: Brunner/Mazel.

Stuart, R. B. 1980. *Helping couples change: A social learning approach to marital therapy.* New York: Guilford.

Talese, G. 1980. *Thy neighbor's wife.* New York: Doubleday.

Toman, W. 1976. *Family constellation: Its effect on personality and social behavior,* 3d ed. New York: Springer.

Visher, E. B., and Visher, J. S. 1979. *Stepfamilies: A guide to working with stepparents and stepchildren.* New York: Brunner/Mazel.

Ware, C. 1982. *Sharing parenthood after divorce.* New York: Viking.

Weiss, R. L. 1978. The conceptualization of marriage from a behavioral perspective. In *Marriage and marital therapy,* ed. T. J. Paolino and B. S. McCrady. New York: Brunner/Mazel.

Wilcoxon, A., and Fenell, D. 1983. Engaging the non-attending spouse in marital therapy through the use of therapist-initiated communication. *Journal of Marital and Family Therapy* 9: 199–203.

Zuk, G. H., and Boszormenyi-Nagy, I., eds. 1967. *Family therapy and disturbed families.* Palo Alto, Calif.: Science and Behavior Books.

INDEX